CYBER
MARKETING

Len Keeler

amacom

American Management Association

New York • Atlanta • Boston • Chicago • Kansas City • San Francisco • Washington, D. C.
Brussels • Mexico City • Tokyo • Toronto

Library of Congress Cataloging-in-Publication Data

Keeler, Len.
    Cybermarketing / Len Keeler.
        p.   cm.
    Includes bibliographical references and index.
    ISBN 0-8144-7879-4
    1. Internet advertising. 2. Marketing—Communication systems—
Data processing. 3. Internet (Computer network) I. Title.
HF6146.I58K43 1995
658.8′4—dc20   95-15141
                                              CIP

Printing number

10 9 8 7 6 5 4 3 2 1

Contents

Introduction

The Networked Marketplace

There's been a great deal of sound and fury generated in the past year or two regarding the so-called information superhighway. The government is promoting it as the "National Information Infrastructure." It's been called, by others, the "I-way," the "Infobahn," the "Databahn" or, simply, "The Grid." You get onto it via "Information Onramps" and choose from an "Information Smorgasbord" or (my personal favorite) "the Information Salad Bar."

Soon after hearing about the info superhighway, we began to hear about the "superhighway wars," as cable and telephone and cellular communications and computer companies quickly announced alliances and mergers and then—just as quickly—called them off. Everyone wanted a piece of the highway pie, but no one was quite sure how to get their hands on it.

Some members of the media elite decided that the superhighway concept was ripe for a backlash, and that started to appear about six months following the initial avalanche of stories. Newspapers started to report on the fact that cyberspace can be a dangerous and chaotic place (true). Industry experts lectured us on the difficulty of merging technologies as divergent as telecommunications and television and computers (true again). Others dismissed the whole thing as a "superHYPEway," referring to it as if it were an illusion or a fad, a passing fancy that would fizzle faster than a sparkler dumped in a fishbowl.

False.

The information superhighway is *here.* In fact, we can now choose from more information superhighways than you can shake a cellular phone at. We've been living in the middle of information superhighways for so long we take them for granted.

Radio is an information superhighway. Television (network or cable, take your pick) is an information superhighway. The telephone system is an information superhighway. Books and newspapers and magazines and newsletters provide information superhighways. Even the much-maligned postal system is an information superhighway. All of these systems deliver information—in vast quantities—and they deliver it a heck of a lot *faster* than you could if you got in your car and went out on the real highway and tried to retrieve that information for yourself.

Some of these information superhighways are one-way, and some of them are interactive. When you talk with someone on the telephone, for instance, you get instant, interactive feedback. Radio, network TV, and cable programs also promote a kind of interactivity with viewer/listener call-in shows. It's clear that we already have plenty of interactive information superhighways.

The New Media Godzilla—The PC

What's really causing all the ruckus is the new kid on the block— the personal computer. The PC represents the potential—and threat—of swallowing up all the other media and spitting them out like used data. The PC snatches power out of the hands of the traditional media and places it squarely on the desktop of the user. The PC, connected to the rest of the world via a modem and telephone line, represents a completely new communications medium that will deftly mix elements of the traditional media such as telephones, televisions, and newspapers, and it will do it at the bidding of the computer user and not the media provider.

No one knows for sure if the computer will eat all the other communications technologies alive. Television, after all, didn't kill radio (but the CD certainly buried the LP, and ink on paper quickly replaced the practice of carving cuneiform characters in stone). Of one thing, however, there is no doubt: computer technology will affect each and every medium it comes into contact with in significant ways.

And one other thing. Computer technology has created—and will continue to create—*new electronic media.* Bulletin board systems. Online services. Interactive CD-ROM discs. Electronic Data Interchange. The Internet.

New media. What do those two words mean? Since this is a book written for marketers, here's a better question: what do the words NEW MEDIA mean to *marketers?* Answer: NEW MARKETING OPPORTUNITIES. Specifically, computer-activated new media will allow more marketers to "digicast" more marketing messages to more customers with greater speed and at lower cost.

That's right. Traditional marketers may not yet understand the importance of new electronic media. They may be intimidated by the technology. Some will angrily resist the need to explore and test the digital waters.

Not you. You're beyond "interested." You want to know *more.* If that means you have to learn something new—so be it. If you have to invest some time and effort getting a basic grip on the technology before it starts paying off—well, you understand that that's the price of admittance to the game. Because you suspect that traditional marketing is, in many ways, a horse and buggy compared to the sleek, aerodynamic Ferrari of Cybermarketing.

This book, of course, is written for you, the soon-to-be Cybermarketer.

Oh, by the way: Cybermarketers *will rule* the marketplaces of the near-term future. Here's a brief history lesson to show you why.

Linking Computers: Trend of the 80s

In the last decade, business made a massive transition from the use of solitary, unconnected mainframe, mini-computer, and PC computers to the adoption of networked systems. Corporations realized that there were major advantages in linking individual systems so that users could share information, so they invested in networking in a very big way. You might even call the 1980's the decade of *networked computing.*

Linking Networks: Trend of the 90s

This decade may well be the decade of *inter-networked* computing. The most significant information technology trend in the last years of this century is the "opening up" of corporate networks by linking them up with other networks, and also the linking of individual computers to the vast "network of networks" that includes the worldwide Internet.

Linking Technologies: 2000 and Beyond

The next step in this transition, the one that everyone was anticipating when talking about the information superhighway, is the linking of different communications technologies into one seamless whole. That means computers combined with telecommunications networks combined with cable TV combined with satellite technology—you get the idea. The obstacles to such a convergence are massive, but they will be overcome sometime early in the next century. The individual media forms that this new "supermedia" will be based on won't disappear completely—there will simply be a much higher level of integration between them. And at the heart of it all will be the supermedia's superbrain: the computer microprocessor.

The implications that these transitions hold for business are nothing short of revolutionary. And the implications for marketing are no less so.

Highways and Marketplaces

Let's talk a little more about highways and superhighways.

Roads are built for a number of reasons, primary among these, commerce. Roads allow goods to be moved from one place to another. Roads allow buyers to get to the marketplaces of sellers, and they allow sellers to pack up their goods and take them wherever buyers are found.

When the automobile was in its infancy, most people would go on trips just for the enjoyment of driving. Going out for a Sunday drive in the country was great fun, even with all the potholes and breakdowns along the way. But soon, automobile technology was being used to move goods from point A to B, and when people took trips in their cars, it was to go to the store or to go to work. I don't know for sure, but I would guess that over 80 percent of automobile travel today has something to do with commerce of one sort or another. Going to the mall to buy something. Driving to work. Taking a trip to the movies or the restaurant. (Yes, that's entertainment, but it also involves spending money.)

I think that's also the way it is with the online world today. Your car is your computer and the modem is the engine—it takes you where you want to go. Right now, most people want to have fun with their "electronic cars," they don't want to think about business, they don't want to see billboards or malls littering "their" online landscape.

The debate rages: Does advertising belong on the Internet? Will it destroy the "ambiance" of the online world? Won't it all be too commercial?

It's a moot point, for several reasons. First, the people who are opposed to business having a presence in the online world have already lost. *We're here.* There's a stampede of businesses going online right now. Second, business is going to create some of the most interesting online information and attractions on the superhighway. (See Chapter 18 for more on that.) And finally, if commercial interests are somehow blocked from doing business on the official information superhighway, they'll just take their business elsewhere. There are already myriad networks businesses are using to conduct different forms of electronic commerce, and there will certainly be more options to choose from as time passes.

The World of Electronic Commerce

Companies are now realizing that there's a whole new world being created online. Individuals and businesses are buying and installing modems at an incredible rate. The membership numbers for online services like America Online and CompuServe are skyrocketing. More and more people are dialing into electronic bulletin board systems to find information and interact with other users online.

This presents business opportunities to those who see these online users as potential customers. They want to know how to reach consumers and business buyers online. They want to know how they can create an electronic "presence" for themselves online—to raise an electronic flag and say, "here we are." They also want to know how the use of interlinked electronic networks can simplify and cut costs from their business processes—turning paper-based correspondence (purchase orders, price quotes, etc.) into *electronic messages.*

As Chris Roeckle, Senior Managing Editor of *Communications Week* magazine, puts it, "What the term electronic commerce implies is that *technology itself* will play a front-end role in a company's selling of products and services . . ."

There are surely going to be winners and losers in the new world of electronic commerce. Some support personnel whose job it was to manage routine marketing and distribution functions are going to see their jobs automated away. There will also be companies who don't respond to these changes who will fall by the wayside.

But there will also be winners as a whole new industry revolving around electronic commerce is born. New jobs and new services will be created—from specialists who design electronic ads, catalogs, and brochures to people whose expertise is in setting up electronic "hypertext" links between documents to companies that buy space on the electronic superhighway and rent or sell storefronts to other businesses.

Marketing and Cybermarketing

Most of us would define marketing as *whatever you do to promote the growth of your business.* It can include market research, publicity, advertising, sales, merchandising & distribution, and customer service & support.

If that's marketing, what's Cybermarketing? The dictionary definition of "cyber" is "the science of the control of complex systems," but in popular usage it has come to have a different meaning—"cyber" has to do with the non-physical "place" where computers and communications meet.

Cybermarketing means: *using the power of online networks, computer communications, and digital interactive media to reach your marketing objectives.*

Traditional Marketing/Traditional Problems

Before we can answer the question of what really makes Cybermarketing unique, we have to take a look at traditional marketing techniques and practices.

• *Traditional marketing is often expensive.* It can cost a lot of money to produce and print brochures, product sheets, and catalogs. It's also expensive to keep support personnel on hand to answer inquiries from customers, and it costs a lot of money in postage and shipping fees to send information to prospects.

• *Traditional marketing can be a very time-intensive process.* Mistakes have to be corrected, revisions have to go back to the ad agency or printer, and you often have to wait months for an ad that you've placed to appear in a publication.

• *Traditional marketing often has a "hit-and-miss" quality to it.* We've all had the experience of playing "telephone tag" with an important customer or contact. Many of us have known the frustration of sending out a huge direct mail effort and receiving a tiny response, or had the sinking feeling that the audience we're reaching isn't quite the right fit for the product or service we're selling.

Cybermarketing, naturally, can't eliminate all of these problems. And, in most cases, Cybermarketing will not replace traditional forms of marketing anyway. Instead, it will both add to and subtract from today's marketing mix. It will add more interactivity. But it will subtract costs. It will add more customer choices. But it will remove marketing's dependence on paper. It will add more "information value" to products and services. But it will take away barriers to starting a business or extending a business into international markets. And frankly, it will turn upside down some old notions we've held of what marketing is all about.

Seven Advantages of Cybermarketing

If Cybermarketing didn't offer tangible advantages when compared to traditional forms of marketing, it would quickly be labeled a novelty or a gimmick, and rightly so. But Cybermarketing does offer bottom-line benefits that tie in directly to the demands placed on organizations trying to make the transition into a new economy. Cybermarketing is not some distant dream. Cybermarketing is for real—and plenty of pioneering companies are already incorporating aspects of Cybermarketing into their day-to-day operations.

Here are some of the real-world advantages Cybermarketing can offer your business.

1. *Cybermarketing can save money and help you stretch your marketing budget.* Electronic versions of catalogs, brochures, and spec sheets don't have to be printed, packaged, stored, or shipped. That's real money. When customers manipulate the delivery of product information, you don't need a secretary or assistant to mail that information out. That's a dollar savings that goes straight to the bottom line. Electronic versions of catalogs, brochures, and product spec sheets can be updated online—you don't have to send them back to the printer for changes. That saves money too. And consider this: the cost to electronically provide *more* marketing information (more "pages" or more detail) to a given prospect is very low, in some cases practically zero. The cost to provide identical information to *more* prospects is also extremely low. Finally, it costs very little to *customize* information that is provided electronically.

2. *Cybermarketing can save time and cut steps from the marketing process.* Cybermarketing eliminates steps from the marketing process. Marketing materials no longer have to wait for the printer. They can be online almost immediately. Cybermarketing saves time. Potential buyers don't have to wait for one of your customer sales reps to return a phone call. They can request the information on their own. Cybermarketing gets you to market sooner. Cybermarketing helps you get your message out quickly. Electronic catalogs, brochures, and product spec sheets can be updated instantly. You don't have to wait until quantities of a printed version are used up. E-Mail allows you to exchange information with potential buyers quickly. Cybermarketing can mean the difference between winning the contract and losing it.

3. *Cybermarketing gives customers another way to buy while enabling them to take control of the purchasing process.* Today customers want more. They want more information about the products they buy, more input into the product itself, and support after the sale. Smart marketers can leverage the inherent interactivity of online communications by encouraging the customer to get engaged in

making decisions about the product. Let them choose the color, select the shipping method, and place the purchase order themselves. The more you can get the customer involved in the process of customizing the product and the selling process to meet their particular needs, the more likely it is that you will get the sale.

4. *Cybermarketing can be information-rich and interactive.* It appeals to information-hungry buyers, analytical buyers. It allows buyers and current customers to search and locate the information they need quickly.

5. *Cybermarketing can offer you instant international reach.* On-line networks have created an instant global community. Cyber marketing erases the time and distance barriers that get in the way of conducting business transactions with customers in other countries. The fax machine did a great deal of the work in knocking down those barriers—and now electronic mail, with its standardized addressing system, is helping to smash them completely.

6. *Cybermarketing can lower barriers to entry and offer equal-opportunity access.* There's a now-famous cartoon from *The New Yorker* magazine showing two dogs having a conversation. One of them is sitting in front of a computer terminal, and he tells the other one, "On the Internet, no one cares if you're a dog." It's also true that when you're doing business online, distinctions related to your ethnic background or your gender or even the size of your business don't seem to matter as much. The online world is a great leveler. And Cybermarketing helps to lower many of the marketplace barriers that have held some would-be entrepreneurs from full participation in the free market system.

7. *Cybermarketing can be continuously available.* One of the nicest attributes of an online information server is that it is always on the job, twenty-four hours a day, 365 days a year. It doesn't take a vacation, doesn't call in sick, and doesn't spend company time making personal phone calls. Your Cybermarketing sales assistant never sleeps—so it can be selling for you while the rest of your company is in bed for the night.

Cybermarketing has a lot to offer when compared to traditional forms of marketing. It's not about to replace traditional advertising, direct marketing, and face-to-face selling—but it will extend it and expand traditional marketing in new directions and in ways that will benefit both buyers and sellers.

Who This Book Is Written For

This book was written for business people involved in marketing a product or service, whether or not they have "marketing" in their titles. You may be a marketing executive, a sales manager, an advertising director, a market research specialist, or a product support manager. You may be an entrepreneur with a tight budget, or a VP for a Fortune 500 corporation. Whatever "hat" you wear, you'll find value in Cybermarketing.

The book has relevance to both business-to-business and consumer marketing professionals. It also has important information for suppliers of marketing support services, including marketing consultants, ad agencies, and PR firms.

Managers of high-technology, information, media, and entertainment industry companies will recognize a good deal of the content included here, because their industries are among the earliest adopters of Cybermarketing techniques. But their low-tech and no-tech brethren will also find a great deal that they can adapt to their businesses as well.

By purchasing this book, you're making a statement that you're not just *interested* in using new media to achieve your marketing objectives, but that you want to *learn how, right now,* and that you're willing to put your money where your mouth is.

Don't worry if you haven't yet started to make the transition to doing business online, there's no need to feel left out. In the following chapters, you'll find out exactly what kind of hardware and software you need to make the online connection. We'll also look at a wide variety of networks and service providers who can help you make the transition from the "digitally disadvantaged" to becoming a *wired* individual or organization.

About This Book

In this book, you'll read case histories of companies who have successfully tested electronic marketing techniques. They will share what worked and what didn't—and why.

The book is divided into three sections. We cover the tools and technologies that you need to be familiar with before you can begin to market online. The second section focuses on marketing tasks you can perform online. The final section is devoted to making it work for you by integrating these new media into your marketing plans.

In practically every chapter you'll find numerous mentions of organizations that can provide additional information and vendors that supply products relevant to the content of the chapter. To help you find contact information quickly and easily, we've included a "Connection Section" at the end of each chapter. There is also a glossary at the back of the book that defines many of the acronyms, buzzwords, and technical terms you're likely to encounter in Cyberspace.

By the way, electronic addresses given in the book are highlighted between angle brackets: $<$ $>$. For example, $<$*charlie brown@peanuts.com*$>$. Filenames are highlighted in boldface like this: **inside-info.txt.**

It's no secret that things are changing fast in the areas of electronic commerce and online marketing. Every day there are announcements of new services, new software and new technologies that weren't available yesterday. *Cybermarketing* is as current and complete as possible at press time. (You may be interested to know that my publisher and I worked together to hyperdrive the normal publication process in order to get the book into your hands as quickly as possible.) This book will provide you with a solid foundation in the applications and technologies associated with Cybermarketing, which can apply to your marketing campaign, today, tomorrow, or five years from now.

Acknowledgments

To Julie, for love and assistance . . .
To family and friends for support . . .
To the editors and marketers at AMACOM . . .
To anyone in the growing digital marketplace who
     contributed in any way . . .
To all of you who buy or read this book . . .
                    . . . my thanks.

Part I

Grab the Keys to the Digital Media Superhighway

The universe of computing, communications, and digital media is divided into three basic parts: hardware, software, and services. Part I covers each of these areas in detail, exploring the vehicles, tools, and technologies that will take you into the online universe.

If you already consider yourself high-tech literate, you may decide to jump to Part II, which focuses on marketing activities you can engage in online. Other readers who are less familiar with computers and communications may need a brief tutorial before diving into deep digital waters and should read the following pages.

First, a quick clarification: *Being online* usually refers to communication between computers via a telephone line or some other telecommunication link. The computers can be situated across the street from each other or across the planet. Another standard interpretation of the word *online,* however, refers to the ability to instantly access database information from your computer, usually from a CD-ROM disc. CD-ROM databases and CD-ROM marketing materials are vital applications for marketers, and this book covers CD-ROM marketing applications.

1

Fire Up Your Engine: Computers, Modems, and Network Connections

In a tiny town in the Sierra Nevada foothills in northern California, the seventy-year-old owner of the local telephone company is getting ready to move his 2,400 rural customers onto the information superhighway. Ralph Hoeper, owner of Foresthill Telephone in Foresthill, California, has approval from the state Public Utilities Commission to begin installing and charging for high-speed ISDN access. The new service will help area businesses connect to the Internet and access a wide variety of online services, including teleconferencing and document sharing. "We're a little ahead of the big boys now," says Hoeper.

If you think the information superhighway is going to take some time to pick up speed, you're betting the wrong way. All around you, all across America, companies and communities are signing up to be part of this information revolution. If you aren't linked up yet, the next few chapters are going to offer you an accelerated course to connectivity, a kind of driver's ed for the infobahn.

This chapter covers the electronic gear required for online and interactive communications. After looking at the computer itself, it reviews the necessary peripheral equipment and the details of the physical communications link. Fasten your seat belts, friends, it's time to kick into hyperdrive.

Computers and New Media

It doesn't matter what kind of computer platform you use—IBM-compatible DOS or Windows machines, an Apple Macintosh, or a UNIX work station—you can conduct business online. And you can reach all but the most remote regions of cyberspace even with an antiquated, outmoded, beat-up computer system and a modem. But don't drag that old Kaypro or IBM PCjr out of the closet just yet. I'm not recommending that you use a dinosaur. With ancient equipment it will take longer to get where you want to go and do what you want to do online; in addition, you won't have access to the best that online networks have to offer.

If you decide to tap into online services that make extensive use of graphics, for example, you'll need a relatively fast computer (one that runs on at least a 386 chip) because graphics require more computing power. Having a faster modem also helps.

Computer manufacturers and resellers are pushing a new category of computers that emphasize multimedia capabilities. These machines have built-in CD-ROM drives, sound cards, and speaker systems. All these extras, of course, add to the price of the system, but it's a good idea to consider making your next PC a multimedia PC. There's been an explosion in the number of CD-ROM discs available for PCs, and many CD-ROM titles provide marketing-related information. (See Chapter 3 for details on CD-ROM technology.) Note that buying a multimedia PC doesn't mean you can produce CD-ROM discs from your PC. You'll need additional hardware and software tools to do that, but if you eventually plan on producing CD-ROMs to support your company's marketing objectives, owning a multimedia PC is certainly a step in the right direction.

Modems for Marketers

The other essential piece of equipment for getting online is a modem. A modem acts as a kind of interpreter to let your computer exchange information with virtually any other modem-equipped computer using regular telephone lines. *Modem* stands for "modulator/demodulator." Computers communicate in digital bits that can't be transmitted over telephone lines, so modems translate these digital bits into electronic signal tones that can be sent over the wires. The modem at the receiving end then changes those tones back into bits for the computer on the other end of the line.

Whether you're using your modem to send a sales report to your marketing rep at an out-of-state trade show or firing it up to cruise the information highway, you need to make sure that it is properly installed and that you understand some basic communication technology. Prior to the development of modems, the only way computer users could communicate with their distant electronically inclined colleagues was by copying disks and sending them through the mail. The biggest engineering challenge for early modem developers was trying to link their modems to many different types of computers. That problem has been overcome with the adoption of industry standards that allow all modems to connect to almost any computer. More on that in a moment.

Modems are either internal (residing on a card within your computer) or external, packaged either as a stand-alone product or rack-mounted for operation in the telecommunications closet of a large computer installation. Internal modems are generally the least expensive, since they don't have a protective case, indicator lights, or a separate power supply.

By 1995 more than one-third of the PCs in the United States, and more than two-thirds of portable PCs, will ship with factory-installed fax/modems. Buying a PC with a pre-installed modem is usually less expensive and more convenient than buying and installing one yourself.

Modem Speeds and Modem Standards

The use of modems has increased steadily since their introduction due to significantly increased data transmission speeds and the ever-expanding range of online services that modem users can access.

The rate at which modems transfer bits of information (bit rate) is usually measured as *bps* or "bits per second." The term *bit*, a contraction of *binary digit*, refers to the smallest unit of information that a computer can use.

Modem speeds range from the ancient 300 bps modems (which transmitted information through a telephone handset) to the merely old at 1200, 2400, and 4800 bps. Most modems sold today transmit data at 9600 or 14,400 bps. Modems which transmit at speeds of 28,800 bps or more are on the market now, and will likely become the new standard sometime in 1995.

If you listen to a modem while it establishes a connection with another modem, you'll hear a variety of tones, beeps, and squawks. This chatter is the two modems trying to find a common "language" so they can speak with each other. The noises are dictated by industry standards that describe every aspect of a modem's signal. The complete collection of international modem standards could fill a bookcase.

Buying the Right Modem

Don't buy a modem slower than 14,400 bps. A slower modem is unsatisfactory if you want to send or retrieve files of any significant size. Higher modem speeds are particularly important to salespeople on the road who want to tap into their company's local area network (LAN) via modem or for marketing managers who need to send large files (like desktop publishing documents) to ad agencies or printers. Some commercial online services add a surcharge to use faster modems, but those charges are usually offset by the savings gained by spending less time online.

Today there are well over 250 companies that manufacture modems. Some of the best known names include AT&T, Boca Research, Hayes, Intel, Microcom, Motorola, Practical Peripherals, Supra, and Zoom.

Installing a New Modem

If you choose to buy an external modem, your first step is connecting the modem to your computer. Macintosh users simply connect the modem's RS232 cable to the port with the phone icon. If you're installing an internal or "board" modem into a Macintosh, the system software will usually recognize the modem and enable your computer to talk to it, although you'll still need a basic communications software program (see Chapter 2) to control your online sessions.

Modem installation in IBM-compatible PCs is somewhat more complex. You'll need to assign your modem to a communications, or COM, port on your PC. You may need to set the jumpers or switches on the internal modem or on the serial card to which an external modem is connected. The instructions that come with your modem will indicate how to do all this, but if you'd rather avoid the hassle, ask your computer dealer to install it for you. Some will do the job for free, and others charge a small fee.

Phone Line Connections

You don't need a fancy telecommunications link to cruise the information superhighway. In fact, a simple POTS (Plain Old Telephone Service) connection will, in most cases, do nicely.

If you have a spare line in your office you can dedicate that line to your modem, or have your phone company come in and install a new line. If you purchase an internal modem, you'll plug that line right into a phone jack located on the back of your PC. If you have an external modem, you'll run the main line to the modem and a short connecting line to your PC.

If you need to share your modem line with your telephone or fax machine, you can buy devices that automatically route incoming calls to the appropriate device. A telecommunications company called Hello Direct carries several products of this type.

Some marketers find that a standard modem will not work in their office environment. That may be because their company uses a special digital telephone service called ISDN (Integrated Services Digital Network, explained later in this chapter). They will need an ISDN modem to access online services.

Others have problems routing modem calls through their office switchboard system. A company called Radish Communications has a product called InsideLine that addresses this need.

Modem Software

Most modems come bundled with a simple version of the software required for them to talk to other modems. This basic communications software will allow you to select modem commands (such as dialing, connecting, transferring files, or hanging up the phone line) from a simple series of menus. You may decide at some point that you need more features, and there are plenty of sophisticated communications software programs on the market that will automate tasks like sending electronic messages and accessing the Internet. See Chapter 2 for a review of some of these programs.

Your modem's software allows you to designate settings for communicating with online services like bulletin board systems. The most common communications settings are as follows:

- Set "auto answer" to NO.
- Set "parity" to NONE.
- Set "data bits" to 8.
- Set "stop bits" to 1.
- Set 45 seconds as the time to wait before terminating a phone call.
- Set "local echo" to OFF.
- Set "terminal emulation" to ANSI.

These settings are appropriate for most dial-up services you'll be accessing. If you dial up a bulletin board system and, after connection, see lines of random characters on your screen, call the service provider and ask if you need to make changes to these settings to access their service.

Getting Your Office Network Online

The simplest way to connect a small office to online services is to purchase a modem for each PC and then supply each user with either a line-sharing device switch or individual phone line for their modem.

If you plan to connect ten users or more, you should begin to look at the option of creating a central access point through which you'll route all of your office's data transmissions. Your local phone company or Internet access provider can explain the kinds of hardware and software you'll need and make recommendations on the type of telecommunications connection that will best fit your communications needs.

New, Faster Ways of Delivering Online Services

Question: How do satellite technology, cable TV, and digital telephone service relate to online computing? Answer: They each hold the promise of delivering faster, more responsive, truly multimedia access to online services.

First, let's look at the satellite angle. Hughes Network Systems is rolling out a high-speed information delivery system it calls DirecPC. DirecPC consists of a twenty-four-inch antenna, coaxial cable, and adapter card attached to your PC. The satellite attaches to an exterior wall of the user's home or office. The system can transmit files, news, information, real-time audio and video, or any sort of digital materials to your desktop at many times the speed of a modem and telephone line.

Another breakthrough could come from delivering Internet and online services access through cable. The cable wiring that delivers cable TV signals can move information up to 1,000 times faster than existing telephone lines. Cable companies are developing the capability to split that cable and attach one wire to your computer and one to your TV, without affecting your cable TV signal in any way. The wire running into your computer will be able to access the Internet and online services at lightning speeds. All that's required is some new equipment at the office of the cable company and a special cable modem or adapter attached to your PC. Zenith already markets what they call the MetroAccess HomeWorks line of cable modems to meet this need. Intel is working on a CablePort line of cable modems as well. Several cable operators are testing services of this type, including Comcast in Philadelphia and Cox Cable (in partnership with Prodigy) in San Diego.

Meanwhile, Pacific Bell is partnering with America Online, CompuServe, and Prodigy to offer subscribers high-speed digital telephone access using PacBell's Home ISDN service. ISDN (Integrated Services Digital Network) uses standard telephone lines to deliver digital (instead of the standard analog) signals and allows you to conduct a phone conversation while your computer uses the same line to simultaneously transmit or receive data. ISDN offers online access speeds up to four times that of a 14,400 bps modem, provided you equip your PC with a digital access device such as ISDNtek's Cyberspace Internet Card or Motorola's TA210 ISDN terminal adapter. ISDN service is available from more and more telephone service providers, and more and more telephone customers—especially customers that use online services—are beginning to ask for it.

HOT TIP: Low-Cost One-Call Voice and Data Sharing

A small company called Radish Communications Systems has created an open communications protocol (i.e., other manufacturers and software companies can adopt it and incorporate it into their products) called VoiceView. VoiceView allows standard modems to switch between voice and data during a single phone call over a single phone line. While speaking, VoiceView users can momentarily mute the voice call to send or receive a stream of data containing audio files, fax, video, or text data. When the file has been relayed, the voice call can resume. Once this technology is in widespread use, you won't have to say, "I'll fax you our price sheet, then call you back once you've had time to look it over." You'll fax it immediately—while the call is in progress—on the very same phone line—and continue with the sales presentation. In some cases, this technology can cut hours, or even days, out of the sales cycle.

VoiceView isn't as powerful as ISDN, but it is less expensive; and it doesn't require specialized ISDN phone adapters. A number of major modem manufacturers have pledged to add VoiceView capability to their product lines, but the real test will be the software applications that will smoothly merge the flow of voice and data. These applications will make online, real-time, computer-integrated sales pitches and customer presentations productive and fun to participate in.

ViewBridge, a Radish product that uses VoiceView technology, is already on the market. You connect ViewBridge between your telephone and wall jack, and another connection links it to your PC. To switch from voice conversation to data transfer, you simply click on a button on your computer screen.

The sooner new access technologies such as these take hold, the better. Consumers and business professionals who are rushing to set up connections to online services and the Internet will soon find that the information superhighway can run at hyperdrive speed right through their desktop PC, while marketers who use the highway to deliver advertising and sales messages will confidently be able to use the full range of digital multimedia to tell their stories.

Summary

This chapter looked at the kind of computer and communications hardware needed to access computer bulletin boards, online services, and the Internet. It touched on computers, modems (what they are, how they work, how to install them), and finally telecommunications connections, including standard phone lines, POTS, ISDN, and other high-speed communications links.

The next chapter reviews the amazing range of software programs available to help you manage your online communications and perform tasks online.

Chapter 1 Connection Section

Contact information for organizations and resources mentioned in or related to this chapter:

AT&T Paradyne, manufacturer of modems, 813-530-2000

Hayes Microcomputer Products, manufacturer of modems, 800-934-2937

Hello Direct, catalog with telephone productivity tools, 800-444-3556

Hughes Network Systems, manufacturer of the DirecPC Satellite delivery system, 301-428-5500

Intel, manufacturer of modems, 503-681-8080

ISDNtek, Cyberspace Internet Card, an ISDN adapter card for PCs, 415-712-3000

Microcom, manufacturer of modems, 617-551-1000 or 800-822-8224

Modems Made Easy, by David Hakala, Osborne/McGraw Hill, 1993

Motorola, manufacturer of modems, 800-426-1212 or 800-766-4883

MultiTech Systems, manufacturer of modems, 800-328-9717

New Riders Guide to Modems, by Esther Schindler, New Riders Publishing, 1994

Practical Peripherals, manufacturer of modems, 805-497-4774

Radish Communications, VoiceView voice and data sharing protocol, 303-443-2237

Supra Corp., manufacturer of modems, 503-967-2410

U.S. Robotics, manufacturer of modems, 800-USR-CORP

2

Check Your
Instrument Panel:
Communications
Software

Your computer's turned on, your modem's plugged in, the phone line is set. Other than an account with an online service provider, what more could you possibly need? Just one more item: communications software to help you navigate your way through cyberspace. This chapter offers a guide to the main categories of communications software you can use to seek out information online, exchange messages with your clients, design electronic marketing materials, and conduct electronic commerce.

What Is Communications Software?

Simply put, communications software helps you perform communications-related tasks, like dialing up an electronic bulletin board from your computer or transferring files between computers. Communications software can assist you in managing the activities you perform online during the time you are "logged on" (connected to) a remote computer in what is known as a "communications session."

It Helps You Get Connected

Some communications programs include the proper settings for many online services (see Figure 2-1). All you have to do is select

Figure 2-1. Crosstalk for Windows from DCA.

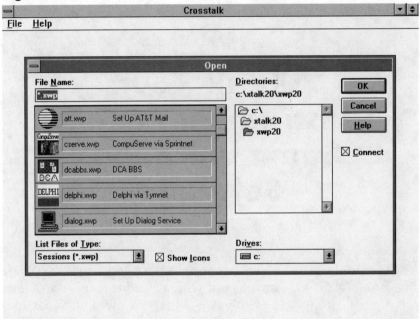

the service you want and hit the *enter* key; the software automatically dials the service and connects you.

It Acts as an Interface

Choosing the right type of communications software is important, because your software should act as a friendly interface between you and the complexities of the networks and computers you're connected to. The software program you're using can either limit or broaden your online options. And it can have a direct impact on your effectiveness as a online marketer. The good news is there are many wonderful communications software products on the market, although it's tough to find a single program that will handle all of your communications needs.

It Manages Communications Tasks

Some communications programs can handle certain tasks automatically, with no assistance from you; for instance, dialing up a remote computer and retrieving electronic mail or automatically sending a file to someone electronically requesting information on your product line.

It Configures Your Modem

When you start your communications software for the first time, a number of settings need adjustment. This process is meant to properly configure your modem so that it can connect with the services you wish to access. The user manual that comes with your modem will explain exactly how to set up your communications program. Here are some of the standard pieces of information you will need to make a connection using your communications software.

- *Phone number.* Simply input the phone number of the modem you want to dial. If your modem needs to dial a "9" to get an outside line, include that here.
- *Port.* This lets the software know which COM port you're using. (Most communications software packages are preset for COM1, so if you're using a different port, you'll have to let the software know.)
- *Transmission speed or baud rate.* Set this to the highest speed your modem can use.
- *Character and data format.* Don't worry about what this means. Just remember that all computers use the standard setting of eight data bits, no parity, and one stop bit (8 + None + 1). Set your software accordingly unless you know the receiving computer uses a different setting or your screen retrieves a lot of garbled information, in which case you probably need a different setting. Contact the operator of the other computer to find out what it is.
- *Terminal emulator.* Different types of computers use various methods for displaying information on the screen. They may use special codes which tell the computer to change screen colors or display certain kinds of characters. Most bulletin board systems use a display method known as ANSI or ANSI BBS. Some computers use the most basic type, called TTY (i.e., teletypewriter) which displays plain text only. If you have a question, contact the system operator to find out what the setting should be.

- *File Transfer Protocol.* This is a standard system of rules by which your computer exchanges files with another computer. If you are going to send files to another computer (uploading) or get files from the other computer (downloading), you need to use the correct protocol. Bulletin board systems (BBS) often let you choose the type of file transfer method you'd like to use from a menu. XMODEM is a slow but reliable transfer method. ZMODEM is faster and allows you to send whole groups of files.

When you're ready to go online, simply tell the software to connect, or dial. Most modems have a speaker or use your computer's speaker to let you monitor their activity. You'll hear the modem dialing the number, making a connection, and then a high-pitched squeal coming from the answering modem. The two modems then quickly work out a common communications protocol so they can talk to each other. At the end of all this, you'll hear a hushed, fuzzy tone called the *carrier signal.* This means the two modems have negotiated successfully and are ready to talk.

When you finish a communications session that transpires without a hitch, save all the communications settings for that particular session in a file after your modem disconnects. Assign a file name that identifies who you were calling, so that you can quickly retrieve the settings the next time you need to dial that number.

What Kind of Communications Software Do You Need?

Communications software can range from very basic programs to highly complex packages packed with features and capabilities. Some programs focus on providing access to one type of communications medium, some to another. A few are designed to execute a single function, such as exchanging electronic messages. Others aim to be all-in-one software solutions. Which program is right for you?

Like so many questions in the world of computers, the answer is, "it depends." It depends on the kinds of online services you want to access; it depends on the kinds of marketing activities you want to engage in online; and it depends on how much money you have to spend on software.

It also depends on the role you choose to play on the information superhighway. The role you play will, to a significant degree, determine what communications tasks you need to perform and which marketing objectives you can accomplish online. See which of these three roles fits you best.

Are You a Seeker?

Seekers look for information and services online. Seekers want to access online databases to gather data and conduct market research. Seekers are looking for answers to specific questions. They typically want access to as many potential sources of information as possible.

Are You a Collaborator?

Collaborators use online resources to work with and communicate with others. Collaborative marketers want to exchange information, share ideas, and propose new projects and partnerships. Collaborators want to make it as easy as possible to get in touch with others, and they want it to be easy for others to get in touch with them.

Are You a Source?

Sources provide information online. Sources want to raise the flag online and say, "Here I am and this is what I do." Sources want to develop a positive online presence for themselves, their products, and their companies.

Do You Wear Multiple Marketing Hats?

Have you decided which role fits you best? Or can you see yourself involved in any one of the three areas? Over the course of a particular project, in fact, you might shift from one role to another.

As an example, let's say your company is opening a new golf resort in Palm Springs. You decide that retired military officers would be good prospects to buy weekend golf packages. As a *seeker* of information, you go online and try to find out if there is an organization or association for retired military personnel. You find that such an organization does exist and that it even has its own bulletin board system. You contact the operator of the system, and as a *collaborator* exchange electronic messages about offering a special rate to the system's users. A deal is set, and now acting as an *information source,* you set up an online response mechanism to handle inquiries about your special golf package.

Sometimes a seeker, sometimes a collaborator, sometimes a source of information. Most marketers are required to wear whatever hat is necessary to get the job done. What type of software works best for each hat?

Focus on Your Objectives

There are general communications software programs that help you handle multiple objectives, and there are other programs that emphasize only one objective. Communications software is further subdivided into programs that focus on a particular communications medium, such as the Internet or CD-ROM.

The key is to focus on what you need to accomplish online. It's not unusual for new users of computer communications tools to be overwhelmed by the technology and the number of choices. You'll be better able to sort through the various options, especially when it comes to software, if you keep your mind set on what you want to accomplish by going online.

Software to Match Your Marketing Objectives

Let's look at some of the different types of communications software available, and see how they relate to achieving specific marketing objectives online.

Programs for Doing a Little Bit of Everything

General purpose communications software is really designed to manage your modem. In fact, most modems come with a simple communications program that has menus for setting up your modem to communicate with another computer. It dials the number of that computer and then helps you manage online tasks. This type of software is very versatile. You can use general purpose communications software to connect with electronic bulletin board systems, share electronic messages with other modem users, and transfer files to your computer.

There are a number of well-known general communication software packages of this type, including CrossTalk from Digital Communications, ProComm from DataStorm Technologies, QModem from Mustang Software, Relay/PC from Relay Technology, SITcomm (for Macintosh users) from Alladin Systems, Smartcom for Windows from Hayes, and WinComm from Delrina. Some of these programs also manage computer fax activity, and a few are beginning to include features that help you access information resources on the Internet.

Programs for Accessing Specific Online Services

The larger online service providers are like super-charged online bulletin boards that typically offer a broader range of services and resources than the average bulletin board system. You can access many of these services with general purpose communications software, although it may not be your best choice. You'll be accessing the service in *terminal mode,* which means that your screen will display plain text only.

That's why some online services offer proprietary software programs that are specifically designed to help you access and navigate their service. This software gives their service a customized look and feel and helps users connect to the service easily and become productive as quickly as possible.

For example, America Online offers their access software in both DOS and Windows versions. CompuServe has CompuServe Information Manager for DOS or Windows. Dow Jones News/Retrieval offers both News/Retrieval Link and TextSearch Plus for Windows users. Apple's e-World service provides access software for Macintosh users on sign-up, and Prodigy has its own graphical front-end.

Programs for Sending and Receiving Electronic Messages

You can exchange electronic mail through a bulletin board using a general communications program. You can also use the proprietary software provided by the major online services as mentioned in the previous section. Some marketers, however, make such extensive use of electronic mail that they want a separate software package to manage their *e-mail*.

There are a number of software programs that streamline the process of sending e-mail. Some programs provide a single mail collection point for people who use a number of different online services. Others include features normally found in computer word-processing packages, such as a spell-checker or online thesaurus. For more on e-mail (including e-mail software suggestions), see Chapter 4.

Programs for Managing Electronic Transactions

Electronic Data Interchange (EDI) is a system used for transmitting business-critical transactions via networks. EDI software is used by major retailers to send purchase orders to their suppliers, by insurance companies to process claims, and by financial services firms to place orders on behalf of their clients. Originally EDI was used by only the largest companies, but as common standards arise and as prices fall for both software and network transmission fees, more mid-size and smaller companies will jump on the EDI bandwagon. EDI is the focus of Chapter 5, and you'll find a list of EDI software vendors there.

Programs for Creating Portable Electronic Documents

Portable electronic documents (PEDs) refer to complex, graphically rich documents that can be transmitted and shared with others, without regard to the software program the document was created in. Designers and publishers have been transferring simple text or binary files over networks for years, but these new tools allow the distribution of documents that include graphics, fonts, charts, etc.

That's big news for marketers, because it means that you can now give customers access to marketing materials online that are colorful, that use graphics, and that employ a variety of type styles the way they're accustomed to seeing marketing information presented on paper.

Acrobat from Adobe Systems allows marketers to distribute complex documents to customers electronically. Using Acrobat, you can send text or non-text files (spreadsheets, documents, graphics) via modem, preserving color and fonts.

Common Ground from No Hands Software and Replica for Windows from Farallon Computing are document exchange systems that allow you to electronically distribute documents to any one, regardless of the type of computer, applications, or fonts the receiver uses. Both programs also allow users to send along a free document "mini-viewer" to everyone on their distribution list. The mini-viewer is a software program that allows recipients to open and view files created in the application program.

Face to Face from Crosswise Corporation allows two computer users (Macintosh or Windows) to collaborate on a multipage document over a network, modem connection, ISDN digital telephone line, or the Internet. Both users must have a copy of the software. If you are working on a long contract or proposal with a major client, you can create it in real-time online instead of faxing revisions back and forth.

TALKShow from FutureLabs allows multiple users to simultaneously exchange, edit, and review computer files (such as marketing materials, sales reports, ads, newsletters, etc.) via any standard phone line and Hayes-compatible modem, or any LAN, WAN or ISDN network. TALKShow has an unlimited guest licensing program, which allows you to send the program to anyone you wish. The program can also be downloaded by your customers from several online services.

Programs for Searching Internet Databases

Although some of the standard communication programs mentioned in this chapter are beginning to include Internet-related communication tools bundled into their software, there are many software programs and providers that focus specifically on Internet connectivity. Internet access and search software are covered in Chapter 10, and some tools you can use to search Internet databases are introduced in Chapter 11.

Programs for Running a Bulletin Board System

A bulletin board system, or BBS, is a computer that's equipped with special software allowing it to act as an information host or server for remote computer systems. The typical BBS consists of a personal computer that has a few phone lines attached to modems running into it. The bulletin board software program manages the requests and interactions of users calling into the system. Many businesses are deciding it's in their best interests to have their own bulletin board service. That way they have control over the design and content of the system.

If you decide to run your own system, you'll need to purchase bulletin board system software. Some of the best known software programs of this type include PCBoard from Clark Development, Synchronet from Digital Dynamics, TBBS from eSoft, The Major BBS from Galacticomm, and Wildcat from Mustang Software. Setting up a BBS is covered in greater detail in Chapter 15.

Summary

This chapter defined the purpose of communications software and challenged you to identify yourself as a seeker, a collaborator, or a source. It emphasized the importance of selecting communication software based on your marketing objectives and examined a number of software programs in relation to these objectives. The key is to decide which services you want to access (bulletin boards, consumer-oriented online services, the Internet), what objectives you want to accomplish (research, information exchange, publicity, advertising), and how much you can afford to spend on software.

Chapter 2 Connection Section

Contact information for organizations and resources mentioned in or related to this chapter:

Adobe Systems, Acrobat document exchange software, 800-872-3623 or 408-562-6767

Aladdin Systems, SITcomm communications software for Macintosh System 7 users, 408-761-6200

Clark Development Company, PCBoard bulletin board system software, 800-356-1686 or 801-261-1686

Crosswise Corp., Face to Face document collaboration software, 800-747-9060 or 408-459-9060

Datastorm Technologies, Procomm communications software, 314-443-3282

DCA Digital Communications Associates, CrossTalk communications software, 800-348-3221 or 404-475 8380

Delrina Corp., WinComm communications software, 800-268-6082 or 416-441-3676

Digital Dynamics, Synchronet BBS bulletin board system software, 714-529-6328

Durand Communications Network, products for adding graphics and photos to bulletin board systems, 805-961-8700

eSoft, Inc., TBBS bulletin board system software, 303-699-6565

Farallon Computing, Replica for Windows document exchange software, 510-814-5100

Future Labs, TALKShow document collaboration software, 800-933-8887

Galacticomm, The Major BBS bulletin board system software, 800-328-1128

Hayes Microcomputer Products, Inc., modem manufacturer and publisher of Smartcom for Windows communications software, 800-934-2937

Imagen, products for adding graphics and photos to bulletin board systems, 604-687-7511

Mustang Software Inc., QModem communications software and Wildcat bulletin board system software, 800-208-0616 or 805-873-2500

No Hands Software, Common Ground document exchange software, 800-598-3821 or 415-802-5800

Relay Technology, Relay/PC communications software, 800-795-8674

TeleGrafix Communications, Inc., products for adding graphics and photos to bulletin board systems, 714-379-2131

3

Spinning Silver Wheels: CD-ROM Technology

Have you ever harbored a secret dream of becoming a big-time Hollywood producer? (Tell the truth. I certainly have, and I'll bet a lot of other marketing types have as well.) Some of us look at CD-ROM as a means of fulfilling that fantasy by putting sound and images and a storyline on a silver platter that spins round and round in your prospect's PC.

Here's the catch: Creating a multimedia production for CD-ROM, like making a movie, can be a sizable undertaking. It can take a team of five or six people six months or more to create the idea and the outline, secure the rights to whatever data are included in the presentation (including text, video, graphics, photos, and music), script the action, create a storyboard, code the database, draw the graphics, create the documentation, and then finally produce a CD-ROM master disc.

To handle this kind of a production, you'll need a fast PC (at least a 486 or Pentium) with as much as 3 gigabytes of storage capacity on a hard drive or tape drive. Finally, you'll have to get top management to approve the production costs, which can range from $25,000 to over $100,000.

But don't let that burst your bubble just yet. There are plenty of CD-ROM marketing projects you can tackle that don't cost *nearly* that much, which in fact can probably even shave a few dollars from your marketing budget. This chapter takes a quick look at the basic technology behind CD-ROM and examines the process of creating CD-ROM applications.

What Is CD-ROM?

CD-ROM stands for "compact disc-read only memory." It's an optical storage medium that a computer can read information from, but can't write information to. CD-ROM technology allows enormous amounts of information to be encoded onto a small disc coated with aluminum film. CD-ROM drives "read" the spinning discs using a laser beam and are able to quickly retrieve the data imprinted on the surface of the disc.

CD-ROM Discs

CD-ROM discs are similar to the audio compact discs we listen to on our home stereos, although they are much more versatile. A CD-ROM platter or disc is capable of holding 660 megabytes of data, which is the equivalent of about one-half million pages of text. CD-ROM discs can also contain sound, animation, and still or moving video images, although these information formats consume significantly more disc space than plain text.

One CD-ROM disc can contain:

- The entire Yellow Page listings for all the phone books in the United States
- A twenty-one-volume encyclopedia, complete with illustrations, sound effects, and video clips
- A multi-vendor, multimedia catalog with thousands of product images and hundreds of pages of descriptive text

CD-ROM Drives

A CD-ROM drive plays CD-ROM discs. The key difference between a CD-ROM drive and an audio CD player is that the drive captures digital information for a digital host (a PC) whereas the audio player translates digital information for an analog machine (a stereo system).

CD-ROM drives are rapidly becoming standard equipment on new computer systems. CD-ROM drives can be either internal, installed inside the PC case, or an external unit that sits on the desk next to your computer.

A major factor in the overall performance of a multimedia computer system is the speed of your CD-ROM drive. Today's CD-ROM drives, including the fastest drives now available, transfer data at a slower rate than any other peripheral on your system. Your computer's hard disk drive is probably ten times faster than your CD-ROM.

The slowest drives on the market, single-speed CD-ROM drives, transfer data at a rate that's fine for retrieving text and low-level graphics, but produces skipping and delays when accessing video and animation. Double-speed drives largely solve this problem. You'll still notice some skipping of frames in passages of video material, but it will be very slight. Triple-speed drives deliver excellent video and audio quality, and quad-speed drives offer super-crisp screen images and resolution.

Laptop computer manufacturers have been somewhat slow to include CD-ROM drives, sound cards, and speakers in the portable PCs salespeople take on the road for presentations. Sooner or later these tools will be standard equipment on "road warrior" machines, because more and more sales teams are incorporating multimedia into their sales presentations.

A number of electronics manufacturers make CD-ROM drives, including Chinon America, Hitachi, JVC, NEC, Philips Consumer Electronics, Procom Technology, Sony, and Toshiba. Tiger Software is a computer distributor that sells CD-ROM drives from a wide range of manufacturers. See the Connection Section at the end of the chapter for contact information.

CD-Recordable Drives

CD-Recordable (CD-R) drives enable business users to publish on CD-ROM relatively small runs of a large database of information, such as product catalogs or customer support manuals.

CD-R burns, or writes, data on a disc medium that is slightly different than mass-produced CD-ROMs, but your customers' CD-ROM drives will nevertheless be able to read the disc pressed by your CD-R system.

Market Acceptance of CD-ROM

One of the best features of CD-ROM technology is the fact that you can quickly search through information stored on a disc to find a specific image or text reference.

For this reason, CD-ROM discs are fast becoming the preferred medium for reference works such as encyclopedias. In fact, the best-selling home encyclopedia doesn't take up much shelf space in a bookcase anymore since it fits nicely on one CD-ROM disc.

The Optical Publishing Association reports that 4.5 million CD-ROM drives were sold in North America in 1993. The installed base has been doubling every year since 1991. There were 7.7 million drives in use in 1993, and the forecast for 1994 is 15 million. Heavy demand will continue as drive performance increases and prices drop. One computer mail-order company recently advertised a CD-ROM drive for under $70.

Computer manufacturers are taking note of the interest in CD-ROM-equipped PCs, and more of them are including CD-ROMs on their computers as standard equipment. When Compaq unveiled its consumer-oriented Presario computers in late 1994, it announced that nearly every machine in the line would come equipped with a CD-ROM drive and be wired for CD sound output.

There's no doubt that CD-ROM technology is here to stay. CD-ROM drives will become faster, CD-ROM discs will become more abundant, and more marketers will be looking for clever ways to put interactive marketing information on these glimmering discs.

Marketing Applications for CD-ROM

Cybermarketers can put CD-ROM technology to use in at least three important ways:

1. They can purchase CD-ROM discs that feature marketing information databases and use these discs as market re-

search tools to track down information on companies, markets, and prospects.
2. They can produce their own CD-ROM discs to use as promotional tools, creating multimedia sales presentations or digital catalogs carrying information on their product lines.
3. They can produce CD-ROM-based manuals as a customer support tool, with technical information that would normally be delivered on paper or over the phone.

Later chapters cover each of these applications. For now, you will have a chance to examine the technology used in creating CD-ROM discs. Keep in mind that the biggest mistake marketers make with CD-ROM is to "CD-ROMify" plain, text-based information without taking advantage of the interactivity and full range of sensory input available in CD-ROM technology.

Reasons for Pressing Your Own CD-ROMs

There are a number of situations where publishing or pressing your own CD-ROM-based marketing materials makes sense.

If you periodically distribute large volumes of data to customers and prospects, and if the printing, storage, and shipping costs for those materials is a significant expense, consider offering the data in a CD-ROM version. If you have a complex sales story that can be told in an interactive, visual format, CD-ROM will help you make the sale. And if your customer support reference materials need constant updating, it will be easier and less expensive to update CD-ROM discs than to send the whole project to the printer each time new material needs to be inserted.

The CD-ROM Pre-Mastering and Mastering Process

The main drawback in the past to recording your own sales, promotional, or technical support CDs was the cost of CD-R (Compact Disc-Recordable) drives. These drives initially cost $15,000 or more. Prices have been falling rapidly, with CD-R drives now available for under $3,000. The software needed to master and pre-master discs will add another $1,000 to $2,500 to the total cost. The price of recordable media (blank discs) used in CD-R drives has also dropped, making the dream of producing marketing-oriented CD-ROM discs more affordable than ever.

A computer company specializing in multimedia computing, Plasmon Data Systems, recently announced a CD-Recorder for under $3,000. With prices falling to more affordable levels, the pieces are in place for companies to quickly and economically produce limited quantities of their own CDs. In fact, you can produce your own CDs for about 5 cents per megabyte of information. A number of manufacturers make CD-R drives, including JVC, Meridian Data, Pinnacle Micro, Philips, and Sony. Most of the major CD-R drives are carried by dataDisc, a CD-ROM service bureau that also sells blank discs.

Pre-mastering is the process of converting your data into a format that is accepted by standard CD-ROM drives. Pre-mastering software requires a significant amount of computer storage space, up to 640 megabytes, to perform its task. Most pre-mastering software packages support tape drive as well as hard drive options for storing that data. Your pre-mastering software will also help you place the most accessed parts of your data on the inner tracks of the disc, where it will be accessed more rapidly. Your software should allow you to simulate exactly how the final product will be viewed and used by your customers before you commit to making a master disc that will be used to reproduce multiple copies for distribution.

CD-Prepare and CD-Record from Dataware Technologies and Tempra CD Maker from Mathmatica are three popular pre-mastering software packages.

Developing Your Own CD-ROM Applications

Dynamic CD-ROM marketing applications depend, more than anything else, on an effective *interface* that helps your customers access the information on the disc. You can't just dump raw information onto a disc and expect your prospects to use it, much less be persuaded by it. Multimedia presentations full of sound, video, and text cry out for a system to transform the cacophony into a useful, valuable tool.

The first decision you need to make is the form your disc will take. Will it be a primarily text-based presentation? Will it include other media only to support the text? Or will sounds, pictures, and images be the main features, with the text merely a supporting player? This is a critical decision, because the software tools for text-based applications are somewhat different than the software tools for multimedia applications.

CD-ROM marketing discs often use a simple format to help the user navigate through the information on the disc. Figure 3-1 shows a menu from a disc from R.R. Donnelley & Sons. If you choose "Electronic Catalogs and Directories" from this menu, the second screen appears (Figure 3-2).

CD-ROM Indexing, Searching, and Authoring Tools

The three main types of tools used to create CD-ROM applications are indexing, searching, and authoring software.

Indexing

Indexing means that every reference to a particular word, subject, or topic in your text is compiled and noted. Let's say your disc is a directory of all the industrial lighting products your company distributes. Your customer can type in *fluorescent* and quickly see all references to fluorescent products listed on the screen. This list comes from the stored, compiled index.

Intelligent indexing makes a big difference in the useability of your disc. Dumb indexing, on the other hand, wastes disc space. For example, you don't want to index "noise" words, words like *a, the, this, which,* and *where.* You also wouldn't want to index the word *lighting* if your catalog is composed of nothing but lighting products.

You also need to consider whether customers will search for information from certain predefined fields only. For your lighting-catalog disc, for instance, you could decide to define searches

Figure 3-1. Menu from a CD-ROM disc.

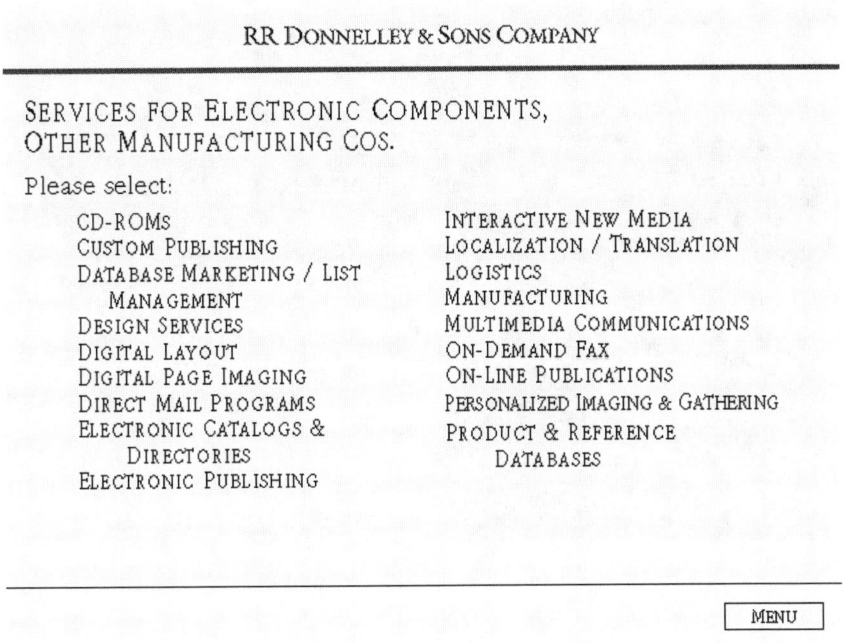

RR DONNELLEY & SONS COMPANY

SERVICES FOR ELECTRONIC COMPONENTS,
OTHER MANUFACTURING COS.

Please select:

CD-ROMS
CUSTOM PUBLISHING
DATABASE MARKETING / LIST
    MANAGEMENT
DESIGN SERVICES
DIGITAL LAYOUT
DIGITAL PAGE IMAGING
DIRECT MAIL PROGRAMS
ELECTRONIC CATALOGS &
    DIRECTORIES
ELECTRONIC PUBLISHING

INTERACTIVE NEW MEDIA
LOCALIZATION / TRANSLATION
LOGISTICS
MANUFACTURING
MULTIMEDIA COMMUNICATIONS
ON-DEMAND FAX
ON-LINE PUBLICATIONS
PERSONALIZED IMAGING & GATHERING
PRODUCT & REFERENCE
    DATABASES

MENU

by type of lighting, name of manufacturer, or part numbers only. In developing your application, you only want to index the elements that the customer will be searching for. That way, you'll create an application that runs faster and is easier for your customer to use.

Searching

After you've indexed the material on your disc, your customer will need a system for retrieving that information. The software tools that perform this function are known as search engines. Some search engines provide users with a list of choices to select from. Others require the user to input a key word that starts the system on a search to retrieve the information. It's usually a good idea to give the user several choices and let them decide how to use the product. Folio Views from Folio, KAware from Knowledge Access, and ROMware from Nimbus are three well-regarded indexing and search and retrieval programs.

Figure 3-2. Screen after choosing from the menu from the CD-ROM disc in Figure 3-1.

ELECTRONIC CATALOGS
AND DIRECTORIES
Digitize text and images to create
a warehouse of electronic information ready to be swiftly updated
and published when needed.
Digitized information also opens
up new possibilities for fast turn-
around of output. Your product
information is now accessible on
your customer's personal computer
through telephone lines anywhere
in the world. ▪

MENU | SERVICES

Authoring

Authoring software usually refers to programs that allow CD-ROM developers to integrate all the different elements of a multimedia presentation into a storyboard with a beginning, middle, and end. The storyboard format allows the developer to view the presentation much as a director would view a film script as it was being created.

Two Windows-based CD-ROM authoring programs are Authorware from Macromedia and Toolbook from Asymetrix. Authorware allows you to create simultaneous events in your application. For instance, a prospect viewing a disc developed in Authorware could request and retrieve pricing information on a golf cart while viewing a video clip of the golf cart zipping across the links. Toolbook provides a set of predesigned templates that allow you to plug text and graphics into attractive screens and menus. Toolbook is a Windows-based program, and you can transfer material from other Windows programs (for example data from a spreadsheet or formatted text from a desktop publishing program) directly into your CD application.

Complete CD-ROM Development Systems

ShowBuilder (from Capitol Multimedia) is an authoring system for CD applications that permits the average computer user to create multimedia marketing presentations on CD. The software helps users create custom marketing presentations that incorporate digital video, still images, graphics, text, and audio, using a simple interface. Capitol packages ShowBuilder with a Sun computer and Philips CD-R equipment.

IPC Technologies markets a CD-ROM mastering system which includes a high-performance Pentium computer, a Yamaha CD-R drive, CD-ROM mastering software, and a 1.7-gigabyte hard drive.

Features That Make CD-ROM an Effective Marketing Platform

Here are a few of the features that have so many excited about the marketing potential of CD-ROM:

- *Multimedia.* CD-ROM marketing discs can include full-color graphics, charts, drawings, and photos for a high-impact multimedia presentation.
- *More multimedia.* CD-ROM marketing discs may also, depending on your budget, include animation, video, music, and sound effects.
- *Customer control.* CD-ROM marketing discs can be organized so that prospects select the information they need from simple menus, even allowing them to see how various options and features affect the price of the product.
- *Flexibility.* CD-ROM marketing discs can be used to achieve a diverse range of marketing objectives: from introducing new products to educating new users, from delivering a complete sales presentation to demonstrating a particular set of product features, and more.

• *Inexpensive shipping.* CD-ROM marketing discs can be mailed for about the cost of a first class letter, far less than the cost of mailing heavy brochures and catalogs.

Design Tips for Creating CD-ROM Discs With Customer Appeal

Avoid the mistake of merely transferring your collateral marketing material sales sheets, brochures, and advertising slicks to CD-ROM. If you're not going to use the inherent capabilities of the CD-ROM medium, stick with your paper-based materials.

If, on the other hand, you're willing to rethink the way you present your marketing message, here are some suggestions that will start you in the right direction.

• *Use the medium.* Use CD-ROM technology's inherent interactivity and multimedia capabilities to create marketing materials that are more valuable to your customers than the printed version of the same materials.

• *Customize information.* Offer your prospects a variety of options for accessing the information on the disc. Some buyers prefer to listen to a narrative, and perhaps others like to read it on-screen. Why not offer both options?

• *Make it quick.* Access to information on disc should be super-fast. Prospects will get frustrated if they have to wait for the disc to retrieve requested information. Some speed issues are out of your control, for example, users may have slow computers or slow CD-ROM drives. But some aspects of access speed are controlled by the software you select to write your program.

• *Offer easy access to data.* Make sure that you offer prospects viewing your disc the opportunity to somehow search for the material they need. Let them type in a key word (product name or product type) that takes them immediately to information on that topic. Or display an index that they can scroll through to highlight and jump to the data they are seeking.

• *Design in upgradability.* As you develop the database of material that will be transferred to disc, keep in mind that at some point you'll probably need to update the information and press a new version of your disc. You'll want to organize information in such a way that it's easy to modify and update.

• *Make a friendly first impression.* Avoid presenting long passages of text as the first "layer" of material the viewer sees. Start with checklists, selector buttons, or brief introductory material that leads to the more complex information.

• *Provide for printing.* If you do include long passages of text on your disc, make sure to position a "print" button on the viewer's screen so that they can print that text and move on.

Three Ways to Squeeze More Value Out of Your Marketing Discs

1. Distribute at trade shows and events.
2. Mail to prospects at a fraction of the cost of a personal sales call.
3. Use as a support tool for a personal sales call and then give to the customer as a leave-behind.

Some Examples of CD-ROM-Based Marketing Applications

Philips Media has helped the distribution division of the Poly-Gram record label create a CD-ROM disc called The Electronic New Release Book. The disc, which will be regularly distributed to music retailers, holds sound samples, video clips, and cover art of all new releases. The disc also includes all product set-up and merchandising information. Retailers can view the information by pointing and clicking on album titles, which reveal more in-depth data. The disc is organized by release date, but record store personnel can zero in on material from Pop, Country, Jazz, or other categories they choose.

Oracle, the major database software company, recently distributed their annual report on CD-ROM. It's a companion to the printed report, with video clips of company officers presenting views of their changing marketplace.

Apple Computer's En Passant CD-ROM project features an electronic catalog showcasing twenty-one mail order and retail companies, including Lands' End, L. L. Bean, Pottery Barn, and Tiffany.

Re:Source Network Solutions is a quarterly "digizine," or digital magazine, produced and distributed on CD-ROM. Pacific Bell Information Services produces and sells advertising on the disc, which is targeted toward users of network equipment and software.

MAX is a CD-ROM product that's sent each month to subscribers of CMP Publishing's *Computer Reseller News* magazine. MAX contains product demos, pricing data, and other detailed vendor information. The first edition of the disc, published in May 1994, carried seventy advertisers, who paid $200 and up to include a product literature page on the disc.

Another publisher packaging information on CD-ROM is *Washington Technology.* The newspaper produces an annual directory called the *Washington Technology Almanac.* The Almanac contains corporate profiles of companies who sell information systems to the government. Participants have the option of including fifteen- or thirty-second video clip commercials or color product animations on their company's profile page.

Printing companies use *The Traveler's Guide to Electronic Prepress* as a presentation to introduce major buyers of printing to the process of planning and executing a complex print project.

Standard Rate and Data Service (SRDS) markets the Electronic Media Kit Library and the Media Planning System for Windows, CD-ROM discs that allow ad agency media planners to review information about thousands of publications, without the mess of having publications and media kits strewn across a desk. The Electronic Media Kit Library is a collection of media kits, updated quarterly, and the Media Planning System is the electronic version of the SRDS guide to publications that allows users to search and locate publications based on up to five different criteria. Each product is updated monthly.

Finally, Seattle, Washington-based Medio Multimedia is launching a national online network, Medionet, which will enable readers of its CD-ROM discs to automatically access sites on the Internet.

The Marketing Future for CD-ROM

CD-ROM burn-units, as previously mentioned, now cost as little as $3,000, but prices are still falling and, at some point, will undoubtedly dip below the magic $1,000 barrier. Then you'll see a significant increase in the number of marketing firms and corporations that decide to create, cut, and press their CDs in-house.

CD-ROM is a technology that is only going to grow. It's based on reliable standards, and CD-ROM discs are simple and fun to use. As more and more consumers become comfortable with using CD-ROM discs in their home computers, and more business users see the value of accessing CD-ROM reference materials in the workplace, smart marketers will seize the opportunity to transfer their sales message to this interactive, entertaining format.

Summary

This chapter looked at the technology behind CD-ROM discs and CD-ROM drives. It noted the rapid growth of the CD-ROM market and the impact that growth will have on certain consumer market segments. It touched on the marketing applications for CD-ROMs and then analyzed the reasons for putting some of your marketing information on disc. Finally, the chapter covered the CD-ROM pre-mastering and mastering process, with a focus on the kinds of hardware and software required for the task. It concluded with a glance at the future of using CD-ROM technology for marketing.

In the next chapter you'll meet a friend of mine and learn why his fanaticism about e-mail could have an impact on the way all of us communicate with customers and clients.

Chapter 3 Connection Section

Contact information for organizations and resources mentioned in or related to this chapter:

AimTech, IconAuthor multimedia development software, 603-883-0220

Apple CD-ROM Handbook: A Guide to Planning, Creating and Producing a CD-ROM, Apple Computer/Addison Wesley, 1993

Asymetrix, Toolbook multimedia development software, 206-462-0501

Capitol Multimedia, Inc., ShowBuilder software for creating CD-ROM-based presentations, 301-907-7000

Chinon America, Inc., manufacturer of CD-ROM drives, 310-533-0274 or, Steve Bosak and Jeffrey Sloman, Que Corp., 1993

CD-ROM: Facilitating Electronic Production, Linda Helgerson, VNR, 1992

CD-ROM Professional, magazine for CD-ROM developers, 800-248-8466

CD-ROM World, magazine for CD-ROM developers and users, 203-226-6967

dataDisc, a CD-ROM service bureau that sells CD-R drives from many manufacturers, as well as QuickSearch CD-ROM search and retrieval software, 703-347-2111

Dataware, CD-Prepare and CD-Record CD-ROM pre-mastering software, 617-621-0820

Designing Interactive Multimedia, Arch Luther, Bantam, 1992

Directory of Multimedia Equipment, Software, and Services, annual directory produced by the International Communications Industries Association

Folio Corp., Folio Views search and retrieval software, 801-375-3700

Hitachi, manufacturer of CD-ROM drives, 914-332-5800

IPC Technologies, Inc., CD-ROM application development system, 800-501-3650

JVC, manufacturer of CD-Recordable drives, 714-965-2610

Knowledge Access International, KAware search and retrieval software, 415-969-0606

Kodak, Kodak PCD Writer CD-R drive, 800-CD-KODAK

Macromedia, Inc., Authorware multimedia development software, 415-442-0200

Mathmatica, Tempra CD Maker CD-ROM pre-mastering software

Meridian Data, manufacturer of CD-Recordable drives and Personal Scribe CD-ROM development software, 408-438-3100 or 800-767-2537

MicroRetrieval Corp., end-to-end CD-ROM development services and re:Search text and image retrieval software, 617-577-1574

NEC Technologies, Inc., manufacturer of CD-ROM drives, 508-264-8000

New Media, magazine for multimedia developers and users, 415-573-5170

Nimbus, ROMware search and retrieval software, 503-626-0595

NowMedia, a CD-ROM disc that explains how to produce CD-ROM presentations, 800-326-4146

Optical Publisher's Association, professional association for CD-ROM content developers, 614-442-8805

Nimbus, ROMware search and retrieval software, 503-626-0595

NowMedia, a CD-ROM disc that explains how to produce CD-ROM presentations, 800-326-4146

Optical Publisher's Association, professional association for CD-ROM content developers, 614-442-8805

Philips, manufacturer of CD-Recordable drives, 800-777-5674

Philips Consumer Electronics, manufacturer of CD-ROM drives, 615-521-4366

Pinnacle Micro, manufacturer of CD-Recordable drives, 714-727-3300

Plasmon Data Systems, manufacturer of CD-Recordable Drives, 408-956-9400

Procom Technology, manufacturer of CD-ROM drives, 714-852-1000

Sony Corp. of America, manufacturer of CD-Recordable drives, 201-930-1000

Tiger Software, distributor of CD-ROM drives and discs, 305-443-8212

Toshiba America Information Systems, manufacturer of CD-ROM drives, 714-583-3111

4

Heavy Traffic:
The E-Mail Express

David Krane, a friend of mine who is a recent graduate of the journalism and public relations program at Indiana University, says there is "absolutely no way" he would have the kind of social life he has without the use of electronic mail. He's able to stay in close touch with family, friends, and fraternity brothers through the use of e-mail, to a degree that he feels would be impossible otherwise. David's dad, for instance, is chairman of the physics department at Oregon State University, and he's a hard guy to reach via phone. But he *always* reads and responds to his e-mail. David finds e-mail messages from former classmates now scattered around the country (and around the world) always popping up on his computer screen at work and at home.

What Is E-Mail?

E-mail, short for electronic mail, is a system for the delivery of digital messages via communication networks from one computer to another. E-mail is the electronic version of the paper memos and letters and envelopes we use to deliver personal and public messages. And just as we use paper-based letters and memos and mailings to promote our products, announce new services, and otherwise communicate with customers, we can now use electronic messages to do the same.

Wired Universities

Why did my friend David become such an avid user of e-mail? His alma mater, Indiana University, started promoting the use of e-mail on their Campus Area Network in 1984 to better link students with faculty and staff. Each student pays a technology fee, approximately $100 per semester, to keep the system up and running. David estimates that of the 38,000 students on the main campus, almost 30,000 are regular e-mail users. Some check their e-mailboxes up to ten times a day, using one of over thirteen hundred PC terminals strategically located throughout the campus. There's a certain level of creative anarchy about the system, including e-mail chain letters, an e-mail dating service, and e-mailed art work from ASCII Michelangelos.

Indiana University isn't the only university to get wired. Harvard, that venerable Ivy League institution, recently spent two years (and several million dollars) to install a super-fast, sophisticated network that allows students to e-mail questions to their Nobel Laureate professors. The network's 10 megabyte-per-second connection (which would allow you to transmit the entire text from this book around the planet in the time it takes to say "tuition increase") now connects 500 freshmen from their dorm rooms to faculty offices, university research libraries, and to the Internet. Before long, the network will create a fiber optic village linking all 12,000 users in a "virtual university."

The Expansion of the E-Mail User Base

If universities are graduating large numbers of students who are heavy users of e-mail and often choose e-mail as their preferred means of sending and receiving information, then marketers should be ready to respond to that preference. These university graduates will be a prime consumer market as well as business buyers and decision makers in the near future.

Recent graduates of wired universities aren't the only ones to catch the e-mail express. Radio personality Rush Limbaugh found love through e-mail. He recently married a computer pen-pal after a whirlwind romance conducted via his CompuServe

e-mail account. Hollywood executives and agents are putting together movie deals by flashing each other electronic messages.
The standard phrase replacing "let's do lunch" is now "do you
need face on that?" (inquiring about the necessity of a person-to-
person meeting).

E-mail is currently one of the computer industry's fastest
growing applications, and millions consider it an indispensable
aid to communications and productivity. The number of workers
using e-mail in Fortune 2000 companies is approaching 15 million, up from 9 million three years ago, according to the Electronic Messaging Association. Companies who have installed
corporate networks are finding that workers soon begin to use e-
mail as the communication medium of choice. A recent poll asked
information systems managers at large and mid-size companies
what they considered the most important application of the information superhighway. E-mail was rated #1 by a wide margin.
One senior manager at a major New York financial services company says that e-mail has reduced his need to initiate international phone calls by over 90 percent.

I've recently met a new group of business people, usually
working in high-technology industries, who actually get a little
miffed if you suggest sending them information via fax or
through the postal system (derogatorily referred to as "snail
mail"). If you have some information to send them, they want it
NOW, unadorned, simple, to the point, and if you can't deliver it
to their e-mail box, they act as if you needn't bother sending it at
all.

Five Advantages of E-Mail Over Other Messaging Systems

E-mail advocates claim that this medium of communication offers
a number of significant advantages:

1. *Digital format.* All information can be managed on screen,
electronically. Recipients can not only read your e-mail proposal,
they can electronically store it, revise it, answer it, or forward it
to other parties, with no hard-copy paper printouts getting in the
way.

2. *Rapid delivery.* Delivery is nearly instantaneous. You can send an electronic message from your office in Chicago to a customer in Australia in a few seconds.

3. *Filtering capability.* The e-mail subject line (a line at the beginning of an e-mail message that highlights the topic of the message, much like the subject line on an interoffice memo) allows users to quickly scan through a list of e-mail messages for critical information. (This certainly beats most voice mail systems, which require you listen to or scan through all of your messages to find out which ones are important.) Cybermarketers can use this subject line like a headline on an ad to grab their prospect's attention with newsworthy information or benefits.

4. *Reliable, secure transmission.* There's rarely an error in transmission, if the addressing information is correct. (Note: e-mail addresses can sometimes be long and fairly complex—full of ampersands @, dots., and underscores __.) Unlike fax machines, which can be out of order, out of paper, or accidentally unplugged (and computer fax modems, which usually require that your computer be turned on to receive a transmission), e-mail systems store your messages for later retrieval. The level of security involved in electronic messages is at least as high, and in most cases higher, than other forms of transmission, including fax and standard mail options.

5. *Low cost.* E-mail messages can be very inexpensive compared to other forms of message transmission (international telephone calls or faxes or overnight document delivery, for instance).

My friend David notes that there's another factor as well, one that he appreciates as a budding public relations professional. E-mail encourages people to use the basics of communication well because it normally doesn't allow the use of visual tricks to beef up a lackluster message. "E-mail forces you to use your command of the language. It tends to level the playing field somewhat between the companies that have access to big ad agencies and graphics departments and companies that just have good ideas. You really have to use the versatility of the English language to get your point across. You can't cut corners with e-mail. It all comes down to " 'how persuasive is your message?' "

Internal vs. External E-Mail

Until recently, most business e-mail has been of the internal, or in-house, variety. It was used to send a note or memo to someone connected to the same corporate network. Although marketers certainly use and value this capability to send messages to other members of their marketing team, they're naturally interested in being able to use e-mail to contact prospects and customers, and to have a vehicle for customers and prospects to contact them as well.

How to Extend Your E-Mail Reach

If your business doesn't yet have the ability to send and receive e-mail outside your company, there are a number of options for you to consider. Your company may choose to set up a gateway that lets users of your internal e-mail system send messages outside the company. Commercial service providers like Compu-Serve, MCI Mail, and Internet can set up this type of link to the outside world.

As an individual user, you can set up a personal account with a consumer-oriented online service like America Online, CompuServe, or Prodigy. Each of these service providers has basic accounts that include e-mail messaging (Chapter 8). You can also access e-mail services when you subscribe to a local bulletin board system (Chapter 6). Virtually all Internet access providers include e-mail services as part of your account (Chapter 10). Or, you can open a single-user account with e-mail providers like AT&T Easylink, MCI Mail, or RadioMail.

As you can see, getting access to e-mail services isn't a problem. You just need to do a little investigation and find out which messaging option best meets your needs.

What to Look for in E-Mail Software

Many online providers integrate an e-mail system with the software you use to navigate their service (see Figure 4-1). You may

Figure 4-1. Typical e-mail software program.

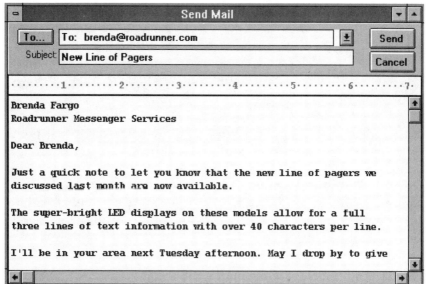

decide, however, that you want or need your own e-mail software package that manages all your electronic messaging activity. If so, here are some features you should look for:

• *Ability to easily manage incoming and outgoing messages.* The best e-mail software systems make it a snap to read, save, delete, and forward messages. Some packages also allow you to categorize and prioritize messages.

• *Ability to send CCs and BCCs.* Marketers need to have e-mail software that allows them to easily send a "cc," or courtesy copy. Sometimes a number of people need to get copies of a particular message—a proposal or new pricing data, for instance. With cc capability, you won't have to retype that message. With "bcc," or blind courtesy copy, capability, recipients won't be informed of the identity of others on the copy list.

• *Ability to edit messages and check spelling.* This feature is more important to marketers than to the typical e-mail user. Since many of your messages will be sent to business contacts outside your company, it's critical to make certain the message is accurate and up to general business communications standards.

• *Ability to create and manage multiple mailing lists.* Marketers often need to divide their direct mail customer lists into categories: current customers versus prospects, big companies versus small companies, and so on. It's the same with e-mail. If you need to send out an electronic message to a particular group of customers, your software should allow you to create a separate list to hold that group.

• *Ability to attach files to messages.* This is critical. You'll often have a document such as a sales letter or price sheet that needs to be included with a message sent to a prospect. Your software should make it easy for you to select that file from your hard drive or floppy disk and attach it to your message. Multimedia Internet Mail Extensions (MIME) enabled software will also allow you to attach graphics, video clips, or other multimedia files to your e-mail messages.

QUICK LOOK: E-Mail Software Programs

E-mail software programs can help you collect your messages from different online services (if you subscribe to more than one), write the text for the new messages before connecting with an online service to send them, and sometimes even allow you to send messages directly from popular word processing or desktop publishing programs. You'll find contact information for the publishers of the following software programs in the Connection Section at the end of this chapter.

- E-Mail Connection from ConnectSoft
- Embla from ICL
- Eudora from Qualcomm
- IMail from Ipswitch
- Internet Messenger from Delrina
- Mail-it from Unipalm
- networkMCI Business from MCI
- Quickmail from CE Software
- Z-Mail from NCD Z-Code

Heavy Traffic 47

How Marketers Can Use E-Mail More Effectively

Once you start using e-mail, you won't be able to stop. You'll be sending out messages to customers, to prospects, and to business partners. It's a good idea to form good e-mail habits early. If you're a veteran e-mail user, the following will be a good review for you. These rules can help ensure that your e-mail messages aren't bozo-filtered out of electronic existence. (A bozo filter is a feature on some e-mail software systems that allows e-mail recipients to automatically delete or refuse acceptance of messages from annoying or irrelevant sources.)

• *Stick to the point.* Keep your messages short and to the point, just as you would in any other form of marketing communication. Remember that e-mail users are even more likely than the typical customer to put a high value on their time. They don't want to waste it on a rambling, unfocused message.

• *Break it up.* Use the return key on your keyboard to break up long blocks of copy into manageable blocks. A computer screen isn't an ideal medium for reading text, and your customers will be turned off by line after line after line of copy in your message.

• *Keep it simple.* Don't use fonts and graphics in your e-mail messages unless you're sure that your customer's e-mail system can accept and translate them so that "what you send is what they get." Otherwise, your client could end up with a screen full of confusing computer control characters. It's usually best to save spreadsheets, proposals, and sales letters you've created in programs like Word or Excel as ASCII text files if you plan to attach them to e-mail messages. That way the files will be more compact and won't take nearly as long to send via modem.

• *Check your mailbox.* If you have an e-mail address on your business card, customers and prospects who send a message to that address will expect a speedy reply. You don't want to miss a key sale because you're too lazy to turn on the PC and check your e-mail.

• *Don't over-copy.* Only send digital copies of your messages to people that really need them. If you're sending routine correspondence to a purchasing agent at a client company, for instance, don't copy the vice-president or president of the company unless it's critical to do so. Otherwise, customers may consider you a nuisance and choose to screen out or ignore your mail (maybe even dragging it, unopened, into the little garbage can icon featured in some e-mail programs. Yikes!).

• *Double check the details.* Check your spelling, grammar, accuracy, and tone. E-mail users sometimes become too informal in their messages. Marketers can't afford to get lazy in any aspect of their communications. Unfortunately, some e-mail software programs don't allow users to go back and correct mistakes or make modifications after the text has been entered. Purchase an e-mail software package that gives you that option.

• *Stay real.* Use e-mail to supplement—not to replace—direct communication with customers. Don't disappear into cyberspace. This may seem obvious, but if e-mail gets to be too much of a habit, you may start wondering why you need to pick up the phone or make a personal sales call to that key customer. That's a great way to turn key customers into former customers.

E-mail offers many of the advantages of both telephone calls and letters. Used properly, it can be a great asset to your cybermarketing tool bag. It's great for reaching people who are hard to reach (you don't have to make an appointment or catch someone at their desk to send an e-mail message) or who do business in different time zones. It also promotes a quick exchange of ideas and suggestions. When time is of the essence, as it so often is in marketing, knowing how to communicate effectively with e-mail can give you a competitive advantage.

As we move toward the age of the decentralized and geographically distributed virtual corporation, e-mail offers the vital link that keeps various elements of the company tied together. As we move further into the future, toward "virtual industry," e-mail will provide the basis for a kind of circulatory system interconnecting webs of customers, suppliers, and trading partners. Why not start preparing to be part of that interconnection now?

Summary

In this chapter we examined:

- The growth of e-mail as a preferred messaging system
- The advantages of e-mail over other messaging systems
- A comparison of internal vs. external e-mail
- Suggestions on setting up an e-mail account
- What to look for in e-mail software
- A list of suggestions on how marketers can use e-mail intelligently and effectively in their marketing communications

The next chapter introduces electronic data interchange (EDI), a method by which companies can exchange transaction-related information without paper documentation.

Chapter 4 Connection Section

Contact information for organizations and resources mentioned in or related to this chapter:

AT&T Easylink Services, AT&T Mail electronic messaging services, 800-242-6005

CE Software, Quickmail e-mail software, 800-523-7638

ConnectSoft, E-Mail Connection e-mail software, 206-827-6467

Delrina, Internet Messenger e-mail software, 416-441-3676

ICL, Embla e-mail software, 714-855-5505

Ipswitch, IMail e-mail software, 617-246-1150

MCI, MCI Mail electronic messaging services, 800-444-MAIL or 202-833-8484

MCI, networkMCI Business electronic messaging software, 800-955-6505

NCD, Z-Code, Z-Mail e-mail software, 415-898-8649

Qualcomm, Eudora e-mail software, 619-587-1121

RadioMail, RadioMail electronic messaging services, 415-286-7800

Unipalm, Mail-it e-mail software, 617-259-1400

5

Data Toll Roads: Electronic Data Interchange

In the future, will your best customers be computers instead of people?

Imagine that you're the sales manager for a sporting goods distributor, and that the buyer that consistently places the biggest orders with your company is a supercomputer at a major national sporting goods chain. The computer practically runs the company. It keeps track of inventory at every retail outlet the chain manages. It knows when stock needs to be replenished, and it knows its suppliers' wholesale prices for every football, catcher's mitt, and sweatshirt the company sells.

At this moment, it knows that the outlet in Tempe, Arizona, is running low on tennis balls, that your company is offering a special deal on tennis balls this month, and how many gross you have in your Arizona warehouse (because your company's computer told it).

This automated purchasing agent sends a short burst of data to your company's computer. The standardized data format includes information on item numbers, colors, quantity, pricing, shipping, handling, billing, and terms. Your company's computer accepts the order, and the deal is consummated.

While all this is taking place, you're savoring a blueberry muffin and a cup of coffee in the company lunch room. You've just hit this month's quota, and you didn't even have to pick up the phone.

That's how electronic data interchange (EDI) works, and how an increasing number of sales transactions will occur in the future. In this chapter, we'll discuss how EDI works and how it can work to your advantage. We'll look at the rapid growth of the EDI marketplace, and then at how specific industries are applying EDI. We'll list some ways you can get started using EDI, and focus on the potential for the Internet to be used as a medium for the transmission of EDI transactions.

What Is Electronic Data Interchange?

Electronic data interchange enables companies to conduct paperless computer-to-computer exchanges of business documents in a structured format, with little or no human intervention. Transactions are conducted over private or public data networks. Using EDI, companies set up electronic trading networks with their business partners, including vendors, major customers, and distributors, in order to reduce paper flow and move product through the pipeline faster.

How EDI Works

EDI is more than simply sending an order form over the Internet or using your computer and credit card to buy a product or service online. EDI transactions demand strict compatibility between the data sent from a buyer to a seller or seller to buyer. EDI-linked trading partners typically engage in a high volume of critical business transactions. For example, a large retailer like Kmart may buy tens of thousands of greeting cards from suppliers such as Hallmark every month. Varying amounts of cards have to be coordinated and shipped to Kmart locations around the country.

Companies have traditionally used paper-based forms to handle these kinds of routine transactions. A typical Kmart/Hallmark transaction might include forms like pricing inquiry sheets, purchasing orders, contracts, order acknowledgments, order status forms, scheduling forms, shipping and receiving documents, invoices, payments, and financial reports.

Transactions like these would bury trading partners in an avalanche of slow-moving paper if it weren't for EDI. EDI was designed to handle this type of critical, high-volume, precise information flow. Here's how: Each category of paper form is "mapped" to an EDI-standard document. Business information is formatted, according to this standard, prior to transmission to the trading partner. The trading partner's computer is ready to accept the data in the pre-determined format.

Who Uses EDI?

Major corporations were the first to use custom EDI systems to manage electronic transactions. Now they expect and are even demanding that their vendors and suppliers link up to these systems, so that they can order products on a just-in-time basis and create a uniform format for exchanging transaction-related information.

Should You Consider Using EDI?

If you sell your products in large quantities to high-volume buyers in virtually any industry, from retail to pharmaceutical to automotive products, you should look into EDI. Even if you're only considering breaking into these markets, it would be worthwhile to learn about this technology. This also holds true for companies that want to become dealers for high-volume products.

Marketing Advantages of EDI

• *Reduces paperwork.* EDI, if properly implemented, can significantly decrease the number of times documents are processed by human beings. The data is entered only once, which eliminates re-keying, reduces errors, and cuts clerical overhead. The data is stored online, instead of in filing cabinets, which means more control over information and faster reports to management. Companies that are opting for EDI are usually switching from fax and telephone-based purchase order systems with surface-mail invoicing. They're able to cut telecommunications costs and achieve higher productivity without increasing staff.

• *Speeds time to market.* EDI has already reduced the cost of doing business among buyers, vendors, suppliers, and manufacturers by ensuring the rapid flow of product, parts, and materials and faster payment of bills and invoices.

EDI can cut the time it takes to move product from the warehouse to the showroom floor by eliminating redundant handling of paper documents and forms. This efficiency leads to reduced inventory, better production cycles, and happier customers.

• *Strengthens relationships with trading partners.* EDI's impact on the marketing function is significant, not only from the standpoint of reducing the paperwork associated with conducting business transactions, but also in the creation of tighter electronic relationships among EDI trading partners. As vendors go through the process of setting up EDI connections with their major customers, they learn more about that customer's organizational style and preferred way of doing business. And customers are probably a little less likely to switch vendors once this electronic purchasing connection is in place. That means that EDI-enabled companies are in a better market position than competitors who don't use EDI.

EDI Market Applications

Companies that want to conduct EDI transactions must first agree to a common format for exchanging data. For example, "Purchase order numbers will consist of seven digits." It generally takes some form of industry consensus on details such as these, as well as the hardware, software, and electronic protocol decisions, to get an EDI project off the ground. Industry members must agree on basic transaction sets (purchase orders, invoices) and data descriptions (cases, barrels, shipment methods) needed to communicate accurately.

The trick is in harmonizing the network connections necessary to hook it all together. Unix work stations at one company have to be able to talk to PCs at another. Mainframes have to be able to communicate with network servers. Some companies choose to use direct dial-up links, while others prefer to route everything through a Value-Added Network (VAN) provider. VANs, like Advantis, specialize in transferring data over networks. VANs typically provide secure storage and forwarding of messages and the conversion of electronic documents delivered under incompatible protocols.

Because of these complexities, various industries have their own approaches to EDI.

The Banking and Financial Services Market

The financial services industry's version of EDI is known as electronic funds transfer (EFT). The primary issue for EFT users is transaction security. While most payment systems are still based on cash or checks, more and more financial service providers are moving toward EFT to control costs, reduce paperwork, increase privacy, and improve cash management. Current EFT systems include interbank transfer networks, such as The Society for Worldwide Interbank Financial Telecommunications (SWIFT); payment networks like Bankwire; settlement systems such as Fedwire; exchange nets that manage the sale of stocks and bonds; and finally automatic teller machine networks that are rapidly evolving into universal debit networks, allowing customers to pay for fast food or gas with bank ATM cards. The brokerage business has ADP and Quotron.

Some banks are creating unique EDI-based systems for their customers. Bank of America has created the Business Connect service to give its business banking customers access to BofA deposit accounts with a PC in order to view account information, transfer funds, and maximize cash flow.

Financial service providers are looking toward the day when customers will conduct financial transactions in their homes and offices via telephone lines, cable TV, and computer networks. Will these various mediums have a common language, electronic standards, and connection protocols to manage these transactions? Will companies who have mastered the technology have a competitive advantage?

The American National Standards Institute hopes to resolve these questions for a number of different industries. It has set up a special panel for the banking and financial services industry to address issues such as data security and customer privacy. Computer, communications, cable, broadcast, cellular, and satellite technology consultants and vendors are attending with the hope of influencing the standards in their favor.

The Grocery Products Market

While large retailers, distributors, and manufacturers have been using EDI for years, the grocery products market, particularly time-sensitive niches like dairy products, has been slow to accept the switch to electronically managed transactions. Suppliers of products with short supermarket shelf lives (e.g., milk, cheese, and butter) felt they couldn't afford to have a computer server go down or a misplaced message wind up in the wrong electronic mailbox.

More recently, however, many of these suppliers are finding that EDI-relayed information can be a powerful marketing weapon. For instance, if you're an ice cream manufacturer like Ben & Jerry's or Häagen-Dazs, it would be nice to have a report (based on EDI-generated information from your grocery chains) showing that your new strawberry swirl is selling better than granola crunch. That data can be instantly conveyed to vendors when stores order more product via EDI.

In other words, if the store is requesting more strawberry swirl, they must have sold out of the product on the shelves. That's the kind of information marketers can use to help plan ad campaigns and guide product launches.

The Power Equipment Repair Market

Shops that repair outdoor power equipment like lawn mowers and leaf blowers may seem like an unlikely group to be leaders in electronic commerce. In fact, their multi-application project, called POWERCOM-2000, showcases some of the best aspects of EDI. It also demonstrate how individual companies within an industry can work together, using technology to streamline the entire marketing process. POWERCOM-2000 connects equipment manufacturers and distributors to their dealers' customer service departments. The system enables the service departments to process orders efficiently, while staying on top of the latest product information. It handles everything electronically from preparing invoices and sales reports to ordering parts electronically to providing catalogs of documentation stored on CD-ROM.

Outdoor power equipment manufacturer Briggs & Stratton got the ball rolling to develop the system, but brought on board a number of other industry suppliers, including American Yard Products, Atlas, and Lawn Chief. Initial research found that only about 15 percent of the nation's 26,000 power equipment dealers were computerized and that only a fraction of those had CD-

ROM drives or the capability to connect to EDI networks. They also found that dealers wouldn't purchase the system unless it incorporated business management applications, like accounting, that would help them justify the expense.

One of the top objectives of the project was to simplify the parts ordering process. Now dealers don't have to find the right manual and then search through it to find the right part. They just push a couple of buttons, find the part, and then simply click on the part number to order it automatically through the EDI system. The system uses direct links, called *hyperlinks*, between listings of related items to help the dealer obtain all the parts needed for a particular installation. POWERCOM-2000 actually alerts the dealer if another part is needed to complete the order.

The graphics capabilities of the system are excellent. Users can print out part diagrams, rotate graphic images of the part on screen, or even zoom in for a closer look. The system can even be set up so that parts are automatically ordered when inventory gets low. The bottom line is that a typical order used to cost about $1.20 to process. Now it costs about ten cents!

The lessons of this project could be applied to many other industries. The POWERCOM-2000 system uses mainly off-the-shelf hardware products available in a local computer store. The users were not oriented toward high-tech solutions to business problems, but they were willing to adopt a relatively low-cost way to reduce their expenses.

The Government Services Market

If you sell to Uncle Sam, it may not be too long before you will make some part of your sales presentation over a network to a government computer. Driven by mandates from the White House and other agencies to streamline and "reinvent," the U.S. Government is aggressively moving away from paper and toward electronic transactions. The Internal Revenue Service already accepts electronically delivered tax returns. The Departments of the Treasury, Defense, and Interior will all have pilot EDI purchasing programs up and running by the end of 1994.

Of greatest interest to marketers is the potential that EDI holds to make it easier to do business with the government, untangling the web of procedures and regulations that have hampered many vendors in their efforts to participate in the $200 billion federal government marketplace.

Government agencies hope to create a single EDI format for registering vendors as government suppliers. They also want to develop one massive database that will hold information on every vendor. Another goal is to use a standard agreement form that details the traffic regulations of this electronic road as it signs up sellers to participate in the system.

The U.S. Department of Defense, which accounts for about 14 million of the 20 million acquisitions the government makes every year, has taken a leading role in the move toward EDI. The Department's goal is to conduct about 80 percent of all business transactions electronically by the end of the century. Civil agencies are also getting in on the act. A pilot program is under way at the government's main purchasing authority, the General Services Administration, which allows computer suppliers to quote prices for hardware and software online. The system doesn't yet allow orders to be processed electronically, but that, reportedly, is the next step. The aim is to allow vendors and agency buyers to communicate with each other directly over computer networks.

The U.S. Postal Service is hungry for a piece of the EDI pie. As its first class and parcel post market share has eroded with the advent of e-mail, fax, and overnight delivery services, the USPS has had to look for new lines of business, and it thinks EDI might be a good fit. After all, the postal service was the nation's first information superhighway. Now it hopes to provide the same sort of orderly support for correspondence on the somewhat chaotic electronic frontier as it did in the days of the wild, wild West.

A senior technology director for the USPS says the service already has access to many of the tools needed to secure electronic transactions, including electronic public keys that encrypt electronic documents, providing them with a time and date stamp and a digital signature of authenticity.

Although this type of public-key encryption is already available to any online user, the postal service may be able to market its version as a simple-to-use, widely available, and government-backed service. The USPS is hoping that its implementation of EDI will become the standard adopted by many industries.

How You Can Get Started With EDI

EDI isn't just for the major players in any given industry. If you do a significant volume of business with a particular customer or group of customers, why not look into starting a pilot EDI program within your company?

Find Out What's Being Done in Your Industry and Marketplace

Ask your industry's trade association if it is aware of any companies already engaged in EDI in your marketplace. Find out if any of your major customers are EDI-enabled. Schedule a visit to discuss their programs, find out about the software they are using, and arrange to participate in their EDI network on a trial basis.

Contact the Data Interchange Standards Association (DISA)

DISA is the organization responsible for developing and monitoring the standards and business-transaction forms used in EDI. It has a publications catalog that provides detailed information on EDI forms and procedures.

Evaluate Current EDI Service and Software Providers

VANs, such as those provided by Advantis, AT&T EasyLink, and General Electric Information Services, have traditionally been the link between participants in EDI networks. They have provided the transmission lines, managed the store-and-forward communications, maintained electronic mailbox services for EDI participants, and even helped EDI users recruit and train new trading partners. But things may be changing as EDI begins to converge with e-mail and new standards eliminate the need for some of the protocol-matching services the VANs provided. Competition is also coming in the form of industry-specific VANs dedicated to a single market, such as the automotive or transportation business.

HOT TIP: EDI Info Site on the World Wide Web

If you have access to the World Wide Web (more about that in Chapter 10), visit the Web server of Premenos, a company that supplies software and services for EDI. (They're also involved in a trial program to transmit EDI data over the Internet.) The Premenos server is packed with information on EDI standards, EDI organizations, EDI providers, and EDI periodicals. You can visit the site at *http://www.premenos.com.*

EDI on the Internet

But the biggest threat to VANs may be the Internet. If users find a way to integrate EDI messages into e-mail packets and send them over the Internet for as little as twenty or thirty dollars a month, VANs will have to quickly reevaluate their pricing.

Researchers at California's Lawrence Livermore Labs have been conducting a pilot program using the Internet as a medium of transmission for EDI, and they are reporting very successful results. The United Nations' Trade Point (profiled in Chapter 17) also has plans to use the Internet as the network backbone for EDI transmission among global business partners.

Before long, a smart software programmer is going to create a simple, standardized, easy-to-use software solution for EDI transactions on the Internet and make a small fortune. The "client" side of the software, the one used by buyers, should be distributed as freeware. (The more buyers using it, the better.) Vendors would purchase the "server" version of the software, which would be used to display their products and accept orders.

Here's how it could work: Buyers would visit the vendor's Internet server; that is, their client software would link up with the vendor's server software. The buyers would browse through the vendor's product listing or online catalog. Buyers ready to consummate a transaction would simply click a few software buttons on the screen, and all relevant purchase information—bill-to address, ship-to address, purchase order number and/or credit card information—would be automatically transferred from the user's software to the vendor's order form.

Here are the advantages of having the transaction take place electronically, via EDI on the Internet. First, it eliminates the time it takes for the buyer to verbally relay transaction information (product number, quantity, etc.) over the phone. That information is frustratingly repetitive, and sometimes the service representatives enter the wrong information. Plus, the clock is ticking while that information is being transferred from the buyer's lips to the service representative's computer screen. Someone is paying for the phone call (either the buyer or the vendor via its toll-free number). Using EDI sellers can trim phone expenses and reassign employees to other tasks.

There's no good reason that this form of EDI can't be standardized so that any consumer with a computer and modem could use it and any vendor who wanted to add EDI capabilities could do so within a short time.

With an Internet ordering system, buyers should be able to search a master directory to quickly locate, for example, all the major suppliers of address labels in the world. Then they should have the option of electronically requesting price quotes for 150,000 one-by-four-inch laser printer labels, with that request being forwarded to all or selected vendors. The adoption of universal product codes would mean that all vendors used identical specifications for their one-by-four-inch laser printer labels. A common format for purchase orders, requests for proposals, and invoices would already be in place. The buyer would be able to accept the price quotes electronically, place the order electronically, be invoiced electronically, and make payment electronically.

Summary

This chapter looked at how EDI works and how it can work to your advantage. It examined the growth of the EDI marketplace and took a look at how specific industries are applying EDI. It suggested some ways for you to get started using EDI and explored the potential of using the Internet as a medium for the transmission of EDI transactions.

In the next chapter you will "log on" to the world of electronic bulletin board systems, looking at the benefits of using existing systems as well as the possibilities of starting your own.

Chapter 5 Connection Section

Contact information for organizations and resources mentioned in or related to this chapter:

> Advantis provides the Information Exchange EDI service, 800-284-5849
>
> American National Standards Institute (ANSI) helps industry move toward EDI standards, 212-642-4920
>
> AT&T Easylink Services provides the AT&T EDI service, 800-242-6005
>
> DISA (Data Interchange Standards Association) manages EDI standards development, 703-548-7005
>
> *EDI Forum* magazine, 708-848-0135
>
> *EDI World* magazine, 305-925-5900
>
> The EDI Group, Ltd., presents an annual EDI Strategies Conference, 708-848-0135
>
> Electronic Data Interchange Association, 703-838-8042
>
> GE Information Services provides EDI Express services, 800-EDI-KNOW or 301-340-4750
>
> Harbinger EDI Services provides EDI software and an EDI network, 404-841-4334
>
> MCI provides EDI Net Services, 800-999-2096
>
> Premenos Corp., provides EDI software and services, 510-602-2000
>
> TSI International provides Trading Partner PC for Windows, 800-EDI-2120

6

Superhighway Service Stations: Electronic Bulletin Boards

The idea is simple. You take a computer, a modem, some software, and a phone line, and bingo!, you have an electronic computer bulletin board system, or more simply, a BBS. A BBS acts as a host system for the client computers that dial in to access information and services. The concept has been around since the first personal computers became popular in the late 1970s (the very first bulletin board system, CBBS, of Chicago, went online in February of 1978) and has grown to the point where today there are an estimated 60,000 public BBSs operating in the United States.

Many BBSs are run out of the basement or den of a computer enthusiast. Some have grown from simple home systems into BBS behemoths, with numerous computer host systems managing hundreds of lines of incoming phone traffic. Most BBS systems are used for a combination of access to electronic mail, repositories of downloadable files, and real-time "chat" between like-minded folks. BBSs can be put to serious business use as well. BBSs are used by hundreds of high-technology companies as technical support systems to assist customers. Other companies use them to extend the core services offered to customers. Some companies have even used the BBS concept to develop unique business applications that provide specialized services to a particular industry or marketplace.

What Is a Bulletin Board System?

A bulletin board system is a computer equipped with special software and telecommunications links. This combination allows the computer to act as an information host, or server, for remote computer systems. The typical BBS consists of a personal computer with one or more phone lines, running into one or more modems. The bulletin board software program manages the requests and interactions of users calling in to access the system.

What's the difference between a BBS and the major online service providers, such as America Online, CompuServe, or Dow Jones News/Retrieval? The main difference is simply one of magnitude. The major online service providers could be termed *super* bulletin boards. They've made big investments in computer technology, telecommunications links, and specialized software to make their services very attractive and easy to use. They've also formed partnerships with other information providers in an effort to offer a well-rounded package of online services to their users.

While the major online service providers have many of the same basic services (electronic messaging, interaction with other online users, etc.) as the hundreds of home-based or regional BBS operators, they do it on a national, or sometimes even international, basis. The larger service providers typically offer local numbers you can use to access their services, while local BBSs do not. If you're in Florida and you want to access a BBS in Oregon, you'll probably have to make a long-distance call to do so.

One online service provider is attempting to address this problem by creating a network that ties together local bulletin board systems from around the country. The CRIS Information and Entertainment Network, from Concentric Research, allows users to access bulletin boards from around the country by dialing into a local access number.

How do you find the phone numbers of local BBS services? Many local computer magazines (the kind distributed in retail computer stores) list the modem number and description of nearby BBSs. Most boards have a small monthly subscription fee, but many will allow you to sign on temporarily as a guest at no charge to explore the system.

Five Ways to Use Local Bulletin Board Systems for Profit

Once you locate one or more boards in your area, here are some ways you can use these boards to accomplish your business objectives.

1. *Messaging.* If you're new to online systems, a local BBS is a good place to familiarize yourself with sending e-mail, posting messages, downloading files, and navigating through online menus. If you get lost, most BBSs have a resident system operator (you can page them from the online menu) who will quickly come to your assistance.

2. *Research.* What better place to gather information about a particular market than from a BBS designed especially to serve that market? If you're a developer of cat food or cat treats, you can bet there's a BBS out there where cat lovers gather to discuss their favorite subject. Do you manufacture after-market products for touring motorcycles? Of course, there's a BBS for touring motorcyclists. Why not log on and see what these enthusiasts are talking about? If you have any customer research questions to ask, feel free to post them. Online enthusiasts are more than happy to discuss their favorite topic.

A few bulletin boards cater to just the sort of special interests we're talking about. The Outdoor Sportsman BBS (modem: 407-635-9590) plays host to divers, hunters, and fishing enthusiasts. The Flightline Aviation BBS (modem: 708-564-0610) is a place for pilots and folks interested in general aviation to gather online and discuss their favorite subject. The Audiophile Network (modem: 818-988-0452) offers a wide range of information on high-end audio components and reviews of new music CDs.

3. *Publicity.* Many bulletin boards allow marketers to place new product announcements in special areas on the board. If your announcement relates to the special interests of the board's users, there's a good chance the board will give your release even greater visibility.

4. *Advertising.* Many local bulletin boards accept text-only classified advertising, while some offer advertising that incorporates photos and graphics as well.

HOT TIP: BBS Lists

Here are a couple of BBSs that provide comprehensive lists of most of the other bulletin boards around the country. These lists provide a good starting point for locating special interest boards that may cater to your market.

Dial up the PDSLO BBS (modem: 516-938-6722) and access THE LIST, a nationwide list of BBS services around the country.

Dial up the Hayes Online BBS (modem: 800-874-2937) and access DARWIN, another nationwide list of BBS sites.

---

5. *Sales.* Many boards are beginning to install software modules that enable users to place credit card orders and purchase products by filling out online order forms.

How Savvy Marketers Can Use Industry-Specific Bulletin Board Systems

Does your industry have an online service dedicated to the needs of professionals in your marketplace? Services like the ones below, based on bulletin board system technology, are springing up in a number of markets. These bulletin board systems, which are typically pretty sophisticated by local BBS standards, are often developed by trade associations or industry publications, and often by entrepreneurs who see a niche and decide to fill it. Industry professionals use these systems to access specialized services and inside information that aren't provided elsewhere.

This is only a sampling of the hundreds of specialized business-oriented bulletin boards available today. Your industry may not be featured here, but keep your eye on industry trade publications for announcements about new online services available for your market. You'll find contact information for each of these services at the end of this chapter.

• *Ampersand (for the Newspaper Business).* Ampersand is an online service for the newspaper and media industry that is being developed by a subsidiary of *Editor and Publisher* magazine. The service is expected to include options for advertisers and their agencies to plan media schedules, to post their news release information online, and to review an online directory of newspaper industry vendors.

• *Billboard Online (for the Music Industry).* Billboard Online is based on the influential music industry publication, *Billboard* magazine. Users of Billboard Online will find a database of all *Billboard* magazine articles from March 1991 to the present, all *Billboard* magazine charts from 1985 to the present, weekly updates on album sales and radio air play charts, concert grosses and touring schedules, gold and platinum recordings from 1958, industry statistics and consumer profile data, Grammy winners, and music video credits.

• *DataQuick (for the Real Estate Business).* DataQuick is a real estate and business property information databank for California and Arizona real estate professionals.

• *Entrepreneurs Online (for owners of growing businesses).* Entrepreneurs Online carries current business news, international trade leads, and information on government-provided small-business support services.

• *HRIN (for Human Resources Professionals).* Human Resource Information Network is an online service that has over one hundred databases covering a variety of human resource issues, including administration, affirmative action, labor and legal issues, safety, health, and training and development. HRIN's databases include information on the Americans with Disabilities Act, collective bargaining, college recruitment, employment and policy guides, fair employment practice cases, labor arbitration databases, and vendors in the training and HR field.

• *Morph Online (for Multimedia Developers).* Morph's Outpost publishes *Morph's Outpost on the Digital Frontier,* a monthly publication for multimedia developers. This bulletin board is a kind of electronic "trading post" for the multimedia developers who read the publication.

• *PressLink (for the Media Business).* PressLink is an online service for the media industry. Users access news databases, digital photos, and digital graphics for their publications through a sophisticated bulletin board system that also acts as a gateway to other information service providers.

How Your Company Can Start Its Own Bulletin Board System

Starting and running your own board means that you can exercise total control over its content. The benefits of board ownership will accrue to you, but of course the responsibilities will as well. You've got to be there to fix it if something goes wrong, and you've got to make the initial investment in software, modems, phone lines, support personnel, consulting, etc.

Companies that are using bulletin board systems are often willing to share their experiences of how they got started and the pitfalls to avoid. Before starting your own BBS, try to talk to a few experienced operators.

BBS Hardware

You don't need a special computer to operate a bulletin board system, but a fast computer will allow users dialing into your system to access information more quickly. You need a fast modem that will automatically downswitch to connect with slower speed modems some customers may be still be using.

New BBS operators often go overboard with their estimates of the number of calls their board will receive. They assume that customers will swamp their system, so they buy lots of modems and set up multiple phone lines.

It's better to start slowly and grow naturally. You can always add modems and phone lines later as the word begins to spread and more users find out about your board.

BBS Software

The most important decision you'll make is which BBS software package you'll use to control your system. As you evaluate the advantages and limitation of various software programs, keep these questions in mind:

- How long has the product been on the market? How many revisions has it been through?
- What kind of a reputation does the software publisher have in the field? (Ask for a list of current customers.)
- Approximately how many of its systems are in operation? What kinds of organizations buy and use its system?
- Does the system allow callers to access information in either text-based or graphical environment, depending upon their computer's capabilities?
- Can system buyers add the option of Internet access to the system?
- Will the system allow online shopping and order entry?
- Can it manage credit card verification?

There are many different BBS programs available (some even distributed at no charge as freeware), but a few products stand out in the field of commercial-grade BBS software.

- Galacticomm is a Florida-based software publisher who produces The Major BBS bulletin board, which is currently one of the leading BBS software packages. It claims an installed base of over 15,000 buyers, ranging from the U.S. Government to corporate customer service groups. The Major BBS supports e-mail, teleconferencing, file transfers, forum areas, file libraries with key word searching, and gateways to other commercial e-mail services. Galacticomm also sells the GalactiBoard, which expands an individual PC's four standard communications ports to eight, so that your board can receive up to eight calls at once. Galacticomm will soon release a new Windows-based BBS software system called Project Victory, which will allow BBS operators to offer users a Windows interface as well as access to the Internet.

- MMB Development Corp., is the publisher of the TEAMate BBS software package. TEAMate was designed for organizations that want to use a UNIX machine as their BBS server. TEAMate software can be used on HP-UX, IBM RS/6000, SUN, and SCO workstations.

- Mustang Software offers the Wildcat! BBS software package and a complete package of BBS tools (which includes Wildcat!)

called BBS Suite. BBS Suite includes an Internet e-mail gateway, a development package for creating specialized applications (like online ordering systems), and a questionnaire editor that allows you to build customized online survey forms.

Other BBS software packages include TBBS from eSoft, CocoNet from Coconut Computing, PC Board from Clark Development, and FirstClass from SoftArc, Inc.

BBS Consultants

Creating a BBS from scratch may involve more time, research, and effort than you're able to invest. If that's the case, consider calling on outside help. There's a growing list of companies that specialize in helping other businesses set up in-house BBSs. One of the largest, Telescan, Inc., of Houston, Texas, is best known for its online financial industry databases. It has also acted as consultant and partner on a number of sophisticated bulletin board ventures, including one for the American Institute of Architects, and two for entertainment industry publications, Billboard Online and The Hollywood Reporter Online.

Another company, Connect, Inc., calls their solution the VPN (Virtual Private Network). Connect's customers set up a virtual BBS on Connect's server. Connect handles the administration of the system and helps the customer create the online information content, customizing it to give the service a unique look and feel for each customer.

SpaceWorks is an online service with a unique concept. SpaceWorks allows organizations to set up a bulletin board-like system within its online service at no charge. SpaceWorks also assists customers in the layout and design of their online site. SpaceWorks is supported by the online connect charges (about ten dollars per hour) incurred by users of the system. SpaceWorks gives back a percentage of that user fee to the client. In other words, the more customers that access your site on SpaceWorks, the more SpaceWorks earns, and the more they'll pay you. Word processing software publisher WordPerfect is one major company that has a customer-support site on the SpaceWorks system.

Other BBS consulting firms include The Business BBS in Los

Angeles, GW Associates of Boston, and NovX Systems Integration of Portland (Oregon). BBS software publishers often provide installation and customization support, or will recommend local technicians who can provide these services.

Responsibilities of a BBS Sysop

Once you decide to run your own in-house bulletin board system, you put on the hat of system operator, the sysop. Managing and maintaining even a small BBS can take many hours. If you have a larger or more complex system, consider hiring an experienced computer operator to take over sysop responsibilities.

The legal issues surrounding the responsibility for information residing on a BBS is still a somewhat gray area. The FBI recently staged early morning raids on a couple of Texas bulletin board system operators as part of a federal investigation into illegal copying of computer programs. It all revolved around a mysterious file, cryptically labeled *TNT6pwal.zip*, which turned out to be a copyrighted commercial software program. The BBS operators claimed to know nothing about the file, and they haven't, as yet, been charged with any crime. But getting a wake-up call from the Feds can certainly put a crimp in your day.

The problem is, as a BBS operator, you may have no idea that your board is being used as a pass-through point for the storage and copying of copyrighted material. You need to maintain tight control over what gets *uploaded,* or copied, on to your board. If you have an unusually active board, it's a good idea to hire a sysop who knows the ropes.

HOT TIP: Iafo for Sysops

If it turns out that you're the one to take the reins as system operator for your own in-house bulletin board system, here are a couple of Internet newsgroups you might want to monitor to soak up wisdom from experienced BBS sysops: *alt.bbs*, which covers BBS systems and software in general, and *alt.bbs.internet*, for BBSs with connections to the Internet. (See Chapter 11 for information on subscribing to Internet newsgroup mailing lists.)

Persuading More Customers to Visit and Use Your BBS

It will probably take some effort and promotion on your part to encourage visitors to visit and try out your BBS. It would be nice if all you had to do was "build it and they will come," but it isn't as simple as that. You may need to advertise the availability of your board with mailers or ads that describe exactly how to use the system and what the benefits are for customers who make the effort. You may decide to create a special software access disk and send free copies to all your customers. You may even consider packaging the disk with every product you sell. (At the very least, make it easy for customers to call and order it from you.)

Once you do get a customer to visit the site, you need to make sure the trip will be worthwhile. Focus on providing the kind of information your customers would find of value, and then keep that information fresh and up to date. Try to utilize your system's graphic capabilities by including pictures, photos, and charts. Design your board so that it's easy for users to locate the information they need and to ask for assistance online (paging the sysop, or selecting a help file).

The success of your board will ultimately be determined by how many customers use it on a regular basis and how many of them share your board's phone number with their colleagues and friends.

Five Marketing Applications for Your In-House Bulletin Board System

1. *Stay in close touch with your sales reps.* An in-house BBS can help to solve some of the toughest problems faced by sales and marketing managers with regional salespeople and representatives that spend a lot of time on the road. A bulletin board system can be used as a repository for information that needs to be distributed to remote offices and sales sites. This can also be a means for those in the field to send call reports and market updates to the home office.

Some companies find it difficult to get their representatives to provide complete contract and sales order information. You can create an online order form on your BBS that the representative must fill out correctly and completely for a sale to be posted.

Need to get hot leads out into the field and into the hands of your representative as quickly as possible? Post them on the bulletin board.

2. *Generate publicity by providing free information.* Does your company have access to information that is valuable to your prospects and customers? Your BBS is a great way to provide access to that information. You can even create a forum for users to discuss issues of mutual interest.

A company that specializes in financial services, for instance, could provide information on mutual funds and an online dictionary of terms used in the financial world. That company could also create a message area where users could post questions about stocks and bonds or other financial instruments which would be answered by company representatives or other users.

By offering this information for free, you'll be building good will and credibility with potential customers and providing a worthwhile service to your industry.

3. *Conduct customer research.* While prospects are visiting your board, why not have them complete a brief survey? You can set up a program that will automatically tally the results and furnish you with a report that will keep you tuned in to the interests of potential customers.

4. *Feature your product information online.* Promotional information online? You can do anything from including a few strategically placed sales messages within other online content to creating a complete electronic catalog with color product shots and online order forms.

5. *Support your customers.* Hundreds of companies are using in-house bulletin boards to answer user questions and provide online documentation. The majority of these companies are in the computer industry, but the concept can be used by any company with a product that requires ongoing support.

Chapter 15, which covers customer support, discusses this option in greater detail. Many, if not most, organizations that launch their own BBS have some form of customer support in mind when they do so.

Summary

This chapter looked into the simple technology that lies behind the typical bulletin board system. It covered ways that you can use a local BBS to reach specific marketing objectives and presented an overview of some specialized BBS services that focus on one industry or market segment. It concluded with a look at how companies can start their own in-house bulletin board systems and reviewed profit-making uses for them.

The next chapter highlights business-oriented database information services that provide a rich source of industry and market intelligence for online marketers.

Chapter 6 Connection Section

Contact information for organizations and resources mentioned in or related to this chapter:

Ampersand, specialized BBS service for newspaper and other media industry professionals, 212-675-4380

Billboard Online, specialized BBS service for music industry professionals, 800-449-1402

The BBS Construction Kit, by David Wolfe, John Wiley & Sons, 1994

Bulletin Board Systems for Business, by Lamont Wood and Dana Blankenhorn, John Wiley & Sons, 1992

The Business BBS, bulletin board system consultants, 310-477-0593

Coconut Computing, CocoNet bulletin board system software, 619-456-2002

Clark Development, PC Board bulletin board system software, 801-261-1686

Concentric Research Corp., CRIS, a nationwide network of bulletin board systems accessible via local phone numbers, 800-745-2747

Connect Inc., a turn-key bulletin board environment, 408-973-0497

DataQuick, specialized BBS service for Western U.S. real estate industry professionals, 619-455-6900

Entrepreneurs Online, specialized BBS service for entrepreneurs, 800-784-8822 or 713-784-8822

eSoft, TBBS bulletin board system software, 303-699-6565

Galacticomm, The Major BBS bulletin board system software, 800-328-1128

GW Associates, bulletin board system consultants, 508-429-6227 or *pwwhite@tbbs.com*

HRIN, Human Resources Information Network, specialized BBS service for human resources professionals, 800-638-8094

Morph's Online, specialized BBS service for multimedia developers, 510-238-4545 or (BBS) 510-238-4554

MMB Development Corp., TEAMate bulletin board system software, 800-832-6022 or 310-318-1322

Mustang Software Inc., Wildcat! bulletin board system software, 805-873-2500

NovX Systems Integration, bulletin board system consultants, 206-447-0800

PressLink, specialized BBS service for media industry professionals, 703-758-1740

SoftArc, FirstClass bulletin board system software, 416-299-4723

SpaceWorks, a turn-key bulletin board environment, 800-577-2235

Telescan Inc., online service provider and BBS consultant, 713-952-1060

7

Information On-Ramps: Business-Oriented Online Services

Consumer-oriented online services like America Online, Compu-Serve, and Prodigy have been generating a great deal of attention recently in the press, on radio, and on TV. There's a lot happening with these services, and some of that excitement is covered in the next chapter.

But here's a statistic that may surprise you: consumer-oriented online services currently make up only 5 percent of total subscriber fees for the online services market. Services that provide business-related information take all the rest of the pie, a full 95 percent of the revenue.

Much of that revenue is generated by online services catering to the financial services market, Wall Street, bankers, and stock brokers. But a significant portion is also invested in massive business databases that specialize in providing marketers and analysts with business and industry news from around the world.

If you'd like to know how you can take advantage of online business research databases to stay on top of consumer trends, track industry news, and keep one step ahead of your competition, read on.

What Are Business-Oriented Database Services?

Business-oriented database services are golden gateways to news, facts, and statistics. These databases make digital versions of business news wires, technical databases, newspapers from your hometown and around the world, and industry magazines and newsletters available for you via modem.

Here's what sets these services apart from the consumer-oriented online service providers covered in Chapter 8 and from the information resources you can find on your own via the Internet and other public-access databases.

- *Focused on business users, not consumers.* These services are definitely focused at the business market and not at the typical online consumer (although individual investors use these services to locate company information).
- *Charge a fee, not for free.* When you use one of these database services, it's not like "surfing" the Internet for random data. You should expect to pay, and in some cases to pay dearly. The fees for these services—from sign-up fees to monthly charges—are higher than those of consumer-oriented services.
- *Focused on information, not communication.* These services usually don't put an emphasis on the exchange of e-mail (Dow Jones News/Retrieval's link to MCI Mail is an exception) or any other type of communication between subscribers. They put the focus on providing facts, statistics, news, and information.

Five Ways Marketers Can Profit From Business-Oriented Database Services

1. *Follow industry news as it happens.* These services provide up-to-the-minute news and information on your industry via news wires and targeted industry newsletters.

2. *Track business and consumer trends.* These services can help you track consumer trends through access to census data and other consumer research. You can track business trends though market research studies and articles in specialized periodicals.

3. *Gain long-term perspective.* Online research can offer historical perspective on industries and markets through access to news and statistics from years or even decades ago.

4. *Nail your competitors.* Find out what they're up to. Which contracts are they bidding for? What new products are they announcing?

5. *Wow your customers.* Don't make a sales call without doing a quick online search for background information that will help you make a more intelligent presentation.

How to Choose the Right Service Provider

There's no right answer, except for the right answer for you and your company. Consider the following guidelines.

• *Evaluate the provider's resource list or source directory.* Ask the service provider to send you a list of source information carried on the service. What kind of publications are included on the list? How many relate to your markets or industry? What kind of news wire sources are available? What about international sources? Are international information sources important to you?

• *Examine the provider's pricing structure.* Many services charge a different rate for each database you access on their system. Others charge a set fee based on the number of characters you access. Some offer a flat-rate monthly fee. You're usually better off paying a fixed rate so that you can relax and spend the time you need to spend to do a complete search.

• *Ask about software.* What kind of software is available to access the service? Rate the service on ease-to-use. Some of the service providers in this category provide you with software that helps you to access and search their service. For example, Dow Jones News/Retrieval has two front-end software options for Windows users, News/Retrieval Link and TextSearch Plus. For DOS users, there's Dow Jones E-Z Online. Datatimes has a software package for their service called EyeQ, which presents a friendly, easy-to-use front end to subscribers.

• *Inquire about training.* Some providers offer free training classes to acquaint you with their services. If you expect to be using the service frequently, the time invested in a seminar will pay off in faster, more productive searches later on.

• *Take a test drive.* If the provider offers a free trial period to put the system through its paces, don't hesitate. Take them up on the offer.

Business-Oriented Database Services: Provider Profiles

The following service providers act as "information gateways" to nearly limitless sources of research information. These providers typically do not offer the e-mail services, forums, or technical support options of the broad-based service providers covered in Chapter 8. If, however, your primary need is comprehensive business news or in-depth industry information, the services listed here are the best place to start.

Claritas Catalyst Connect

Claritas Catalyst Connect is an online market research database provided by Claritas/VNU Business Information Services. Claritas specializes in demographics, census data, and business and retail sales information. Claritas Catalyst Connect segments the data it provides by industry and subject matter. Here is a sample of some of the data segments offered: Census Data, Consumer Lifestyle Information, Business Information, Restaurant Industry Information, Shopping Center Data, Consumer Purchasing Data, Media: Cable TV and Yellow Pages, Banks/Savings & Loans/ Credit Unions, Financial Segmentation, and Crime/Environment/Schools Data. The Windows-based Catalyst Connect software is licensed to users on an annual basis.

Data-Star

Data-Star is an online research databank that is very strong in European news and information, and it has a search tool called Star-Search that allows users to repeat searches in multiple databases; and another called Cross, which is an online index to databases—users enter search terms, and Cross scans its list of databases and reports which ones produce matches. Data-Star has over 300 databases, fifty-four of which are unique to the service.

Here's a sampling: Frost & Sullivan, market report summaries; Hoppenstedt, directories of companies in Germany, Austria, and the Benelux; ICC, financial file on all U.K. limited companies; Predicasts, market research databases; and Tradstat, import/export statistics. Data-Star doesn't charge an annual fee. Sign-up is free. It also offers free search time for new users and on new databases. Data-Star is co-owned by Radio-Suisse and American database provider Dialog Information Services.

DataTimes

DataTimes provides access to over 3,500 information sources from around the world, including news wires, newsletters, broadcast transcripts, and the largest online database of newspaper information (140 daily newspapers) offered anywhere. DataTimes carries the major business news wires, including Dow Jones News, PR Newswire, and Business Wire; business periodicals, including *Forbes, Business Week, Barron's,* and hundreds of industry newsletters; domestic newspapers, including *The Wall Street Journal, The Washington Post, The Los Angeles Times,* and *USA Today;* international newspapers, including *The Times of London, South China Morning Post, The Financial Post,* and *The Jerusalem Post.* You can use any standard communications software package to access DataTimes. Note: DataTimes also provides an online gateway to the text information in Dow Jones News/Retrieval.

Dialog

Dialog was the one of the first (and is probably the largest) database provider of its kind. Here's a representative sampling of some of the business-related information you'll find on Dialog: ABI/INFORM, Accounting and Tax Database, Brands and Their Companies, Business Dateline, Company Intelligence, D&B, Donnelley Demographics, Datamonitor Market Research, DMS/FI Contract Awards, DMS/FI Market Intelligence Reports, Foundation Grants Index, Industry Trends and Analysis, Insurance Periodicals Index, Jane's Defense and Aerospace, Journal of Commerce, M&A (Mergers and Acquisitions) Filings, Moody's Corporate News, PIERS Imports and Exports, Standard and Poor's Daily News, Tax Notes Today, Textline Global News, Thomas

Register Online, Trade and Industry ASAP, Trade and Industry Index, TRW Business Credit Profiles, U.S. Patents Fulltext. Dialog has a front-end software package, called DialogLink, available in DOS, Windows, and LAN for Windows versions. The company is working on a Macintosh version of DialogLink.

Dialog has also created a World Wide Web site (see Chapter 10 for more on the Web), which includes a list of all Dialog databases and a screen for ordering information from Dialog via fax-on-demand. You can visit the site at the following address: *http:// www.dialog.com*. Dialog intends to eventually make its entire database available to subscribers via the Web.

Dow Jones News/Retrieval

Dow Jones News/Retrieval's (DNJ/R) strength is in business news, business research data, and financial information. Subscribers can also utilize Clip, an electronic clipping service that scans over 1,300 sources, clipping and automatically delivering news items based on key words, symbols, or news codes. Its best resources include the Business Library (over 200 business and trade publications online), DataTimes (over 180 regional, national and industry publications), Business Dateline (business news from over 330 regional U.S. publications, including Dow Jones news wire, *Barron's,* and *The Wall Street Journal*), international news (*The Asian Wall Street Journal Weekly, The Wall Street Journal Europe,* and seventy other publications), major U.S. newspapers (*The Los Angeles Times, The New York Times, The Wall Street Journal,* and *The Washington Post*), the McGraw-Hill Library (over thirty-five industry publications), Predicasts Newsletters (over 550 trade and industry periodicals), and press releases wires (Business Wire, Canada NewsWire, and PR Newswire). Note: DJN/R has a flat-rate thirty-dollar-a-month pricing plan (called Market Monitor), which is designed for individual investors. Market Monitor allows users to access a limited range of services after 7 p.m. weekday evenings or all day weekends.

Global Report

Citibank's Global Report is a service whose strengths are in the areas of financial information and international news. It can provide company news and profiles, country news and profiles, financial markets information, foreign exchange data, global stock market data, industry news, money market information, top news headlines, and world news. Note: CompuServe (see Chapter 8) provides a gateway to Global Report.

Information America

Information America specializes in information on business-related legal filings: bankruptcy records, liens and judgments, lawsuits, etc. It also provides the Info AmeriCall search service for clients who don't have the time to perform a search themselves. Sleuth finds relationships between people and businesses; Asset Locator locates real property, property transfers, aircraft or watercraft ownership, etc.; Executive Affiliation connects individuals to the businesses in which he or she is an owner or key executive; Business Finder contains information on over 15 million companies in the United States and Canada; People Finder contains information on 111 million people, 92 million households, and 61 million phone numbers; Corporate and Partnership Records determines the name of record for a company, address, date of incorporation, names of officers and partners, etc.; County Records for California, Georgia, Pennsylvania, and Texas only; Bankruptcy Records for California, New Jersey, Texas, and parts of Georgia and Pennsylvania only; Liens and Judgments uncovers liabilities or encumbrances of assets for businesses and individuals; Lawsuits provides selected state-level court records with information on defendant, plaintiff, case number, filing date, and type of case; Dun's Business Records Plus lists a variety of reports on over 7.7 million public and private businesses; and SEC Filings contains reports filed by over 6,000 public companies with the Securities and Exchange Commission.

Knowledge Express

Knowledge Express is an online information service that specializes in commercial uses of technology. It focuses on news sources that cover research in progress and hosts a number of databases that list new technologies available for licensing. If you'd like access to information on little-known products and inventions developed in government and university laboratories, this is a great place to start.

Lexis/Nexis

Lexis is a legal research database, and Nexis a business research database. Nexis divides its databases into convenient "library" groupings. The following library-grouped databases are available on Nexis: the Accounting library, which includes the annual reports of selected corporations and government agencies plus accounting literature; the Asia/Pacific Rim library; the Banking News library, which features over eighty banking industry news and article databases; the Computer and Communications library, with over forty infotech information sources; the Company library, with over 230 files of business and financial information, including thousands of company and industry research reports; the Consumer Goods library, including over forty trade publications covering cosmetics, drugs, electronics, food, retail, and apparel industries; the Energy library; the Entertainment library, featuring news, litigation, film credits, grosses, company profiles, etc. for the entertainment industry; the Environment library, covering environmental hazards, EPA ratings, site responsibilities, company investigations, etc.; the Europe library; the Executive Branch library, with White House and federal agency news, including federal procurement, federal regulations, and the text of the Federal Register; the Insure Library, with leading insurance industry news sources, legal and regulatory materials, and analyst reports; the Invest-Analyst Research library for investors; the Legislative library, covering legislative activity in the U.S. Congress and 50 state legislatures; Lexpat, the U.S. Patent and Trademark Office Library (full text of U.S. patents issued since 1975, including the Manual of Classification and Index); the Marketing library, which includes information sources on advertising, market research, public relations, sales, promotions, consumer behavior, demographics, product announcements and product reviews; the Merger library, with data on merger and acquisition research, including SEC filings; the North/South American library; the People library, which concentrates on biographical information about people in the news; the Transportation News library, with more than twenty sources concentrating on aviation and automotive news and issues; and finally the World library, which covers international information and events.

NewsNet

NewsNet focuses on business news and industry newsletters. NewsNet carries over 700 newsletters and other news and information services. Here's a sample of what you'll find on NewsNet: American Business Lists Online, AP DataStream Business News Wire, Comline Japan Daily, Defense Daily, Investext, TRW Business Profiles, Xinhau English Language News Service.

Reuters NewsMedia

Reuters NewsMedia markets Reuters online services, including Reuters Business Briefing, Reuters Business Alert, and Reuters Corporate World News.

Summary

This chapter explained what sets business-oriented database service providers apart from other online services: They are strictly for business, for-fee services that focus on providing information rather than communication services. There are a number of ways that marketers can take advantage of this kind of service, from tracking business trends to monitoring the competition. It included a checklist for selecting the right service provider and profiled most of the major services in this category. (If you're ready to learn some procedures for conducting online searches, jump to Chapter 11.)

The online services in the next chapter are definitely *not* for business only. So, take off your shoes, loosen your tie, and get ready for the world of consumer-focused online services.

Chapter 7 Connection Section

Contact information for organizations and resources mentioned in or related to this chapter:

Claritas, provider of the Catalyst Connect online market research service, 607-257-5757

Data-Star, an online research databank with focus on European news and information, 215-687-6777

DataTimes, an online research databank including over 140
online versions of daily newspapers, 405-751-6400

Dialog, one of the first and largest online research databanks,
415-858-3785

Dow Jones News/Retrieval, an online research databank
with a focus on business news and financial information,
609-452-1511

Global Report, an online research databank with a focus on
financial information and international news, 212-657-3597

Information America, an online research databank with a focus on business-related legal filings, 800-235-4008

Knowledge Index, an online research databank with a focus
on commercial uses of technology, 215-293-9712

Lexis/Nexis, an online research databank with information
grouped into electronic "libraries," 800-346-3947

NewsNet, an online research databank with focus on business news and industry newsletters, 215-527-8030 or 800-
952-0122

Reuters NewsMedia, online research databases focusing on
corporate news, 212-603-3587

8

Digital Destinations: Consumer-Oriented Online Services

At first glance, consumer-oriented online services don't look very businesslike. (They're not supposed to.) In fact, what you'll find online when you visit America Online or Prodigy, or Compu-Serve are people *having fun.* They're playing online versions of multiuser video games. They're downloading megabytes of free software. They're sharing recipes and reading movie reviews and checking baseball stats. But don't be fooled—there's also a great deal of business activity going on behind the scenes. Users are buying products in online shopping malls, swapping electronic messages with business contacts in Munich or Mexico City, and looking up trademark information for a new product launch.

Consumer online services are *hot*; they're hot with users and with high-tech investors who are eager to grab a piece of the on-line action.

This chapter introduces you to the major consumer-oriented online players, as well as some recently announced services.

Read on if you want to find out what attracts marketers, as well as modem users, to consumer-oriented online services.

What Are Consumer-Oriented Online Services?

Consumer online services typically use simple point-and-click software to give users easy access to a wide variety of entertainment and information services. Consumer-oriented online services focus on the consumer market by providing a mix of online services that attracts recreational users. These services can include electronic games, free software, online shopping, discussion groups with other members, and technical support for computer products.

Although these services primarily target recreational users, they can also carry a good deal of value for business users; and many business owners and managers are active users of e-mail, file transfer, technical support services, and interaction with other subscribers. Online services used to be capital-intensive businesses that required wheelbarrows full of money for software and systems development, but now it's rapidly becoming easier and less expensive to enter the online marketplace. Suddenly the playing field is beginning to fill with new players. Around the time this book appears in stores, a division of Disney is expected to be up and running with a science-related service called Discover Online. Sony has just announced Sony Online, the first online service of its kind to be freely available on the Internet, and Prodigy followed quickly with the announcement of a new service called AstraNet for the World Wide Web.

Meanwhile, Apple Computer is bundling access software for its e-World online service into every new Macintosh computer. Microsoft reportedly will do the same when it packages its planned online service, The Microsoft Network, with every copy of Windows 95. That means that before long virtually every computer sold in North America will come equipped to easily access an online service.

Smart marketers are keeping tabs on developments in the consumer-oriented online service area because:

- A few of these online services (see the service provider profiles later in this chapter) provide valuable market research information within the databases and news services they carry.
- Others give you the opportunity to reach their subscriber base with advertising, publicity, or by becoming a member of their online shopping malls.

Anyone considering starting their own corporate online service, be it a bulletin board system or an Internet marketing site, should first evaluate how these consumer-oriented online services have designed their systems in order to attract users. They've spent millions of dollars testing what appeals to online users, what works and what doesn't. It makes sense to take advantage of that experience when you design your own system.

How to Choose the Right Service Provider

If you decide to see what all the fuss is about and become a member of one or more of these online services, follow these steps:

• *Evaluate the provider's list of resources.* Call the provider and ask for a list of the information databases it hosts on its system. (You'll also find a list of some of the best business-related resources for each provider in the profiles following this section.) Also ask about Internet connectivity. What kind of Internet services does the provider offer? (Fast forward to Chapter 10 for a complete list of Internet information tools and services.)

• *Examine the provider's pricing plans.* What does it cost to open an account? What does it cost on a monthly basis? Is there a two-tiered pricing plan for "basic" services and "advanced" services? What's included in the basic plan, and what will you have to pay extra for? How much extra?

• *Ask about software.* Does the provider give you software that allows you to access the service, or do you have to buy your own? Is the software available for your computer system (DOS, Windows, Macintosh)?

• *Take a test drive.* Ask the provider if it offers a free trial period to put the service through its paces, to see how it works for you, and to evaluate what kind of business benefits you can derive from it.

• *Look at the membership numbers and the membership profile.* How many people subscribe to this service and who are they? Does it appear that they could be colleagues of yours? prospects? customers? Get as much information about the service's user base as you can from the customer service representative and the provider's promotional material.

Profiles of the Major Consumer-Oriented Online Services

The online services listed in this section are multi-faceted: they usually provide electronic mail services, electronic forums where subscribers communicate with each other; games; free software; and sometimes business research databases. Some Cybermarketers will find services like these to be a good value and a good place to get an introduction to the world online. They are usually easy to learn and often offer a simplified user interface in the form of a DOS or Windows front-end software package.

The information provided in this section is as current as possible, but things change quickly in the online marketplace. Please contact providers for updates on their information resources, pricing, and membership.

America Online

With a membership of slightly over one million users, America Online (AOL) offers a friendly and easy to use interface that will be very familiar to users of the Microsoft Windows operating system. The e-mail system is intuitive and robust. The best business-related resources on AOL include the Cowles/Simba Media Information Network, Home Office Computing Magazine Online, Hoover's Handbook (company profiles), and the Microsoft Small Business Center (see Figure 8-1). AOL has been the most aggressive of the consumer online services in rolling out Internet-related applications, which now include an e-mail gateway, access to Usenet newsgroups, and WAIS and Gopher searches, as well as an Internet forum. AOL has recently merged with Redgate Communications, a privately held company that develops CD-ROMs and other multimedia products. Speculation is that the merger will spur AOL to move into new media markets, including interactive advertising.

Compuserve

CompuServe Information Service is the largest of the consumer-oriented online services, with nearly 2.5 million subscribers. Com-

Figure 8-1. Screen from America Online.

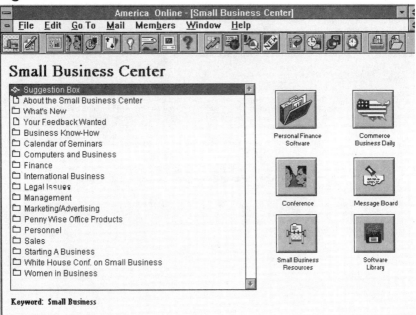

puServe is a broad-based service that offers a lot to attract both business and recreational users. It has an easy to use software interface for Windows called WinCim, its e-mail system is fairly easy to use, and its forums are a good place to interact with other business owners.

CompuServe's best marketing resources include: Biz*File, a database of 10 million U.S. and Canadian businesses (see Figure 8-2); Business Database Plus, with access to over 450 business and trade periodicals; the Business Demographics database; CEN-DATA, with statistics from the Census Bureau; Commerce Business Daily, the online version of this periodical listing of government contracts; vendor and special interest forums, including the Computer Consultant's Forum, the Entrepreneur's Small Business Forum, and the Public Relations and Marketing Forum; the IQuest Business Management InfoCenter; the Marketing/ Management Research Center; Neighborhood Report demographic data; Business News, including AP Online; Business Wire; the Dow Jones News Service; Executive News Service, an

Figure 8-2. Screen from CompuServe showing Biz*File database.

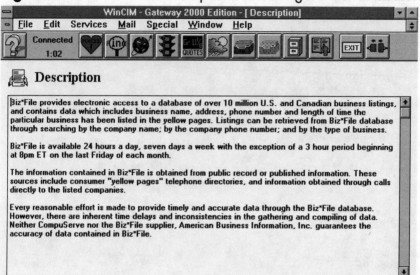

electronic clipping service, NewsGrid; US Newspaper Library and UK Newspaper Library; NTIS-Government Sponsored Research; and the Patent Research Center. CompuServe offers Internet e-mail, access to Internet mailing lists and discussion groups, an Internet forum, and the ability to access the service from the Internet. It plans to add more Internet services in 1995.

Prodigy

Prodigy is a partnership of IBM and Sears, Roebuck & Company, and it is the second largest service provider in this group, behind CompuServe. It has focused its marketing efforts on families who own home computers, so until now it hasn't put an emphasis on providing resources for business users. That may change in 1995. Prodigy recently announced that it will add a number of Internet services to its lineup and has started a new set of services called Prodigy for Business, which will include an online gateway to Dun & Bradstreet financial databases and to the Lexis/Nexis databases. It already offers a section called Company News, an Entrepreneur's Exchange, several columns from *Home Office Com-*

puting magazine, and a bulletin board for people running home-based businesses.

E-World

Apple Computer designed its e-World as an "electronic village." Users navigate from point to point on the service using the visual metaphor of a town complete with a Library, Newsstand, Community Center, Computer Center, eMail Center (including Internet e-mail gateway), and an Arts and Leisure Pavilion. E-World isn't divulging membership numbers, but Apple is bundling e-World software with all new Macintosh computers.

HOT TIP: A Note to Cybermarketers Who Can Provide Interesting Electronic "Content"

Many online service providers, and especially the newer ones like e-World, are rushing to outdo each other in trying to offer the best and most interesting kinds of information online. They're open to proposals from marketers who can make the connection between the service's subscribers and their information, particularly if that information is oriented toward entertainment, cultural, or leisure activities. (More on these opportunities in Chapter 12.)

GEnie

General Electric Information Service's GEnie is a low-cost way to buy a "window," or gateway, into the huge databases of research-service providers Dialog and Dow Jones News/Retrieval. Keep in mind that GEnie users do pay charges above and beyond normal service fees to access these advanced services. Any basic communications software can be used to access GEnie. GEnie is working on a "GEnie for Windows" software package to be released later this year.

But GEnie has promised to upgrade from basic Internet messaging to full Internet access for its users. GEnie's best business resources include access to Dow Jones News/Retrieval; access to Dun & Bradstreet's Company Profiles database; access to Bid-Board (a Department of Defense purchasing marketplace); the GEnie NewsStand, a searchable database of articles from over 900 publications; the Home Office/Small Business RoundTable; the Tax Roundtable (see Figure 8-3); the Thomas Register of companies; and the TRW Business Credit Profile Database.

ImagiNation

ImagiNation is a "strictly-for-fun" online network. It emphasizes multi-participant online games. If you're thinking about developing interactive products with an element of entertainment, check out the action on ImagiNation.

Coming Soon: Electronic Marketplace Systems

High-technology information provider International Data Group's Electronic Marketplace Systems (EMS) was under con-

Figure 8-3. Screen from GEnie listing features of the service.

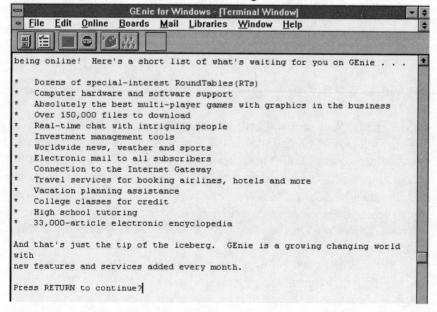

struction at the time of this writing. The purpose of EMS is reportedly to allow computer users to buy computer and electronics equipment online.

Coming Soon: Interchange

AT&T recently purchased from computer publisher Ziff-Davis their Interchange Online Network, targeted toward avid computer users, and promising to employ an easy-to-use Windows-based user interface. The creators of this service are attempting to push the capabilities of currently available online services through the application of "hyperlinks" that allow subscribers to skip from one related document or service to another.

Coming Soon: The Microsoft Network

Software giant Microsoft Corp., is planning its own online service and hopes to corner the market by supplying easy dial-up access to the service for all users of the upcoming next generation of its Windows PC operating system software, Windows 95 (scheduled for delivery in the Summer of 1995).

Microsoft chairman Bill Gates promises that his service will make it easy and inexpensive for users to browse the Internet, send e-mail, and access news and other information. Some analysts believe that Microsoft's entry into the online market could be great news for the online industry, invigorating innovation and stimulating demand.

But other online competitors such as CompuServe and America Online are understandably nervous. Buyers of Windows 95 will be able to subscribe to the service directly with a click of the mouse. That, combined with the Microsoft name, could give the company a big advantage in capturing market share from other online players.

There are other important marketing implications for the introduction of this particular online service. For one, businesspeople will be able to easily reach most of their prospects, customers, and suppliers through the same standard interface used for desktop computing. The service's most important feature will be the ease with which people will be able to communicate with each other. Also, the service may be offered at a very low fee or even be free, supported entirely or in part by online advertising sponsorships.

Here's the bottom line: The Microsoft Network could quickly double or triple the current number of users of consumer-oriented services (now estimated at between 5 million and 6 million subscribers) while blurring the distinctions that separate consumer-oriented from business-oriented online networks. If Windows 95 becomes as common as today's Windows operating system (now over 75 million computers), some industry observers say The Microsoft Network could make online computing nearly as universal as phone service.

On the Horizon

Here are three fairly safe predictions on trends that will continue within the consumer-oriented services arena:

1. *More and better Internet access.* The larger service providers can't afford to ignore the public's fascination with the net. The ability to send e-mail across the Internet will lead to access to Internet search tools like Gopher, participation in Internet mailing lists and discussion groups, and access to the Internet's multimedia World Wide Web.

2. *Faster connections.* When it comes to online services, faster is better. It's no fun waiting for files to transfer from the service's database to your computer or for graphic images to be slowly "drawn" on your computer screen. So online providers are looking for ways to speed up subscriber connections. Two of the most promising possibilities: ISDN (Integrated Services Digital Network) digital phone service and cable modems.

3. *More attention to the business market.* Look for more business news and industry databases to appear on the consumer-oriented services. These services are realizing that a significant number of their users aren't dialing in just for fun and games, but also to conduct research and network with other business professionals. Online providers are more than ever on the lookout for new ways to help marketers create a presence online that will not offend subscribers.

Summary

This chapter looked at the unique aspects of consumer-oriented online services and listed some steps to take before selecting a service provider. It reviewed each of the major services in this category, and provided a "sneak peak" at some services which weren't available to the public at the time of this writing, as well as a look at what the future holds for these services.

The next chapter offers some insights, opinion, and speculation regarding the future of interactive shopping via TV. Don't touch that dial! Stay tuned for interactive TV.

Chapter 8 Connection Section

Contact information for organizations and resources mentioned in or related to this chapter:

> Apple Computer Corp., provider of the e-World online service, 800-775-4556 or 408-974-1236
>
> America Online, provider of the America Online service, 800-334-6122 or 703-448-8700
>
> AT&T Corp., provider of the ImagiNation! online service, 800-618-1494
>
> AT&T Corp., provider of the Interchange online service, 800-595-8555
>
> CompuServe, provider of the CompuServe online service, 800-848-8199 or 614-457-8650
>
> International Data Group, to provide the Electronic Marketplace System online service, 415-286-6700
>
> General Electric Information Services, provider of the GEnie online service, 800-638-9636 or 301-251-6415
>
> Prodigy Services Company, provider of the Prodigy Interactive Personal Service online service, 800-776-3449 or 914-448-8000

9

The Five Thousand Channel Chunnel: Interactive TV

Many, if not most, of America's major media, cable, computer, software, and telecommunications companies are currently fighting to be the first to run a fiber-optic wire right into Joe Consumer's den. Attached to that wire will be a buzzing box to intelligently manage the incoming and outgoing stream of data generated by Joe Consumer's new-found interactive power. The amazing result? TV on Steroids! InfoSurfing for Sofa Spuds!

The obstacles appear overwhelming to many industry observers, but just look at the formidable armada sailing into these uncharted waters. You'll find names like Microsoft, EDS, Hewlett-Packard, Oracle, Bell Atlantic, US West, Silicon Graphics—it's a roll call of America's technology elite. If they can't do it, who can? You'll also find some not-so-familiar names, companies like IT Network, daVinci Time & Space, and CyberLab 7 that have staked their fortunes and survival on the fervently held belief that the future of TV will be interactive.

What Is Interactive Television?

At its visionary best, interactive television (I-TV) means that the TV screen becomes a window into cyberspace. With I-TV, consumers have access to whatever entertainment, information programming, or content their hearts desire. The TV set acts like a computer, perhaps roaming the Internet in search of information from the Library of Congress. Kids use the screen to hold a quick teleconference with their teachers. Home shoppers find suppliers of products and services using multi-level directories that provide information on store hours, prices, and availability. And you, the mighty cybermarketer, use this tool to inform and interact with your customers in their own homes.

That preceding description represents the dream of interactive television. The reality is that I-TV is still in a developmental test stage. Some experts think it may never emerge from that stage. Others are certain that successful tests will lead to a rapid roll-out of I-TV services nationwide.

Let's take an inside look at the technology, the applications, and some of the tests going on around the country, so you can decide for yourself.

Set-Top Boxes

A set-top box is a computer-based control unit that lets you determine what you watch on your television set. If you subscribe to cable TV, you may now control your set using a cable TV converter box.

A new generation of set-top boxes that will allow viewers to access interactive video services is now under development. The main job of these boxes will be to convert incoming digital signals into analog signals that can be accepted by your TV set. This transformation takes a great deal of computing power.

Future set-top boxes are also likely to offer links to other "communication appliances" such as telephones and fax machines. Either the local cable or telephone company will supply the digital feed running into the consumer's home. A single digital wire will deliver I-TV, phone calls, fax, and perhaps even Internet access. Links to home computers will allow online subscribers to access their accounts at speeds that leave today's analog modems in the digital dust.

The first set-top boxes are being built by computer hardware and software companies who are betting that I-TV will soon represent a huge market. Unfortunately, each of the major challengers (including Scientific-Atlanta, General Instrument, and others) has its own idea about the hardware and software requirements needed to create the ultimate set-top box. Eventually, there will have to be some sort of agreement on a standard protocol.

Another challenge is keeping the price of this "smart box" low enough so that consumers will be willing to buy or rent them from the local video-services provider. In order for I-TV to be effective, there will have to be a lot of computing horsepower built into set-top boxes. That additional power will be expensive to deliver, and consumers may not be willing to pay the price. Finally, the box will have to be easy to use, or consumers will reject it.

Two-Way Wiring

The cable TV wire running into your home has an abundance of data transfer (or bandwidth) capacity to spare. You may remember that the current standard for modems is 14,400 bits per second. (See Chapter 1 for details on modems.) Well, the average cable connection can handle 9,600,000,000 bits per second. That's 9.6 *billion* bps, in case you missed it. But that cable is basically a one-way street, funneling video data into the consumer's home, but not allowing the consumer to talk back to the network.

One of the primary goals of the information superhighway is to combine the two-way communications capability of the telephone system with the massive bandwidth capacity of the cable-TV system. When consumers have two-way capability, they can request a movie or other programming content and have it delivered immediately to their set.

Video Servers

How does the I-TV service provider store all the digital information and entertainment content that consumers will request? That's where video servers come in. Video servers are powerful computers running complex database programs. These computers are connected to the I-TV network via communication switches.

When a consumer's set-top box "calls" in from the network to request a particular piece of information or programming, the server retrieves the file containing that material and sends it out over the network. Because the storage format is digital, multiple users can request the same content at the same instant in time, with the server sending a digital copy to each user.

Among others, Apple Computer, Digital Equipment, Hewlett-Packard, IBM, Silicon Graphics, Sun, and Tandem are working on the hardware requirements for video servers, while Microsoft and Oracle are tackling the database software challenges.

Video-on-Demand

With smart set-top boxes offering two-way communications capability, consumers are ready for video-on-demand (VOD). VOD allows I-TV viewers to select movies, interactive games, television shows, educational videos, special interest programs, promotional videos, or other video content. The requested material appears on their screens in seconds.

Transaction Technology

How will the I-TV provider manage the tens of thousands of content requests, product purchases, and credit card transactions that will occur every day?

This is the logistical nightmare that gives I-TV technologists cold sweats. Managing billing for a regular cable system is a major undertaking. When you add the complexity of running credit checks, fulfilling product orders, and tracking the purchase activities of consumers who can pick and choose programs and products at will, the industry is facing a hurdle some experts think can't be overcome. But there are many high-tech wizards eagerly working on solutions to this problem.

Perhaps the promise of interactive TV will be the 1990s' version of putting a man on the moon. In other words, it's a challenge too good to pass up.

Five Marketing Applications for Interactive TV

Here's one major factor in favor of I-TV as a marketing tool: Consumers are very comfortable with their televisions. They don't have to learn a new technology to use it, as they do with online services based on computers and modems. Most households have at least one TV set and are already familiar with the concept of shopping via television from the success of services like the Home Shopping Network and QVC.

Assuming the technical and logistical problems will eventually be ironed out, let's take a look at some potential marketing applications for I-TV.

1. *Sponsored content.* This takes us back to the days of early television, when almost every show had a primary sponsor (e.g., Texaco Star Theater). Then television shows became increasingly expensive to produce and networks hiked ad rates as viewership increased. Marketers began to share the costs of sponsorship by running short "spot" ads during commercial breaks.

With the advent of I-TV, it may become possible for marketers to again become sole sponsors of individual television programs. As I-TV audiences gain more control over the shows they select, marketers will sponsor programs that project the image they desire in the marketplace. Single sponsorship of a program delivers the twin benefits of exclusivity and greater input and control over the content of the show.

2. *Targeted home shopping.* I-TV will multiply the opportunities to create "narrowcasting" content programming that zeroes in on the special interests of a single group of viewers. Imagine, if you will, The Sports Car Channel, The Perfume Channel, or The Skateboard Channel. These channels will be like video-based special interest magazines, watched by the hard-core enthusiasts and opinion leaders who also happen to be the most likely buyers of the sponsor's products.

3. *Electronic directories.* Let's say Jack Cyberconsumer wants to see the new hit movie *CyberMarketing II* at the multiplex, but he's not sure what time it's playing. He's looking for the entertainment section of the newspaper, but can't find it. He considers calling the theater's prerecorded announcement, but he

doesn't want to have to listen to the schedules for seven or eight other movies. So, he turns on his I-TV and uses its menu system to find "local attractions." He selects "movies" and then "multiplex." He reads a brief synopsis of the story, checks the time and the price, and then prints a copy of the information on his laser printer.

That was an example of an electronic directory in action. The consumer "drills down" through a menu system to get exactly the information or services he or she needs. And if this sort of video-based information selection process works for movies, it would work just as well for someone needing information on sporting events, concerts, or plane tickets.

4. *Video catalogs.* Jack's wife, Janice Cyberconsumer, is shopping for a new car, but she can't decide between the Accord or the Taurus. So, she uses her touchpad remote to request ten-minute video presentations on each model. These mini-movies are like low-key commercials, offering Jane background information on gas mileage, engine performance, and customer satisfaction ratings. At the end of each program, the local dealership gets a short plug. Jane is also invited to complete an interactive application for an auto loan.

5. *Interactive infomercials.* Have you ever had the humbling experience of wanting to buy one of those household gadgets (like a juice machine) from a TV infomercial and finding there was no credit available on your credit card? Or perhaps your spouse convinced you not to make the purchase at that particular time. But later, when he or she has left the house and/or the Visa is reactivated, you decide to treat yourself to (pick one) miracle thigh creme, a super sponge mop, or the incredible stain remover. You use your set-top box to request the half-hour infomercial and sit back to enjoy it with your credit card in hand.

With video-on-demand, consumers will be able to request any type of content, including commercials. If you can create an infomercial that is interesting and informative, that will attract viewers browsing through video-on-demand directories, maybe they will watch your infomercial instead of *Casablanca* or *Gone With the Wind*. Wouldn't that be an accomplishment!?

Those are a few thoughts on using I-TV to sell more products and services. Now let's look at some actual I-TV trials.

Testing Testing: Profiles of Several I-TV Pilot Projects

Trials of interactive TV concepts are taking place in living rooms all across the country. Consumers are getting a chance to sample the future of television as cable, telecommunications, and entrepreneurial I-TV start-ups put in place their visions of interactivity for the masses. From these initial tests, one or more winners should emerge.

And by the way, would you like to place *your* bet? Most of the companies spearheading these tests are anxious to find corporate sponsors willing to participate (i.e., advertise) in exchange for getting some early feedback on the marketing potential of I-TV.

• Telecommunications provider Bell Atlantic is testing an interactive in-room video directory at hotels in Atlanta and San Diego. Hotel guests can key in numerical codes from a directory menu on a TV to view and hear about local advertisers, events, and services.

• Another Bell Atlantic I-TV project offers video-on-demand and other services in northern Virginia. Stargazer uses a graphic "shopping mall" to help users navigate though the system. Bell Atlantic has convinced clothing catalog marketer Lands' End and retailer Nordstrom's to be early participants in the interactive mall.

• The daVinci Channel is an I-TV experiment being developed by daVinci Time & Space of San Mateo, California. This twenty-four-hour-a-day, advertiser-supported service will be targeted at children ages three to twelve.

• Interactive Network of San Jose, California is charging customers about $200,000 to test interactive video advertising in San Francisco, Chicago, and South Bend, Indiana.

• U S Avenue is an ambitious project from Interactive Video Enterprises in San Ramon, California. IVE is a division of US West, the Englewood, Colorado-based regional phone company. Two hundred households in Omaha, Nebraska, will be hooked up to the service in late 1994. The roster of advertisers includes

J.C. Penney's catalog division, Hallmark, Nordstrom's, Virgin Records, FTD, Richard Wolffers (sports collectibles and memorabilia), and Ford Motor Company.

The U S Avenue concept is that I-TV content should be "layered." The first layer that the viewer sees should contain entertainment or information. For example, in the *first* level, a documentary-type program on the history of the Jaguar could lead to a *second* level that provides information on the local Jaguar dealership. A *third* level could allow the viewer to request a product brochure. As another example, a first-level video on the creation of a Garth Brooks album could lead to a second level where the viewer could order the CD using a separate hand-held device. The viewer's credit card information would already be preapproved and on file in the cable companies' computer databases, captured when the consumer signed up to use the system.

• Pacific Bell had planned on an I-TV trial in Milpitas, California, but announced that it will skip the trial phase and immediately begin to build a statewide interactive network. It's estimated the network will cost $16 billion and take over seven years to build.

• Time Warner's Full Service Network I-TV trial in Florida will begin with a few consumers who have $6,000-dollar "home communication terminals" hooked up to their TV sets. These early I-TV guinea pigs will try out digital services like movies on demand, multi-player games, and electronic catalogs from direct mail merchants such as Eddie Bauer. The second tier of services (to be offered later) includes news on demand, sports stats on demand, access to library resources on screen, and a broader range of interactive shopping options.

Summary

This chapter looked at the technology that makes interactive television possible, including set-top boxes, two-way networks, video servers, video-on-demand, and transaction technology. It considered some of the marketing applications that are being used in current I-TV trials and speculated on some of the ways that I-TV could be used once services are in place. It also took a quick look at some of the interactive TV projects being tested around the country.

The next chapter looks at a phenomena that already offers many of the interactive, multimedia services the I-TV industry is hoping to put into place, the international network of computer networks known as the Internet.

Chapter 9 Connection Section

Contact information for organizations and resources mentioned in or related to this chapter:

Bell Atlantic, 215-963-6531
daVinci Time & Space, 415-525-2880
Interactive Network, 408-325-5000
Interactive Video Enterprises, 510-355-2980
Pacific Bell, 415-542-9000
Time Warner, 212-598-7200

10

The Incredible Infobahn: Business on the Internet

Have you heard the story of the wired Coke℗ machine? The "customers" of this particular vending machine were students at the Carnegie Mellon University Computer Science Department. The machine was on the first floor, and the students were on the third floor. They quickly tired of making the long trip down a few flights of stairs only to discover that the unit was empty. So these enterprising students connected the machine to a nearby computer linked to the Internet. They could then send electronic messages to the machine to check whether its chutes were full of cans or empty, saving themselves an unnecessary trip. That was the one of the earliest examples of the electronic commerce on the Internet.

Although this chapter briefly examines the business side of the Internet, its primary purpose is to supply a background on the technical and logistical issues involved in getting connected to the Internet. It starts with a brief overview of the Internet, how it got started, and the impact it may have on your marketing plans. You'll also find a list of companies that provide access to the Internet and a review of software tools and applications that will help you navigate the net. Later chapters examine specific marketing applications for the Internet, i.e., market research, advertising, conducting sales transactions, in greater detail.

What Is the Internet?

The Internet is a worldwide "network of networks," connecting thousands of computers and millions of users. Once the exclusive domain of university academics and researchers working for government agencies, the Internet now connects, via telecommunications lines, some 40,000 central computer "nodes" at universities, government labs, and corporations. Each node may include hundreds of computers, which in turn can be connected to thousands of individual users. Some experts estimate that as many as 30 million people worldwide have some access to the Internet through a direct connection, an online service provider, or their company or organization.

How Did the Internet Start?

The Internet started as a U.S. Department of Defense project in the 1960s. Its original purpose was to provide a decentralized, fail-safe connection for military researchers and computer defense networks that could function even in the event of war or other disaster.

It grew with remarkable speed as government agencies, university campuses, libraries, and businesses all set up links to the growing network. As it began to spread its tendrils to other parts of the world, the overall value of the net grew along with its user base.

Who Owns the Internet?

The Internet isn't owned or managed by any single individual, corporation, or organization. In fact, the Internet isn't a single communications network—it's a "super-network" made up of connections between many, many other networks. There are committees (the Internet Architecture Board, the Internet Engineering Task Force, the Internet Society, etc.) that evaluate and make recommendations on technical issues related to the network, but the Internet itself is governed more by a set of guidelines and codes of behavior than by any specific regulations.

Although the U.S. Government's National Science Foundation (NSF) has been providing about $24 million a year in subsidies for the Internet, a major transition is now in the works. The NSF will be withdrawing most of its funding of the Internet's backbone network, and major communications service providers will begin to replace what was a patchwork of regional networks with a more secure, reliable, and technologically state-of-the-art system.

Who Uses the Internet?

The Internet's overall user profile is changing radically due to its explosive growth (as many as 100,000 new users a month). A large portion of that growth is coming from the commercial sector, which accounts for about half of all network traffic. About 35 percent of the traffic is from universities, educational institutions, and researchers; the rest is government or military-related.

According to the Internet Society, about half of the Fortune 500 companies are on the Internet, and nearly two-thirds of Internet users work for major corporations. In many companies, engineers and researchers have used the Internet for years. But access is quickly extending to users in marketing, sales, and customer service departments.

The Internet is an open electronic community where information is shared freely and where geographic boundaries can be crossed with a flick of your computer's mouse. As such, it's a wonderfully flexible business resource. In 1991, a decade-old ban on commercial use of the Internet was lifted, and in the very near future, most businesses, as well as most libraries, schools, and city halls, will have Internet connections.

How Big Is the Internet?

The Internet blankets the entire planet. There are connection points in over 150 countries, and that number increases every month. From Algeria to Antigua, from Brussels to the Bahamas, countries are rushing to set up Internet links.

The number of Internet users is an open question, and will probably remain so. The most commonly quoted figure is from 20 to 30 million users. Some estimates focus on the United States; others are worldwide. Some estimates are of the core Internet, which includes only hosts using the Internet's TCP/IP protocol to connect to the backbone network operated by the National Science Foundation. Others include anyone who can exchange e-mail through Internet gateways like America Online, CompuServe, or local bulletin board systems.

The Internet connects about 3.2 million computer hosts (about two million of those are in the United States). Some guess that as many as ten computers are connected to each host (that's where the 30 million figure comes from). Others say that many of those "hosts" are really just individual PC users. The key factor may not be exactly how many users are accessing the Internet at any point in time, but whether or not the Internet user base is of a significant size and whether that base is growing.

It's clear that the Internet offers an important and attractive new medium for information and communication. And it's only going to get easier to access. New software and service packages are making it a snap to navigate the Internet. Online service providers like America Online and CompuServe are offering their users limited gateways to the Internet, which will soon be transformed into full-access connections. The real wild card may be the Internet's World Wide Web, which offers a whole, new multimedia Internet experience that is absolutely irresistible. (More on World Wide Web later in this chapter.)

How Does the Internet Work?

The Internet is set up in three "tiers." The top tier is the National Science Foundation Network. Regional networks and major access providers make up the middle tier that acts as a link to the final tier. That tier includes smaller access providers, corporations, organizations, universities, and individual users.

The Internet naming system divides Internet sites into "domains." If you're with a business organization, you'll fall into the commercial domain, which uses .com as the last part of the address, for example "ford.com." Other domains include .mil for military-related organizations: "army.mil," .gov for government agencies: "whitehouse.gov," .org for non-profits: "red-cross.org," and .edu for educational institutions: "yale.edu."

Internet e-mail addresses have a @ symbol in the middle. The characters on the left side of the @ represent the user's identity on the system, while the characters to the right refer to the domain server or network where the user's e-mail box is located.

In computer terminology, a *protocol* is a set of guidelines that computers use to communicate. There are two major protocols for the Internet: TCP, Transmission Control Protocol, and IP, Internet Protocol. TCP divides data files traveling on the Internet into smaller chunks of information called packets. Each of these packets is numbered to that they can be reassembled when they reach their destination. Special Internet computers, called routers, examine the packets and find the most efficient path for them to travel, relaying them from router to router over various networks. IP handles the addressing and delivery of data to the right destination. The IP protocol marks each packet with its source and destination address.

The Internet, contrary to some media reports, is not a UNIX-only system, using a series of arcane and complex commands that no one except software programmers can understand. Although based on UNIX, the Internet is a network that is very flexible in terms of the computer operating systems that can use it. (Windows, fine. Macintosh, no problem.)

Another common misconception about the Internet is that when you hook up to it, your company's computers automatically become information servers on the net, allowing anyone and everyone access to your computer and its files. Quite to the contrary, you have to put forth some effort to allow access to your computer system; it doesn't happen automatically. Your computer and its files can't be accessed directly from the Internet unless you set it up that way.

QUICK LOOK: Worried About Internet Security?

There's been a lot of discussion about the relative lack of security for companies who want to do business on the Internet. Scores of network hardware and software vendors, sensing that concern, are quickly filling the security void with products that enable secure access, file transfer, and communications on the Internet. Following is a list of some of those vendors.

BBN Internet Server from Bolt, Beranek & Newman, 617-873-3000

DEC S.E.A.L. service from Digital Equipment Corp., 508-952-3266

EnTrust public-key security system from Northern Telecom, 800-667-8437

FasTraq Security Modem from LeeMah Data Security, 510-786-0790

FireWall IRX Internetwork Router from Livingstone Enterprises, 510-426-0770

FireWall-1 from Internet Security Corp., 617-863-6400 or *info@security.com*

Netra Internet Server from Sun Microsystems, 800-786-0785

NetSite Secure Commerce Server from Netscape Communications Corp., 415-254-1900

PGP software for Windows or Mac from ViaCrypt, 602-944-0773

RSA Sign, RSA Check, and MailSafe from RSA Data Security, 415-595-8782

SecretAgent software from AT&T Secure Communications, 800-203-5563

SecureNet Key, Defender Series access control units, and Windows Defender Management Software (WinDMS) from Digital Pathways, 415-964-0707 or sales at *digi-path.com*

Secure / IP security cards from TGV, 408-457-5200

Security Router from Network Systems Corp., 612-424-4888

SecureWeb Toolkits from Terisa, 415-617-1836

Sidewinder secure server from Secure Computing, 612-628-2700

TIS Gauntlet and TIS Trusted Mail from Trusted Information Systems, 301-854-6889

Veil encryption software from TECSEC, 703-506-9069

WebFace Challenge/S server from Silicon Graphics, 800-800-7441

Five Marketing Applications for the Internet

Here's the bottom line on what the Internet means to you as a marketer: increased productivity. Specifically, the ability to retrieve information and communicate with your market faster and at a lower cost. Here's how:

1. *Sending Messages.* In Chapter 4, we covered the benefits of electronic mail in detail. One of the Internet's primary functions is to act as a worldwide exchange medium for e-mail. So much e-mail, in fact, that the computers which commercial service providers use to support e-mail sometimes get overwhelmed with the sheer volume of traffic. On a typical day, over 25 million people use the Internet, either directly or indirectly, to exchange e-mail. You can use Internet e-mail to send and receive messages from your customers, colleagues, or business partners. You can also use your e-mailbox as a delivery point for marketing and industry information provided by commercial news services. You can even set up e-mail boxes that automatically respond to customer inquiries with a predetermined marketing message reply.

2. *Transferring Files.* You can use the Internet not only to exchange mail, but also to transfer files from your computer to another computer or to retrieve files from someone else's system. The Internet has a standard means of transferring files, called file transfer protocol (ftp), which you can use to transfer files from an Internet host computer to your computer. Many Internet hosts support anonymous ftp, which means you don't need to have a password or account set up on the host machine in order to transfer files.

3. *Monitoring News and Opinions.* The Internet is also a place for online discussion and interaction. It's used by millions of people to share ideas and interests in a town hall atmosphere. Thousands of discussion groups, or newsgroups, cover multitudes of topics, ranging from juggling to kite-building to gun collecting to lucid dream research to creating paper sculptures using origami techniques. Like newsgroups, mailing lists link people with similar interests. Contributions to the mailing list are channeled through an individual or automated mail-list software and periodically routed to subscribers.

4. *Searching and Browsing.* The Internet is a repository of vast amounts of digitized information in the form of books, manuals, technical data, reference works, government publications, and so

on. You can use Internet software tools like Archie, Finger, Go-pher, Mosaic, Veronica, WAIS, and the World Wide Web to search for these files and databases.

5. *Posting, Hosting, or Presenting Information.* There are nu-merous ways to present information on the Internet, from posting short articles and company news items in Internet newsgroups to setting up an ftp site where customers can retrieve useful files to creating a multimedia business site on the World Wide Web. We'll cover your marketing options in greater detail later in the book.

The World Wide Web and Mosaic

The World Wide Web (WWW or Web) is a hypertext system re-siding on the Internet. Hypertext is a software-based technology used for linking files and documents. The Web allows Internet users to view and present information in a variety of media (text, graphics, audio, even video) on the Internet. A browser program enables Internet users to view documents and files on the Web. Anyone with a browser program, like Mosaic, can use the hyper-text capability of the Web to easily "mouse click" from one linked document to another, no matter where the documents are located on the net.

When you're on the Web, you see "pages" of information on your computer screen that look somewhat like pages in a maga-zine. These pages can contain text, full-color images, and icons that enable you to access audio and video files. A typical Web page will have selected items (called hyperlinks), usually text, which are linked to other files or documents. By clicking your mouse on these "pointers," the linked information is retrieved so that it can be viewed on your screen—even if that information resides on a computer server located halfway around the world.

In fact, Web servers are located everywhere on the planet. There are thousands of Web servers, and more servers are going online each day. You could spend days "cruising" the Web and barely scratch the surface of the information found there.

The Web has quickly evolved into a very popular Internet application. There are art galleries and magazines on the Web.

There are even Web sites dedicated to icons of popular culture such as Elvis and Barney the purple dinosaur.

Business is getting involved in the Web in a big way. Fortune 500 companies are creating sophisticated Web sites that present information on their products and services. Small-business owners are putting up Web pages that feature everything from the menu of a Chinese restaurant to the price schedule for a dry cleaning establishment. Entrepreneurs are creating Web "cyber-malls" shared by merchants of all kinds. A few brave individuals are even starting businesses that are based on selling products (such as music CDs) exclusively via the Web.

All you need to access the Web is the right kind of Internet connection and an Internet software program that includes a Web browser. We'll cover how to get both in this chapter.

Choosing the Right Internet Service Provider

A variety of online service providers can offer you limited or full access to the Internet. Some offer Internet access as an extension of their primary service, and others specialize in Internet access. Some market their services only to users in a particular geographic region, while others sell Internet access services to users throughout the country.

You can open an account with a local bulletin board system. Some offer Internet e-mail services, but most are limited in terms of their access to Internet search and retrieval tools like Gopher, ftp, and Telnet (see Figure 10-1).

You can also access some Internet options through a consumer-oriented online service provider like America Online or CompuServe. These services also have their limitations when it comes to offering the full range of Internet possibilities, but all the major services are moving toward the objective of offering full access.

You can set up an account with a local or regional Internet access specialist. Most major metropolitan areas have one or more providers who offer connections to businesses and individuals in their service area. You can also set up an account through a national Internet service provider. These companies typically offer

Figure 10-1. The Telnet address books.com on the Internet.

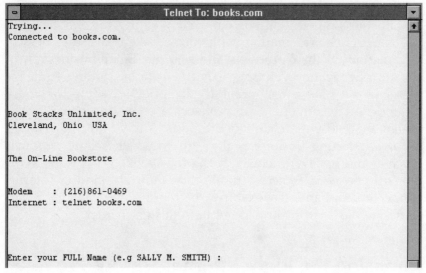

either local dial-up numbers in major cities or the ability to dial in through a toll-free number.

There are four main levels of connection offered by Internet service providers:

1. *Gateway.* A bulletin board system or consumer-oriented online service like America Online or CompuServe can provide you with this type of account. As mentioned earlier, you can use services such as Internet e-mail and Internet mailing lists, but (at least for now) you won't have access to the full range of services provided by companies that specialize in connecting users to the Internet. With a gateway account, you aren't "on the Internet" in the strictest sense. Instead, you're using the service provider's computer as a host, and it's serving as a kind of window onto the net for your computer.

2. *Dial-up, terminal, or shell accounts.* This type of Internet account is typically the base-level account offered by Internet access specialists. Although inexpensive (around $10 per month for an individual user), accounts of this type typically confine the user to viewing only text files on the Internet. Like the gateway connection listed above, dial-up account users are also not on the

Internet as a host computer, and instead are using the service
provider's computer as the host system.

3. *SLIP, compressed SLIP, or PPP accounts.* This type of Internet account is a little more expensive, but it's also a faster,
easier way to access the Internet. It also offers the capacity, when
using a browser program like Mosaic, to view graphical files on
the World Wide Web. The great majority of new Internet accounts
for individual users are of the SLIP variety. Some office networks
are connected to the Internet via SLIP as well, but most office
systems administrators choose one of the higher speed options
described below.

4. *High-speed dedicated lines.* Connecting an office network to
the Internet is usually a more complex and expensive process
than setting up an individual connection, and a wider variety of
options are available. Decision factors include the speed of data
transmission, whether the connection will be full-time (continuous) or on-demand (periodic), and which Internet services will be
available to which users on the network. Special higher-speed
phone lines (56,000 bps and up) are leased from the telephone
company. Since a regular modem can't handle these higher-speed
lines, special hardware is required as well.

Here's a strong recommendation: Choose an Internet service provider and connection option that gives you full access to the
World Wide Web. There are strong indications that the Web is
rapidly becoming the medium of first choice for marketing activities on the Internet. It's easy to see why: The Web is colorful and
exciting, and it makes Internet navigation simple and straightfor-
ward. What's more, there are virtually no objections being raised
to companies advertising or selling on the Web.

HOT TIP: Mac Users, Heed This

If you're a Macintosh computer user, find out if your service provider has some familiarity with Mac Internet connectivity. The
software issues are a little different from those for PC users, so
finding a service that has had some experience with Mac connections would be a big plus.

Questions to Ask Potential Service Providers

Select the right Internet service provider, and you'll be up and running on the Internet without too much time, trouble, or expense. Choose the wrong Internet service provider, and you may find yourself frustrated and bogged down in arcane and complex technical issues. Here's a list of questions that will help you find the right match.

• *What Internet services are available?* Your provider should offer access to the full range of basic Internet applications including e-mail messaging services; access to Internet mailing lists and newsgroups; easy access to information search tools like Archie, Gopher, Telnet, Veronica, and WAIS; and the ability to access the graphically rich, multimedia World Wide Web.

• *What special services are available to business users?* If you're connecting your office to the Internet, find out if your service provider can put limits on the kinds of services your office receives. (Some limits of this kind are good. You may not want employees getting on strange Internet newsgroup mailing lists, for example.) Ask if they can assist you in obtaining an Internet domain name for your company, which identifies your company as a node or site on the Internet.

• *Are there any restrictions on business use?* A few Internet access providers, particularly some regional nonprofit networks, have tighter restrictions on business use of Internet than commercial Internet service providers. Check the fine print of your agreement, and if the restrictions appear too confining, take your business elsewhere.

• *What specific marketing-related services do you provide?* Some service providers put extra emphasis on attracting business accounts and realize that one of the key reasons companies connect to the Internet is to use it as a vehicle for marketing communications. These providers offer special services with a marketing focus. For example, ftp drop box services allow you to set up a company file directory with open public access. This allows you to store files for customers to pick up and lets others deposit files there for you. Gopher servers allow you to set up a text "page" on the Internet with a table of contents-like menu systems that identifies text that file users can select and immediately view on screen (see Figure 10-2). A growing number of service providers are now offering World Wide Web services, which assist you in creating a graphically rich "home page" or "site" for your company on the Internet. (For more information on Internet marketing options, see the chapters on advertising and sales.)

• *What is the rate structure?* Request a price sheet with a cost breakdown. Charges should be clearly spelled out and categorized according to the type of connection and the kinds of services provided. Will you pay a flat monthly fee or only be charged for the time you're on the Internet? Are most services covered in your basic monthly fee, or are extra charges tacked on for every additional service you use?

• *What type of technical support is available?* If you're an individual user, will they help you set up your modem and software? If they're attaching your office network to the Internet, will they help you by installing the required hardware and by making arrangements with your local telephone service provider, or do

Figure 10-2. Gopher server screen from NYSERnet.

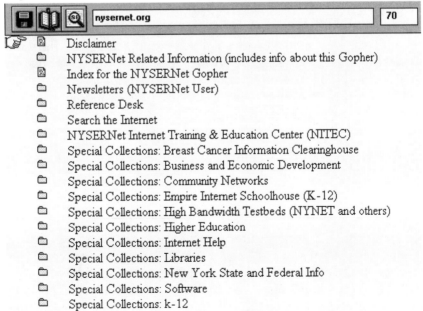

they leave it up to you? Do they offer on-site support (few do) or a phone support line (a must)? Will they provide you with Internet software programs (on disk or on their server for you to download) and will they help you configure those programs? Do they provide any training or classes for new users? What about documentation—what kind of information materials do they provide after you sign up?

HOT TIP: Register Your Domain Name—Now

If you're already doing business on the Internet (or plan to), don't wait to register your company name or product name as an Internet domain name.

Your domain name uniquely identifies your company as a node (or site) on the Internet. Most companies choose the name of their organizations as their domain name (xerox.com), but others come up with creative alternatives. (Harley-Davidson, for example, recently registered "hog.com" as their domain.)

The actual registration for a domain name goes through the InterNIC, a nonprofit consortium that provides Internet-related services. There's been a population explosion of commercial sites (the InterNIC has received as many as 1,200 domain name requests in a single month), so it can take two weeks or more to research the availability of your name and register it. The InterNIC's home page on the Web <*http: // www.internic.net*> includes information on domain name registration.

There have already been scuffles over the ownership of several domain names. In a couple of instances, companies have even registered the names of their competitors. So don't get caught napping. Start the registration process ASAP.

• *How reliable is the technology backing up my connection?* This could be a critical issue, particularly if, over time, the Internet becomes the key communications medium for your company. If your service provider isn't able to deliver reliable and consistent service, you could experience the sinking feeling of having your network connection being down because your service provider isn't equipped to handle the volume of transmissions its customer base generates. The explosive growth of the Internet has strained the resources of some providers. Try to find out if they have enough phone lines to accommodate their users. Continual busy signals or slow response from the host machine could be a warning sign that the provider's system is overburdened.

Selected Internet Service Providers

This following list isn't meant to be an exhaustive directory of Internet service providers. There are scores of providers located throughout the world, and new service providers open shop every week. The companies listed here are some of the largest and most active Internet connection services in the U.S., and most of them provide connections on a nationwide basis, with local dial-up numbers throughout the country. (Some even have access numbers in other parts of the world, so that you can log on to the Internet when traveling internationally.)

If you live in or near a major metropolitan area, you can often find a locally based Internet access provider simply by picking up a copy of your local computer magazine and paging through the ads. Soup to nuts Internet access (e-mail, Gopher, ftp, Telnet, and World Wide Web access) for individual users is now available from some service providers for as little as $20 per month.

ANS provides a wide range of Internet access services nationwide, 703-758-7700 or *info@ans.net*

Alternet provides Internet access nationwide, 703-204-8000 or *alternet-info@uunet.uu.net*

CompuServe Network Services provides connections for office networks through this division, which is separate from the consumer-oriented CompuServe Information Service described in Chapter 8, 614-457-8600

Delphi Internet provides access to all Internet services except the Web, and working to quickly provide Web access as well, 800-544-4005

IBM Global Network provides Internet access primarily to users of IBM's OS/2 Warp operating system software, 813-878-3000 (see Figure 10-3)

Figure 10-3. Home page for IBM's Internet service.

Internet Express provides dial-up service in many major cities or toll-free access nationwide, 719-592-1201 or 800-592-1240 or *service@usa.net*

internetMCI will provide service/software package beginning early 1995, 800-898-4979

Netcom provides the NetCruiser package, which includes easy access software, 408-983-5950 or *info@netcom.com*

Performance Systems International (PSI) provides Explore OnNet with the PSI InterRamp Internet access service, 703-904-4100 or *info@psi.com*

Pipeline provides Pipeline Internet access software for service users, 212-267-3636 or *info@pipeline.com* (see Figure 10-4)

SprintLink provides high-speed leased lines for office networks, 703-904-2680

If you'd like a more complete list of Internet access providers, contact the InterNIC, an organization that offers free Internet guidance and information, at 800-444-4345.

Software for Navigating the Internet

The following software programs were all designed with a single idea in mind: to make it easy for the typical computer user to access the Internet. There was a good deal of negative press recently about the Internet being difficult to access and navigate. That's incorrect. With the right kind of software, navigating the Internet can be a breeze.

Here are the elements you're looking for in an Internet software program (or programs):

- Internet e-mail support
- A newsgroup reader for organizing and viewing postings to Internet mailing lists
- A Gopher client ("client" meaning "tool" or "module") for locating and viewing informational text files on the Internet
- An ftp client for transferring files from the Internet to your computer's hard drive
- A Telnet client for logging on to a computer as a remote user
- A graphical browser for viewing documents on the World Wide Web

Figure 10-4. Pipeline's Internet interface.

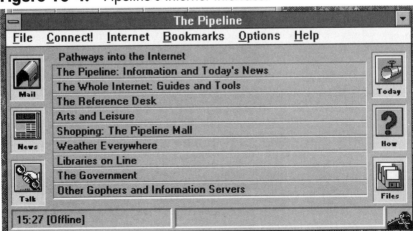

The software vendors listed below are engaged in a heated competition to provide the fastest, easiest, most productive software for accessing the Internet. The likely result of this battle will be innovative approaches to Internet navigation and a further growth in active users of the Internet, even among the ranks of computer novices. Marketers can't help but benefit, both as users of Internet resources and as presenters of marketing information on the Internet.

Where do you go to get the software?

Several of these programs are available as shareware on the Internet, which means you can retrieve copies of programs to try out before making the decision to actually purchase them. If you have access to the tools needed to retrieve files on the Internet (ftp), you can get working versions of InternetWorks Lite at *ftp.booklink.com/lite* and NetScape at *ftp.mcom.com.*

Some of the programs are available in larger computer stores (such as Internet Express), and a few are available in major bookstores (e.g., Internet in a Box).

Some are available direct from the provider (internetMCI and NOV*IX Internet for NetWare).

A couple of the software programs listed here are meant to be used with a specific Internet access service: Netcom's Netcruiser and MCI's internetMCI, for instance. Other programs are packaged with free trial sign-ups with a particular service provider, but still give you the option of using whatever service provider you choose.

Recommended: We've already covered why marketers must have access to the Web, so either select a software package that includes a Web browser as one of its component parts, or get your hands on a stand-alone Web browser like NetScape to complement software that includes the other Internet tools. Your Web browser will also give you access to the resources listed throughout this book by their URLs (Uniform Resource Locators), which are the Web equivalent to Internet e-mail addresses.

You'll find contact information for each of the companies listed here in the Connection Section at the end of this chapter. Call them for further information and directions on how to best obtain copies of their programs.

- BW-Connect NFS from Beame & Whiteside
- Explore OnNet from FTP Software
- Internet Anywhere from Mortice Kern Systems
- Internet Chameleon from NetManage
- Internet Connection from the Morris Group
- Internet Express from Phoenix Technologies, Ltd.
- Internet in a Box from Spry/O'Reilly & Associates
- internetMCI from MCI
- InternetWorks and InternetWorks Lite from BookLink Technologies
- IWare for NetWare from Internetware, Inc.
- NetCruiser from Netcom
- NetScape from NetScape Communications Corp.
- NOV*IX Internet for NetWare from Firefox
- Pipeline for Windows and Macintosh from InterCon Systems
- Quarterdeck Mosaic from Quarterdeck Office Systems
- Reflection Mosaic from WRQ
- Smartcom Internet Explorer from Hayes MicroComputer Products, Inc.
- SuperHighway Access for Windows from Frontier Technologies
- Super Mosaic from Luckman Interactive
- WinGopher Complete from Ameritech Library Services
- WinWeb and MacWeb from EINet

Summary

This chapter included a brief overview of the Internet: who uses it, the kinds of activities you can conduct on the Internet, and the tools that help you find information and perform specific tasks. It listed vendors who offer commercial Internet access software and services and explained how to avoid problems that can crop up when you first get connected.

That's the end of this section of the book, covering the basic tools you need to go online. The next section, Part II, covers marketing tasks you can engage in using digital media.

HOT TIP: New Operating Systems Ready to Tap
the Power of the Net

Computer operating systems with built-in Internet utilities virtually
guarantee the continued growth of the Internet. The newest versions of all the major computer operating system software programs include (or will include) Internet access tools.

The current version of IBM's OS/2 operating system (OS/2
Warp) includes a choice of bonus applications, one of which is
IBM's Internet Connection for Windows, with a browser called
Web Explorer.

The current version of Apple's System 7 operating system
also includes the TCP/IP Internet communications protocol.

Most importantly, Microsoft's next Windows upgrade, Windows 95, will sport a custom version of TCP/IP, a list of Internet
service providers and one-button access to Microsoft's new online service, the Microsoft Network.

Chapter 10 Connection Section

Contact information for organizations and resources mentioned
in or related to this chapter:

Alternet, Internet access services, 703-204-8000 or *alternet-in-
fo@uunet.uu.net*

Ameritech Library Services, WinGopher Complete software,
800-556-6847

ANS, Internet access services, 703-758-7700 or *info@ans.net*

Apple Computer, Apple System 7 software, 800-795-1000

Beame & Whiteside, BW-Connect NFS software, 919-831-8989

BookLink Technologies, InternetWorks and InternetWorks
Lite software, 508-657-7000

CompuServe Network Services, network connection services,
614-457-8600

EINet, WinWeb and MacWeb software, 512-343-0978

Firefox, NOV*IX Internet for NetWare software, 408-321-8344

Frontier Technologies, SuperHighway Access for Windows software, 414-241-4555

FTP Software, Explore OnNet software, 508-685-4000

Hayes MicroComputer Products, Inc., Smartcom Internet Explorer software, 404-840-9200

IBM, OS/2 Warp with software, 800-3 IBM-OS2

IBM Global Network, Internet access services, 813-878-3000

InterCon Systems, Pipeline software for Windows and Macintosh, 703-709-5500

Iternet Business Association, a trade association focused on commercial use of the Internet, 703-779-1320 or *info@iba.org*

Internet Express, Internet access services, 719-592-1201 or 800-592-1240 or *service@usa.net*

internetMCI, internetMCI software and Internet access services, 800-898-4979

Internet Society, an organization fostering the growth of the Internet, 703-648-9888

Internet World, a monthly magazine covering the Internet, 203-226-6967

InterNIC, a consortium offering Internet guidance and information, 800-444-4345

Internetware, Inc., IWare for NetWare software, 408-244-6141

Luckman Interactive, Super Mosaic software, 818-548-2880

Microsoft Corp., Windows 95 software (available late Summer of 1995), 206-882-8080

Mortice Kern Systems, MKS Internet Anywhere software, 519-883-4372

Morris Group, The Internet Connection software, 800-843-3606

Netcom, NetCruiser software and Internet access services, 408-983-5950 or *info@netcom.com*

NetManage, Internet Chameleon software, 408-973-7171

NetScape Communications Corp., NetScape software, 415-254-1900 or *info@mcom.com*

Performance Systems International (PSI), Internet access services, 800-PSI-3031 or *info@psi.com*

Phoenix Technologies, Ltd., Internet Express software, 617-551-0120

Pipeline, Pipeline software and Internet access services, 212-267-3636 or *info@pipeline.com*

Quarterdeck Office Systems, Quarterdeck Mosaic software, 310-392-9851

SprintLink, high-speed leased lines for office networks, 703-904-2680

Spry/O'Reilly & Associates, Internet in a Box software, 206-447-0300 or *info@spry.com*

Ventana Communications, Internet Membership Kit software, 800-743-5369

WRQ, Reflection Mosaic software, 206-217-7500

Part II

Use Digital Media to Pinpoint Your Marketing Targets

Now that you have you have finished Part 1 and learned how to get online and about the resources available to you in cyberspace, it's time to take a closer look at what you can actually do, from a marketing standpoint, once you're there.

First of all, let's define again the term *marketing*. If marketing is whatever you do to promote the sale of your products or services, then it should include:

- *Market research* from competitive information-gathering to industry awareness to soliciting customer opinions and preferences
- *Publicity* from press releases to the positioning of your company and its offerings in the marketplace
- *Advertising* that is text-based (classified) and graphic-based (display)
- *Sales,* including distribution and merchandising
- *Customer service* and customer support

It's difficult to create strict boundaries between these areas, because you can easily use one digital media tool to accomplish so many different marketing tasks.

Let's say, for example, that you decide to set up a bulletin board to handle routine customer-service inquiries. Then you decide to post a survey questionnaire that customers can answer and realize that your BBS is also a great place to conduct customer research.

Then you start posting press releases on the system and conclude that it is also a wonderful publicity tool. Finally ("but wait, there's more!"), you create an online order form and display photos of all your products. Before you know it, your BBS has become an advertising and sales tool as well.

Digital media can surprise you with the diversity of roles it can play in your marketing plan. Part II explores how digital media tools can add something of value across the entire marketing spectrum—and hold the potential to completely transform the way you execute some aspects of your marketing strategy.

11

How to Locate Priceless Business Information Online

When you go online looking for market research information, you never really know for sure what you're going to find. Recently a market research specialist was trying to locate information online about the market prospects and profit potential for a hot air balloon business. Online databases make extensive use of key word searching, and when she typed in the key word *hot air* her screen immediately filled with magazine articles and news items related to that key word. The trouble was that instead of retrieving information on hot air ballooning, that particular key word produced nothing but articles about politicians being full of "hot air."

The best thing about using online resources for market research is that you don't even have to leave your desk. Your computer and modem can take you around the planet in seconds, sifting through volumes of research data, thousands of specialized periodicals, and complete libraries of reference materials—and that's not hot air.

This chapter will show you how to quickly get started doing research online. You'll find out why it makes sense to include electronic research on the menu of strategies you use to obtain business information. You'll be introduced to a number of online research projects that you can start on immediately, and you'll find out how to prepare yourself before going online. Along the way, you'll be exposed to the wide array of search options available, and you'll get a preview of the wide range of information you'll find online. Finally, you'll be presented with specific tactics that will allow you to engage in more efficient and productive electronic market research.

Real-World Benefits of Using Online Market Research

Research is the art and science of locating information, and market research is finding information that will help you gain a business advantage. Online market research is the practice of using online databases and information sources to conduct market research, the act of retrieving information electronically. And if information is power, then online information clearly leverages your power to find and use information to your advantage. Here's how:

- *Be the first to know.* Information that's available online today won't be in newspapers, magazines, or professional journals until tomorrow. In fact, some of that information won't be available for days or even weeks. In a business environment that moves as rapidly as the one we find ourselves in today, enjoying an inside edge of as little as an hour or two can sometimes make a critical difference in winning a customer or closing a contract.

- *Get control of the information flow.* Although most of us at times prefer to receive information in a prepackaged format (like the nightly television news), having access to unfiltered information can often be a real asset. Having that access gives you the opportunity to be your own news editor, to spot trends before others do, and to make up your own mind on the significance of a particular tidbit of information.

- *Make better customer presentations.* Customers appreciate sales pitches and marketing proposals that are tailored to meet their needs. The majority of the information you need to personalize your pitch comes from direct contact with your customer. Online research can help fill in the details, giving you perspective on your customer and positioning you as a savvy and well-informed vendor.

- *Create tighter marketing plans.* One of the most difficult jobs of any marketer is forecasting the future. Online databases can act as your crystal ball. They can bring into view the opinions of experts, statistics from the past, and projections for tomorrow. These databases combine reports, research, and commentary related to your industry, plus, of course, the constant stream of news that you can analyze to detect the currents of the future.

• *Save valuable staff time.* You can use the industry grapevine. You can make a trip to the library. You can wait for the next trade show or conference. Or you can go online this minute. If you need the answer *now*, online research is fast and efficient. It lets you avoid telephone tag and voice mail. So forget the plane ticket. Don't worry about the library's hours, or whether it will have the particular reference book you need. Just log on and start looking.

• *Cut research costs.* Obtaining market research information can be an expensive process. If you add up the dollars spent by a typical marketing department at a mid-size company on industry reports, consultant's fees, trade journal and newsletter subscriptions, etc., the total outlay would be significant. Online research won't eliminate all those expenses, but online databases can put many of those same resources at your fingertips on a fixed-cost or pay-as-you-need basis.

• *Gain access to a broader range of information.* It would be next to impossible for even the best-stocked corporate library to obtain the hard copy versions of all the information digitized in the aver-

---

QUICK LOOK: Market Researchers Play the Cyber Name Game

What are we going to call the market researchers of the future? In the past, business research analysts depended on libraries of printed books, periodicals, and documents to satisfy corporate information requests. Now, they're shifting to online resources to answer questions faster and more reliably. Some of them feel it's time that their titles change to better reflect this new reality. In fact, instead of titles like "Corporate Research Specialist," "Company Librarian," or "VP/Market Research," I'm beginning to see business cards sporting titles like "Digital Information Analyst," "Cybrarian," and even "Knowledge Navigator."

age online database. Even if it could, you wouldn't be able to access that information using the industry codes and key words most database publishers provide to make it easier for you to search and find the information you're seeking.

As you can see, there are a number of good reasons to start using online research immediately. Let's dive in and take a practical look at the type of information you can uncover in an online market search.

Seven Online Searches That Deliver Meaningful Market Data

1. *Locate current industry facts and figures.* One very successful salesperson I know informed me that a major factor in his success was his commitment to taking advantage of change. "I'm always looking for news about my customers' and prospects' businesses. When something changes in an organization, especially when a new person comes on board, I always use it as an opportunity to be the first one in the door to introduce myself and make a positive impression. When I'm using online services to track industry personnel changes, I'm more likely to be the first one in to make a presentation to a new decision maker." You and your organization can be first, too. The online wire services carry news of promotions, new hires, and transfers within hundreds of organizations every day. Why not track that information and distribute it to your sales team? Business-oriented online databases can provide in-depth, up-to-date information on markets and industries (see Figure 11-1).

2. *Conduct a quick market analysis.* If you need information fast on a new market or product opportunity, one of the first places you should look is an online database. The government has conducted studies on hundreds of industries and market niches. Many of them are available online. Market research firms are constantly conducting research about traditional and emerging industries. Highlights of their research reports are also available online.

3. *Uncover competitive secrets.* A surprising amount of information about companies that you wouldn't expect to be public is available online. Industry newsletters, market experts, and company personnel are making statements about your competitors

Figure 11-1. Dow Jones News/Retrieval screen.

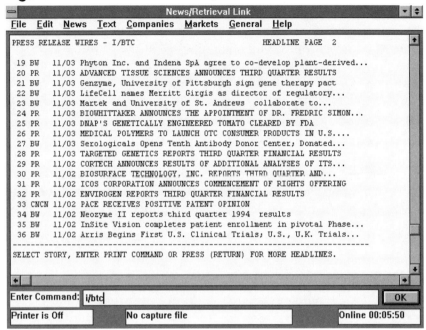

every day in the news media. You can't follow each of the hundreds of print and broadcast sources, but you can funnel that information into an easy to use package online.

HOT TIP: Download Mailing Lists via Modem From American Business Lists Online

This service from American Business Information (ABI) allows users to create and download their own customized mailing lists by specifying type of business, geographic location, size of business, and other variables from ABI's lists of 10 million U.S. businesses. Users can also access "special selects" from the main list (for example: Growing Businesses, Big Business, Small Business Owners, etc.). ABL Online is a dial-up service that you can access using any basic communications software. The subscription fee is $95 per year, but there's a $100 free-usage bonus for new subscribers.

---

4. *Reveal business-to-business customer preferences.* One great way to find out who's buying what in your industry is to scan the online newswires for announcements of major purchases and contract activity. Many public companies also announce sales re sults, from which you can detect what kinds of products and services your target customers are buying, and why.

5. *Unearth nuggets of consumer data.* American Marketplace, a twice-monthly publication you'll find on DataTimes, Dow Jones News/Retreival and NewsNet, summarizes new statistical data issued by the Census Bureau and private companies with a focus on consumer marketplace trends. CompuServe carries Neighborhood Demographic Reports (GO NEIGHBOR), which includes basic demographic data by U.S. zip code, and the Cendata service, which provides census information directly from the U.S. Census Bureau (GO CENDATA). You can also find a fat electronic file full of consumer statistics on the U.S. Department of Commerce's Census Bulletin Board (301-763-1568 with your modem).

6. *Conduct online focus groups.* A few progressive market research experts are starting to conduct focus groups online. Online users are often willing to share more information online than they would in person, because of the relative anonymity of the experience. Many of these focus groups have garnered a higher level of response than expected, and participants seem to enjoy the experience of interacting in an online research experiment. If your company commissions or conducts consumer research of this type, you may find that online services offer a very convenient and effective format for asking people their opinions.

Note: Don't miss the item about ad agency BBDO's online consumer surveys in Chapter 12.

7. *Do some digital "dumpster diving."* You never know what you'll end up with in the electronic flotsam and jetsam of cyberspace. That's why it's a good idea to periodically trawl through the online backwaters and seek out unrelated bits and pieces of information about your industry that can add up to a trend or opportunity.

It's clear you can accomplish a number of valuable, real-world market research tasks online. But if you've never accessed online databases before, you might be wondering, what exactly will I find when I go online?

HOT TIP: Monitor Research Activity With Best-North America

Best-North America is an online inventory of ongoing scientific and technical research at 110 North American universities. The database includes contact information and a description of the research projects of 75,000 research scientists, engineers, and physicians.

Business Information Available Online

If it's business or news-related information and it's in print, it's probably available in a digital version, too. For example:

• *Industry Magazines, Newspapers, and Newsletters.* On News-Net, you'll find one of the largest databases of industry newsletters available anywhere. Data-Times, on the other hand, carries a more complete line of local, regional, national, and international newspapers than you'll find in any library.

QUICK LOOK: Get Industry News Delivered to
Your Computer Desktop

If your company doesn't have its own market research department, and if you don't have the time to seek out online information yourself, don't worry. You can get your own automatic, customized online news feed from a number of different service providers. Electronic clipping services monitor multiple information sources, including newswires and digital versions of magazines, newspapers, and journals, "clipping" selected news items that match your pre-selected information profile, and then, for a monthly fee, send them to your fax machine or e-mail address. America Online (their clipping service is called NewsHound), CompuServe, and Dow Jones News/Retrieval all offer clipping services as an option for subscribers. As a participant, you're equipped with an electronic "folder" that clips and holds whatever news items are retrieved within the guidelines you select.

You can choose a topic, an industry niche, a group of companies, or almost any combination imaginable.

A service called HeadsUp will deliver seventeen to twenty headlines of news items each morning to your e-mail box (or fax machine) from industry categories you've selected in advance. If you want the text of the entire article, you just call an 800 number and key in a code for the news item to have it delivered immediately. HeadsUp, from Individual, Inc., provides targeted news coverage for a number of key industries, including: Automotive, Business and Finance, Computer and Information Services, Defense and Aerospace, Energy, Environmental Services, Healthcare, Imaging and Video, Mass Communications and Media, Semiconductors, Telecommunications, and Transportation and Distribution.

Other services of this kind include BusinessWire's IndustryTrak service, Comtex customized news via e-mail, Farcast's e-mail news service (which uses "intelligent agent" technology to seek out news items at your command), and Mainstream Newscast, a satellite-delivered news feed direct to your PC or office network.

It's a great feeling to start your day at breakfast scanning all the top news items that affect your market and your industry. That way you can call your clients and pass on some snippet of news ("Did you hear that Amalgamated Industrial just bought out Allied International?") that they might not have heard about until you filled them in.

• *General Business Publications.* Most major online services carry text versions of popular business magazines and newspapers such as *The Wall Street Journal, Business Week,* and *Forbes.* America Online has an electronic version of *U.S. World & News Report,* complete with graphics and sound.

• *Industry research data.* Log on to Data-Star and you'll find market report summaries from major consulting firm Frost & Sullivan. Dow Jones News/Retreival carries the *Marketing Research Review,* an analysis of commercially available marketing research.

• *Consumer research data.* Visit the U.S. Department of Commerce's Economic Bulletin Board on the Internet and you'll find thousands of data files (over 700 of them updated on a daily basis) covering purchasing statistics for hundreds of product categories. On a more specific level, The Boomer Report (available on NewsNet) is a monthly review of the buying habits of the nation's 77 million "baby boomers" and their spending habits.

  • *International data and statistics.* International newswires, such as China's Xinhau English Language News service and Japan's Kyodo News Service, carry breaking information on international products and markets. Specialized news databases and newsletters, such as the Africa Intelligence Report and Brazil Watch, are also available online.

Hot Tip: Review Contract Awards With BidNet

BidNet monitors listings of government contracts, screens those that pertain to the user's business or industry, and then forwards relevant contract information. Access is via online or fax. Call for national, regional, or state-by-state rates.

Online Options for Business Research

There are a number of online options available to market researchers, and the best choice in each case really boils down to the task at hand.

CD-ROM Discs

Innovative CD-ROM discs can save marketers valuable time, effort, and money. Three discs that should be in every marketer's toolkit are DirectPhone, SelectPhone, and FreePhone from ProCD. The DirectPhone disc lets you quickly search and retrieve individual phone numbers from 80 million residential and business phone directory listings. SelectPhone allows you to create your own lists of consumer or business prospects by defining a geographic area, zip code, or Standard Industrial Classification (SIC) code. FreePhone contains all of AT&T's 250,000 toll-free directory listings. PhoneDisc Business is a defined business listings disc, like SelectPhone.

Allegro Business 500 provides extensive information, including contact listings, revenues, and product information, on 500 major U.S. companies. Another disc, Government Spending, can fill you in on what your competitors are selling to the government and when their contracts come up for renewal. It also includes exactly how much agencies are spending with certain suppliers. There are over 425,000 records on the disc. You can order the ProCD Products and PhoneDisc Business from TigerSoftware or other CD-ROM dealers. You can get Allegro Business 500 from Online Computer Systems and obtain Government Spending from CD Publishing. American Business Information offers credit reference information on 10 million U.S businesses through a CD-ROM online service package.

Consumer-Oriented Online Services

If you need to access research information using a friendly, easy-to-use interface at relatively low rates, one of the major commercial services like CompuServe, America Online, or Prodigy is probably your best choice.

Business-Oriented Database Services

These services really have only one reason for being, and that's to provide users with information that will help them make more money. They provide background information on companies and markets for marketers and financial investors. If you need a range of research information that's both broad and deep, one of these services will probably be your best choice.

Specialized Bulletin Board Services

Bulletin boards often have a cozy, local flavor. A wide variety of specialized boards are springing up that focus on a particular industry or marketplace. If your research needs are localized in nature or involve a single industry or area of interest, one of these services may best serve your needs.

Your Own Bulletin Board System

If you operate your own bulletin board system, what better way to conduct fast market research than by posting questions on the board? While a focus group can take months to set up, you can have nearly instant feedback from a busy customer-support bulletin board. BBS operators have a definite advantage when it comes to developing useful customer research quickly. The online connection puts them in close touch with the most active segment of their user base.

Government Databases

Federal, state, and local government agencies operate hundreds of online computerized information systems. One of the best is FedWorld, an electronic information service operated by the National Technical Information Service (see Figure 11-2). FedWorld is special because it's an online gateway connected to over 135 different government bulletin board systems. FedWorld has over 90,000 registered users and receives over 3,000 contacts per day. You can reach FedWorld via modem by dialing 703-321-8020. (You can also reach FedWorld on the Internet via Telnet at *fedworld.gov* or on the WWW at *http://fedworld.gov*.)

Here are a few of the best government bulletin board systems for obtaining useful business and marketing information:

Figure 11-2. Table of contents page of the FedWorld website.

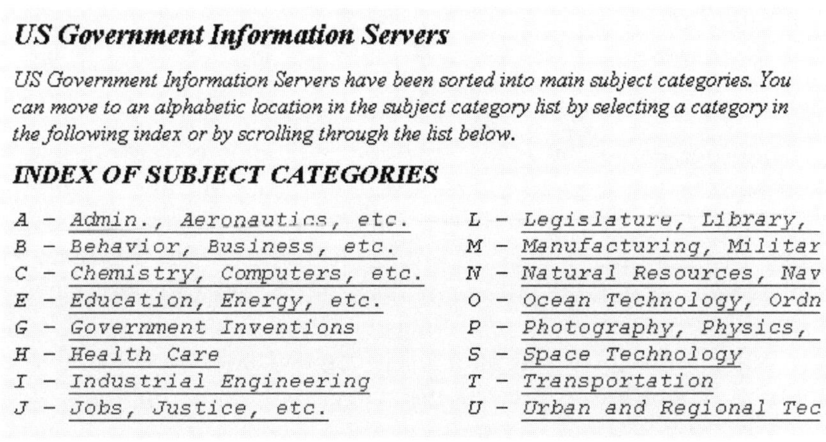

US Government Information Servers

US Government Information Servers have been sorted into main subject categories. You can move to an alphabetic location in the subject category list by selecting a category in the following index or by scrolling through the list below.

INDEX OF SUBJECT CATEGORIES

A — Admin., Aeronautics, etc.	L — Legislature, Library,
B — Behavior, Business, etc.	M — Manufacturing, Militar
C — Chemistry, Computers, etc.	N — Natural Resources, Nav
E — Education, Energy, etc.	O — Ocean Technology, Ordn
G — Government Inventions	P — Photography, Physics,
H — Health Care	S — Space Technology
I — Industrial Engineering	T — Transportation
J — Jobs, Justice, etc.	U — Urban and Regional Tec

- *Air Force Small Business BBS.* For small business contractors who want to do business with the Air Force. Voice: 800-638-9636. Modem: 800-638-8369.
- *Business Gold.* Locate federal laboratories who are conducting research available for commercial licensing. Modem: 304-243-2560. Login at "guest."
- *Census/Bureau of Economic Affairs Forum.* This board offers trade opportunities and economic and census statistics. Voice: 301-763-1580. Modem: 301-763-1568.
- *Federal Highway Electronic BBS.* Requests for proposal announcements. Modem: 202-366-3175.
- *GSA Information Resources Service Center.* Information for companies who want to sell to the Federal government. Voice: 202-501-1404. Modem: 202-501-2014.
- *National Science Foundation.* Federal budgets for research and development. Voice: 202-634-1250. Modem: 202-634-1764.
- *OASYS.* Information on Navy contracts available to outside suppliers. Modem: 804-445-1121.
- *VA Vendor Bulletin Board System.* Data for companies who want to sell to the Veterans Administration. Voice: 800-735-5282. Modem: 202-233-6971.

The Internet

The Internet is a vast, ever-shifting repository of facts, information, and opinion. Thank goodness there are tools to help us sift through mountains of data to locate the diamonds buried just beneath the surface.

Newsgroups and Mailing Lists

Internet newsgroups and mailing lists enable Internet users with similar interests to share ideas, information, and opinions with each other via e-mail. If you subscribe to a list, you'll receive copies of messages that are "posted" (sent to the list's central e-mail server) and then automatically distributed to everyone on the list.

What kinds of discussion lists can you subscribe to on the Internet? There are lists covering every imaginable hobby, issue, industry, and subject area. The list server at The World online service plays host to many, many lists. You can request their "List of Discussion Lists" to get a quick overview of the diversity of mailing lists you can subscribe to. Send an e-mail message to *majordomo@world.std.com* with the command **lists** in the the body of the message.

The procedure for subscribing to most Internet mailing lists is very simple. You send an e-mail message to the address of the mailing list's list server with the following command in the body of the message:

subscribe *name of list your e-mail address*

Here are some examples of marketing-related lists you can subscribe to:

- *Directmar.* This list hosts discussions related to direct marketing. Send subscription command to *majordomo@world.std.com.*
- *Free-Market.* This list has postings related to Internet marketing. Send subscription command to *listserv@ar.com.*
- *HT-Marcom.* This list covers the marketing of high-tech products. Send subscription command to *listproc@usa.net.*
- *Inet-Marketing.* This list is focused on marketing on the Internet. Send subscription command to *listproc@einet.net.*
- *Newprod.* This list zeros in on the new product development process. Send subscription command to *majordomo@world.std.com.*

Gopher

Gopher is a wonderful multi-level menu system for organizing files of information stored at thousands of servers throughout the Internet. When you visit a Gopher server, you'll see a page filled with one-line descriptions of files, groups of files, or other Gopher servers you can visit. Depending on which you choose, either a text file or new group of choices will pop up on your screen. (You don't need any special software to access Gopher. Just about any Internet software package will connect you to Gopher and the other services listed below.)

Some Gopher servers contain highly specialized information resources, while the menus on other servers are general in nature. Once you become familiar with "Gopherspace," you'll start finding favorite spots. But you have to start somewhere. Three great Gopher launching pads include the Library of Congress Gopher *marvel.loc.gov*, the InterNIC's Gopher *rs.internic.net*, and the NYS-ERnet Gopher *nysernet.org*.

There are thousands of Gopher servers on the Internet. How can you possibly keep track of them all, and how can you find the specific information you need if you're in a rush? Just use the Very Easy Rodent-Oriented Net-Wide Index to Computerized Archives, better known as Veronica. Veronica is an Internet utility that indexes the file descriptions listed on Gopher menus. Veronica servers enable searchers to type in a key word or key words, such as *European Trade,* and within a minute or so receive a list of all Gophers with menu lines that contain those words. You can access Veronica servers from almost any major Gophersite (including the NYSERnet Gopher, listed above). If Veronica isn't on the main menu, select "other Gophers," and a few Veronica servers will be listed.

Jughead, like Veronica, indexes key words from Gopher menus, but it doesn't go as deep into the layers of a Gopher menu; it sticks with the first few menus of a Gophersite. (Some researchers refer to it as "Veronica Lite.") On the plus side, Jughead completes a Gopher search a little faster than Veronica.

World Wide Web Search Tools

The Web abounds with search programs and directories, including resources like the SUSI Search Engine, the WebCrawler, and the highly regarded Yahoo list. The directories usually include lists of websites, usually organized into subject categories. The search programs typically allow you to type a word or two of text into a blank field. The program's search engine then looks for references in web files that match your terms, presenting you with a list of "hits" if successful. The resulting list of references is hyperlinked, so all you need do is click on the name of a file and you'll be transported to the Web server where the file is located.

Many websites, especially those of Internet service providers,

Figure 11-3. Page from the IBM Network website for linking to Web search tools.

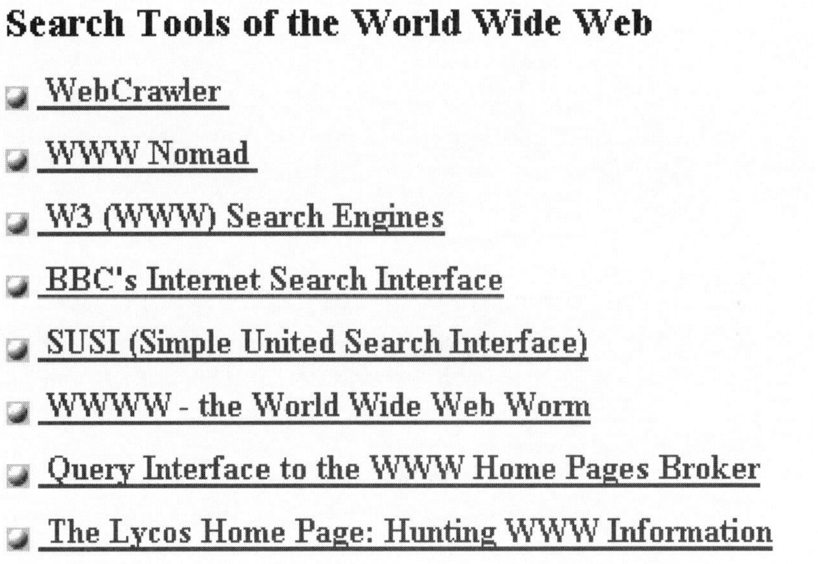

Search Tools of the World Wide Web

WebCrawler

WWW Nomad

W3 (WWW) Search Engines

BBC's Internet Search Interface

SUSI (Simple United Search Interface)

WWWW - the World Wide Web Worm

Query Interface to the WWW Home Pages Broker

The Lycos Home Page: Hunting WWW Information

have pages that include links to one or more of these search tools. The IBM network website has a resource page of this type (see Figure 11-3). You can access it at *http://www.ibm.net*.

HOT TIP: Best Government Websites for Business Researchers

There has recently been a major thrust in government policy toward making more information available to the public, particularly through the use of online applications such as bulletin boards, Gopher servers, and CD-ROM discs. Many government agencies are also making information available on the Web, and several of these government websites stand out in their usefulness to marketers looking for industry data, regulatory information, and insights into the process of selling to the government.

- The FedWorld website at *http://www.fedworld.gov* provides a central link to hundreds of government information resources. Also available in the form of a BBS.

- The FinanceNet website at *http://www.financenet.gov* provides a link to information about sales of federal, state, and local government assets to the public and also has resources related to government management of private resources.
- The SBA Online website at *http://www.sbaonline.sba.-gov* carries information on starting and growing a business. Business owners and entreprenuers loved the BBS version (it logged over one million calls in its first year online) and the website is expected to attract even more users.
- The Stat-USA website at *http://www.stat-usa.gov* features information on industry statistics, international trade, and consumer demographics. (This service, unlike most online government information sources, carries a subscription fee.)
- The U.S. Patent & Trademark Office website at *http://www.uspto.gov* includes information about what constitutes a patent or trademark, how to file, and data on researching existing patents and marks.

Ten Easy Steps to Planning and Executing Online Market Research

Online marketing information isn't a static property, like a book or newspaper article. It exists in a number of different dimensions: You can search and retrieve information based on the name of a company, on an industry category, on a market niche, on a product type, or on a chronological timeline. I like to think of online databases as "information cubes," and there are many different ways to slice and dice those cubes in order to secure the information you need.

Online services use a variety of methods for organizing and retrieving the information buried in their databases. Many services use codes that are unique to the world of online information. Here are some suggestions for familiarizing yourself with the interfaces you'll encounter when you seek information online.

Before you begin your search, you need to have a plan of action. That plan will guide your search, keep you on track, and save valuable time. Here's how to plan your search.

• *Determine what you need to know.* Start with a broad statement of purpose that covers the topic. Make a checklist of every question you'd like answered.

• *Formulate your questions carefully.* Next, refine your general information needs into a specific question. A well-designed question not only saves time online; it increases the likelihood that you'll get a data match that meets your information requirements.

• *Review potential sources of information.* Create a binder containing the database source guides for each of the online services you use regularly. The guides are usually cross-referenced to help you locate the databases that will best meet your needs.

• *Select the right source.* First of all, try to pick a service provider that presents its information in a format you're comfortable with. Many service providers offer new users a free trial to get comfortable with the service. Use that opportunity to evaluate not only the type of information available, but the method of organization and retrieval, as well.

• *Study database instructions.* Before you begin an actual search, print a hard copy of commands used to access data.

• *Take a test drive.* If you have the time (and if the service provider offers it) take a training session or workshop offered by the provider. Some providers even offer online "practice" databases, where you can work on your search skills for free or at very low rates.

• *Conduct the search.* Set aside a reasonable period of time to conduct the search. Have a legal pad at hand to note interesting pieces of information you come across that aren't directly tied to your current search. Otherwise, you'll get sidetracked and lose the focus of your search.

• *Use key words and codes.* Experiment with combinations of category codes to slice the information cube in new ways. Dow Jones News/Retreival, for instance, uses industry codes as well as business-news codes. For a product launch I recently worked on, I used the codes *I/CPR* (for computer industry) and *N/CTC* (for non-government contracts) to obtain newswire releases on major purchases and contract signings within the computer industry.

• *Back out and take a breather.* Make special note of the database's escape command. If you get frustrated, lost, or bogged down in the middle of a search, it's better to use that trigger to escape and catch your breath, rather than lose your composure and put your fist or foot through the monitor screen. Some databases have access fees running fifty dollars per hour or more, and canceling a search that's going nowhere will allow you to regroup without the meter running.

• *Organize and compile the results.* The rough data collected from a successful search will have limited value. That same information, after it's analyzed and organized, will be much easier to understand, draw conclusions from, and act upon.

Although it is a lot of fun to experiment online, trying new search techniques and making surprise discoveries, the reality of online research is that it costs money. Practically every minute you spend online is running up your bill, not even taking into account the value of your own time. With that in mind, it makes sense to find ways to trim the costs associated with your online market research.

HOT TIP: Use UnCover to Search Millions of Articles Online

UnCover is an online periodical article delivery service (see Figure 11-4). UnCover indexes nearly 15,000 English language periodicals. Over five million articles (primarily science, technology, medicine, business, and the humanities) are available through a simple online ordering system. Articles located in the UnCover database can be sent to your fax machine within twenty-four hours. Searching the database online is free—you only pay for articles ordered, which cost $8.50 each, plus a copyright royalty fee. You can access UnCover via the Internet by Telnetting to database .carl.org or via modem at 303-756-3600.

Figure 11-4. Main menu for UnCover.

```
                          Welcome to
                           UnCover
             The Article Access and Delivery Solution

UnCover contains records describing journals and their contents.  Over
4000 current citations are added daily.  UnCover offers you the
opportunity to order fax copies of articles from this database.
Type  ?  for details.

For information about a new service, UnCover Complete, type ?C



         Enter   N   for   NAME search
                 W   for   WORD search
                 B   to    BROWSE by journal title
                 QS  for   QUICKSEARCH information
                 S   to    STOP or SWITCH to another database
         Type the letter for the kind of search you want,
         and end each line you type by pressing <RETURN>


                 SELECTED DATABASE:  UnCover

ENTER  COMMAND (? FOR HELP) >>
```

Three Easy Ways to Hold Down Your Online Research Costs

Keep in mind that, unless you're paying a flat monthly fee to access your service provider's database, your time online is costing you money. In otherwords, the meter is running. Here are some ways to cut the cost of online research.

1. *Narrow your search.* This means formulating your questions with care. Try to limit each search to a specific objective (e.g., to obtain a list of all the major suppliers of automotive after-market products for the European market). Keep a notepad handy for jotting down interesting bits of information that you encounter during your search so you can keep moving forward on your primary objective without getting sidetracked.

2. *Make use of special pricing offers.* Online vendors sometimes set up special promotions designed to promote usage of a particular database for a limited period of time. Others offer discount rates or flat rates if you use the service in off-peak hours. The

best way to keep track of these promotions is to read the newsletters and newsmagazines most services send to their subscribers (e.g., DowLine from Dow Jones News/Retrieval).

3. *Search at the fastest modem speed available.* Some services charge more when you use a faster modem. In most cases, it's still less expensive to use the hot-rod modem. Your searches will be faster, and you'll zip through the process of downloading a file from the service provider's database to your hard drive.

Some marketing executives may find that they simply don't have a spare minute to spend online conducting marketing research. Let's face it, not everyone has the time, or the desire, to do the electronic legwork required to prospect for choice nuggets of information buried in huge mountains of data. Fortunately, there are a growing number of vendors in the online arena that will supply you with a continuous stream of updated industry information, tailored to meet your specific needs.

QUICK LOOK: Let Intelligent Agents Seek Out Information on Your Behalf

Wouldn't it be nice if you had your own personal research assistant to locate information for you on the net? That's not a pipe dream. Electronic news clipping services (profiled in this chapter) do just that, monitoring news wires and capturing relevant news items based on your pre-selected requirements. But that concept is in the process of being pushed a little further with recent announcements. Not only will these new electronic agents keep an eye out for information you think is important and grab it as it goes by, they will actually go out onto the network, on a reconnaissance mission of sorts, in a quest to return with just the right bit of news or data.

Network software publisher Novell, Inc., is working on a program that promises to give PC users easier ways to wade through the wealth of information available on corporate networks, as well as public networks like the Internet. Code named Corsair, the program will work with Novell's widely used network operating system, Netware, as well as Microsoft Windows and other programs. Corsair will be teamed with an information browser program, code named Ferret. Using Corsair, marketers will be able to click on familiar icons in order to retrieve data. Simulated office buildings, business parks, and virtual cities are some of the metaphors the software will use. Selecting a hospital building, for example, would retrieve healthcare industry information. Selecting a government building would begin a search for government regulations or trade data.

Software developer General Magic recently announced the first application of their intelligent agent network protocol, called Telescript, incorporated into AT&T's PersonaLink public online network. Telescript technology includes the use of mobile "information agents" that go out onto a network and perform tasks on behalf of their users. In the future, these agents will be able to search publications and databases for personalized information and deliver it back to the user's computer screen or electronic mailbox.

AT&T and others are working on combining voice recognition with intelligent agent technologies. Someday soon you may be able to say to your computer, "Get me that article on biotechnology from yesterday's journal," and it will understand and do just that.

Summary

As you can see, online market research isn't quite as complicated as you may have suspected it to be. In fact, it's getting easier and easier to find those valuable needles in the digital haystack as service providers rise to meet the challenge of making their databases easier to access.

This chapter looked at the benefits of online market research and proposed several online searches to help get you started. It charted the type of information you'll find online and looked into the digital media that provide that information. Several examples of specialized sources of industry information were highlighted, as well as a list of the steps involved in organizing and conducting an online search. A number of automatic news feed services were described, and the chapter finished by looking into some software-based tools for sniffing out valuable data online.

As you become proficient at finding out all about other companies online, you'll probably decide it's time to get your company's name on the wires. Putting your name online is the topic of the next chapter.

Chapter 11 Connection Section

Contact information for organizations and resources mentioned in or related to this chapter:

American Business Information, American Business Lists Online, targeted mailing lists online, 402-593-4593

American Business Information, credit reference information on CD-ROM, 402-593-4593

Business and Legal CD-ROMs in Print, an annual review of CD-ROM titles, 203-226-6967

Cartermill Inc., provider of Best-North America database of government and university research projects, 800-BES-TNA-1

CD Publishing, publisher of the Government Spending CD-ROM disc, 800-460-2371

CompuServe, consumer-oriented online service with a significant number of business-oriented databases, 800-848-8990 or 614-457-0802

ComTex Scientific Corp., Comtex customized news via e-mail, 800-624-5089 or 203-358-0007

DataTimes, business-oriented online service, 800-642-2525 or 405-751-6400

Dialog, business-oriented online service, 800-334-2564 or 415-858-3785

Dow Jones News/Retrieval, business-oriented online service, 609-452-1511

DowVision on the Internet, service providing business news and information via the net, 609-520-4685

Entrepreneurs Online, specialized online research service for entrepreneurs, 800-784-8822 or 713-784-8822

Farcast, Farcast customized news via e-mail, 415-327-2446 or *info@farcast.com*

Finding It on the Internet, by Paul Gilster, John Wiley, 1994

General Magic, MagicCap software and Telescript information agent protocol, 415-988-2565

InfoSeek, Internet search system, 408-982-4450 or *info@info seek.com*

Individual, Inc., HeadsUp customized news via e-mail, 800-414-1000 or 617-354-2230

International Data Base Corp., provider of BidNet government contract database and alert service, 800-677-1997 or 518-438-0092

Knowledge Express, business-oriented online service, 215-293-9712

Mainstream Data, Newscast for Windows software and FM receiver for customized news via e-mail, 800-299-2278

Online Computer Systems, Allegro Business 500 CD-ROM disc, 800-922-9204

TigerSoftware, sells ProCD phone directories and other CD-ROM discs, 800-238-4437

The UnCover Company, Uncover, an online periodical article delivery service, 800-787-7979 or 303-758-3030

12

How to Gain Instant Visibility Through Positive Online Publicity

Joe Boxer, a San Francisco manufacturer of designer underwear, is posting its Internet address, *joeboxer@jboxer.com*, on billboards throughout the country. I know this not because I saw one of its billboards, but because a writer mentioned this marketing ploy in an article in a local newspaper, which was later picked up on a national newswire and relayed around the country.

The moral of this (brief) story is this: Using new media puts your company in a good position to gain attention and publicity. In this case, Joe Boxer will probably get more value out of the thousands of dollars of free national publicity it has received than it will from customers sending e-mail inquiries about briefs vs. boxers, but I may be wrong.

You're looking for ways to give your commercial enterprise some visibility in cyberspace, right? Whether you personally handle your company's public relations efforts or hire a public relations agency or specialist, there are many routes for generating awareness, gaining credibility, and making a statement about who you are on the net.

This chapter examines several of them, including how to use online wire services, how to host an online event, how to share your knowledge and expertise online, how to publicize what you do on the Internet, and some suggestions about developing a presence online. There's a simple reason for doing this: The online universe is a good place to be seen.

An Online Presence Is Good Public Relations

Some businesses choose to create a presence online just to be there. It's somewhat like a Hollywood agent wanting to get a good table at a trendy, new restaurant. After all, it pays to be seen in the right places, doesn't it?

The legendary rock group The Rolling Stones certainly think so (and don't tell me they're not a business—they're a conglomerate!). The Stones have a site on the World Wide Web which features information on upcoming concert dates, video and audio clips from their most recent tour, a library of band photos, and a place for fans to purchase tour merchandise. Computer manufacturer Sun Microsystems and M.I.T. Media Lab spin-off Thinking Pictures, Inc., helped the Stones put up their Web server. All parties benefit from the media glow surrounding the site. If you have access to the World Wide Web (see Chapter 10), you can visit it at *http://stones.com.*

Miller Brewing Company has created an online "pub" on the Web called the MGD Tap Room from its Miller Genuine Draft beer. The site is designed to be something like a real bar, where people get together, find out what's going on, and share information. Miller will host lifestyle-related information at the site, which will be provided by reporters at alternative newspapers from around the country, including Chicago's *NewCity*, Los Angeles's *Reader*, and San Francisco's *Bay City Guardian*. Visit the taproom at *http://www.mgdtaproom.com.*

Where did the new United Paramount television network go when they decided to promote the "Star Trek: Voyager" series? Not where no man has gone before, but to a site on the World Wide Web. The interactive site invites visitors to become members of the crew, assigning them roles on the starship. First task: Learn all about the Voyager: her mission, personnel, and technology. The site also features audio and video created by the series' stars. Visit the Star Trek: Voyager site at *http://voyager.paramount.com.*

Sport marketer Reebok contracted former MTV video jockey-turned Internet entreprenuer Adam Curry to create the "Planet Reebok" site on the Internet's World Wide Web. Planet Reebok, unlike many commercial websites, isn't an advertisement for Reebok's product line. Although the site gives visitors access to research information on the company's shoes and a corporate history of Reebok, one of its key features is a group of Web pages that covers community projects Reebok is involved in. Visit Planet Reebok at *http://planetreebok.com*.

State tourism boards are also looking for visibility in cyberland. Utah's site mirrors the information in brochures sent by the state's Travel and Tourism Bureau to interested travelers who respond to Utah ads in travel magazines. (The ads, by the way, include the website's Uniform Resouce Locator (URL) address.) The site includes an introduction to Utah, a map of Utah's regions, a guide to national parks, monuments and public lands, and suggestions for Utah "adventure plans." See the "sites" at *http://www.netpub/utah!*.

Hawaii's home page on the Web proclaims: "Hokeo Hawaii: Welcome to the Islands," offering visitors the option of learning more about the islands, checking out island activities, and brows-

---

QUICK LOOK: Entertainment Celebs Seek Virtual Visibility Online

Live on Prodigy is a feature on the Prodigy online service that includes over 100 "chat rooms" where TV, music, and movie celebrities participate in online discussion sessions with fans. Prodigy's online "auditoriums" can now hold up to 500 participants, and the service claims that they will soon have auditoriums that can accommodate 20,000 participants. Stars and celebrities such as Tim Allen, Tom Clancy, Jay Leno, Meat Loaf, and Jerry Seinfeld have all participated in Prodigy online chat sessions, where typed thoughts fly back and forth in real time between them and their fans.

The book publishers, record companies, and television networks that promote these personalities are eager for online bookings. Online service users are rightly perceived to be opinion leaders whose influence, through their use of digital communications, extends well beyond that of the typical consumer.

Figure 12-1. Hawaii Visitors Bureau home page.

The Hawai`i Visitors Bureau welcomes you to our Hokeo Hawai`i Web Server!

ing a calendar of events (see Figure 12-1). There are also links to information about three Hyatt hotels and twenty-six Outrigger resorts in Hawaii (see Figure 12-2). Make sure you visit Hawaii's website at *http://www.visit.hawaii.org*.

In each of these examples the subject of the online attention wins by gaining increased visibility and possibly new buyers or viewers or both. The service provider wins by adding interesting content to its service, retaining current subscribers, and perhaps attracting new users. The online subscribers and surfers win, because they find something fun to participate in.

How can you take advantage of this type of publicity for your product or service? If you have an entertainment-oriented product, consumer online services, such as Prodigy, are more

Figure 12-2. Another screen from the Hawaii Visitors Bureau.

Figure 12-3. Home page on the net for the Seattle Mariners base-ball team.

Welcome to Mariners Headquarters!

This new service of the Seattle Mariners will keep you up to date with Mariners news, schedules, information, and in contact with the members of our administrative offices.

The information and services that this Web site will begin to offer over the next few months will include player and team information, game reports and schedule information, official Mariners

than happy to provide interactive links from their membership to your program. Prodigy even has a "TV hub" where you can find programming highlights for television and cable networks such as CBS, ESPN, CNN, The Disney Channel, and the American Movie Channel.

But even if your product is less glamorous, there are ways you can provide value for online users in the form of useful information or interaction. The entertainment and media companies are early adopters of this kind of publicity opportunity, so take your cues from them. Find something interesting or useful that you can share with online users, and then make an arrangement with an online service provider to host that content on the net. Before you know it, cybermarketers from all kinds of industries and professions will be finding creative ways to attractively position their products online. Figure 12-3 shows the home page developed by the Seattle Mariners baseball organization, offering information to fans.

How to Create and Host an Online Forum, Event, or Attraction

A forum is a distinct area where people of similar interests congregate within an online service. Forums can include a library

Figure 12-4. Screen showing schedule for "chat" session with television host Conan O'Brien.

area where forum participants can download files of information related to the topic of the forum. They can also "chat" with each other online and post questions and comments that other forum members will respond to (see Figure 12-4).

If you have an idea for an online forum that you think might be appropriate for one of the consumer-focused online services, like Prodigy or America Online, write a proposal that covers your expertise in that area. The service provider will want to know how you'll gather information to keep the forum site current. You should develop some ideas on subtopic areas that could support the main topic. The service provider will want some suggestions on regularly scheduled conferences that could be held in that area, and it will want to know how you intend to promote the forum to the membership.

Hosting a forum can require a good deal of time and effort. The forum area has to designed and created, and then kept up to date on a regular basis. The rewards of hosting a forum, however, can be significant. As a forum administrator, you have the opportunity to interact with serious enthusiasts who are often very influential in the marketplace. You have access to constant feedback from them on trends in the market, their likes and dislikes, and what really matters to them. It's hard to put a price on that type of information.

The New York office of international ad agency BBDO started a forum called Trendsetter Hotline on CompuServe. The forum has five areas, including a monthly survey for measuring online users' opinions on various subjects, an electronic magazine, an advertising I.Q. test, a contest area, and a conference room where BBDO reps discuss topics like interactive media and getting a job in the ad business.

Companies that host forums or who participate as advertisers or vendors in online malls often have opportunities to get involved in special online events that other companies don't have access to. Ford Motor Company, for instance, recently had a chance to host a heavily promoted event on CompuServe. Ford, which sponsors an Indianapolis 500 racing team, arranged to have members of the team available to take live questions from CompuServe members. The event was promoted on CompuServe for weeks before the event date and generated a great deal of interest and goodwill for Ford.

QUICK LOOK: Sega Reaches Fans With Online Forum

Here's how video game marketer Sega of America uses its forum on CompuServe:

> Users can view or download text files with tips and hints from game developers on how to master popular game titles.
>
> Regularly scheduled interactive conferences with Sega execs, game developers, producers, artists, and celebrities are held.
>
> There are online fan club meetings and get-togethers where game enthusiasts from around the country can "meet" each other online, discuss their favorite games, and share ideas with each other.
>
> News releases and regular updates on the progress of new game titles are posted.
>
> There are feedback opportunities (via e-mail or online postings within the forum's feedback area) for users who want to influence the development of new titles and new directions for current favorites.

It's possible to make this type of splash on the Internet as well. Sun Microsystems, which was the official computer supplier to the 1994 World Cup of Soccer, created an online Internet database for the Cup. The server provided a wide variety of statistics, images, game results, and other information for soccer fans around the world. The Sun server was eventually "hit," or visited, more than three million times during the games.

How to Share Your Expertise Online

When you go hunting for new customers, you don't necessarily have to look any farther than your own computer. You can dial up a bulletin board system, access an online service, or cruise the Internet to share ideas and information with potential prospects and customers. A growing number of consumers and business professionals are using online services to get fast answers to pressing questions. If you're the one giving the answers, that free advice may lead to profitable business relationships somewhere down the line.

You can gain credibility by providing good advice even when you can't profit directly. Start participating in online discussions and share information when someone asks a question related to your area of expertise. Respond to public information requests and questions (for example, ". . . does anyone know a company that can set up a videoconference between London and Washington D.C.? . . .") with a brief description of what you do or what you have to offer along with a phone number if that bit of publicity is truly relevant to the request. Don't use a hard sell or brash hustle, just as you wouldn't in a face-to-face encounter.

Another technique is to post files online that highlight your specialized knowledge. Users will often read these messages and request more information. It helps to boost your standing as an expert in your field and, who knows, you may even become an online guru.

As a marketing professional who is an active user of online services, you have a significant advantage over marketers that don't. You're always tuned in to what's happening in your field. You have a broader range of contacts you can turn to for information and support. And you have a higher level of visibility than your unwired colleagues. Don't forget, many newspaper and magazine writers and editors are avid users of online services. When they're looking for experts on a particular topic, one of the first places they'll look is online.

How to Use Online Wire Services

While we're on the topic of writers and editors, you've probably heard of the Associated Press (AP) and United Press International (UPI) wire services. These services distribute up-to-the minute news stories and feature information to media outlets worldwide.

But you may not be aware of Business Wire and PR Newswire, two specialized wire services that will guarantee distribution of your company press releases and product announcements to many of the same media outlets as AP and UPI, for a price. All you need to do to take advantage of these services is to relay your press release, via e-mail or fax, to these services, and they will distribute your message to hundreds of TV and radio stations, newspapers, and magazines. It's kind of an online version of "Meet the Press."

Business Wire and PR Newswire sell media coverage based upon geographic circuits that can be as small as a single U.S. city or county. The larger the circuit, the higher the price tag.

Here's a bonus you'll really like: Your release will also auto-

---

HOT TIP: Newswire Headlines

Write newswire headlines with care before an online reader selects your electronic press release for review. Initially only its headline will be visible on the user's computer screen, and often only a limited number of words of that headline can be displayed. Make sure your headline clearly describes the critical elements of your press release in the first few words. Keep it brief and to the point, or your release could easily be passed over by someone who should be reading it.

matically be carried on several major online services, including Dow Jones News/Retrieval and CompuServe, giving you extensive extra coverage at no extra cost.

Advantages of Sending News Announcements Online

There are a number of advantages to using online publicity services as an alternative to the usual process of writing and copying a press release, developing a mailing list, and then stamping and mailing out hundreds of releases.

1. *It's faster.* You can quickly broadcast your message to a wide range of media outlets. In fact, the services listed here can get your press release out onto their news wires within a few hours after they receive your text.

2. *It's more effective.* More and more editors and reporters are finding that they prefer to use online services as a way to track developments in their industry or area of interest, because it saves them time. They can access the releases that relate to their needs, without opening hundreds of envelopes and scanning their contents for relevant information.

3. *It saves time and money.* You can eliminate some of the time, effort, and uncertainties involved in developing a press release database and then managing the mailing effort. The cost savings can be significant when you compare your actual "in-the-mail" expenses to the coverage delivered by an online publicity service.

At times an online press release can actually contribute to sales. A friend of mine recently placed a print ad in a specialized business magazine for a new Internet-related information product. She simultaneously sent out an electronic press release on Business Wire. She generated three times the number of responses from the print ad (which, incidentally, cost about three times as much as the Business Wire release) but the electronic press release ultimately produced (along with a significant amount of editorial coverage) twice as many actual sales, and eventually ended up being four times more profitable than the magazine ad.

Who Provides Online Business Publicity Services?

Here's some basic information on the online press services mentioned in this chapter. You'll find contact information for each of them in the Connection Section at the end of this chapter.

Business Wire is a wire service that can deliver your press release to hundreds of media outlets (TV stations, newspapers, magazines, specialized periodicals, and online databases) on a local, regional, national, or international basis. Business Wire charges a seventy-five dollar annual membership fee. Press release charges are based on your selection of a geographic circuit which may cost less than fifty dollars to several hundred dollars per release. High-tech marketers, take note: Technology-oriented press releases carried on BusinessWire are automatically relayed to the editors of International Data Group (IDG) newspapers and magazines. IDG is one of the world's largest publishers of computer and high-technology magazines and newspapers with over 172 titles worldwide.

PR Newswire is a wire service that delivers press releases to hundreds of media outlets (TV stations, newspapers, magazines, specialized periodicals, and online databases) on a local, regional, national, or international basis. PR Newswire charges a one hundred dollar annual membership fee. The cost per release ranges from less than one hundred dollars to several hundred dollars, depending on the geographic reach.

NewsBytes is a daily online news service that covers developments in the computer and communications industries. Many of the major commercial online services carry NewsBytes, including America Online, Dialog, and GEnie. There is no charge for sending a relevant press release or news announcement to NewsBytes.

QUICK LOOK: PR Firm Sets Up Site on the Web

San Francisco, California-based high-tech public relations firm Niehaus Ryan Haller (NRH) recently unveiled a site on the World Wide Web. The firm's home page provides information on a service called NRH Mailbot, which automatically delivers press materials for the firm's clients to anyone who inquires via e-mail. The site also features background materials on NRH clients and direct links to the clients' Web home pages. Visit at *http://www.nrh.com:8400*

Spreading the Word via the Internet and Online Grapevine

The Internet is a great place for online discussion and interaction. Millions use it to share ideas, interests, and information. Thousands of discussion groups, or newsgroups, cover a multitude of topics, ranging from juggling to kites, from guns to origami.

Some lists offer open enrollment to anyone, and others are for members of an organization or business group. After you subscribe to an Internet list, which is often as simple as sending an e-mail message to a particular address, the "list server" software will begin e-mailing copies of all messages posted to the list directly to you. Some lists generate as many as thirty or more messages each day.

You can also post messages to the list. Some lists are moderated by someone who checks postings for relevance and appropriateness of content, others are not.

If you're interested in starting your own list, ask your Internet service provider about adding this capability to your account.

The media know a good publicity outlet when they see one. That's why TV stations, radio stations, and magazine publishers are rushing to develop places on the net (see Figure 12-5).

Figure 12-5.   A TV station's home page on the net.

You're Online with NewsChannel 5!

You've reached the top page of NewsChannel 5's menu of services on the World Wide Web. More people in Middle Tennessee and Southern Kentucky turn to NewsChannel 5 for news and information than to any other source. Now you can turn to NewsChannel 5 Online.

News, including Today's Top Stories, Larry Brinton's Street Talk, and more.
Sports, with Hope Hines' Inside Sports.
Weather: Forecasts for Nashville and the World.
Entertainment Report, including Chris Clark's Movie Reviews

QUICK LOOK: Connected Customers Flex Online Muscles

Intel, a major U.S. manufacturer of computer chips, was caught by surprise recently, when a flaw in its flagship Pentium chip blossomed into a major public relations and customer service crisis.

The first public announcement of the chip's flaw was a message posted to an online discussion group by a mathematics professor. Other discussion group members soon joined in, along with a major Intel customer (as well as competitor), IBM. IBM posted the results of research tests on the Internet, which disputed Intel's claims that the flaw was a minor one that should be overlooked or ignored.

Before long, the storm of protest became so loud that Intel was forced to capitulate by offering free Pentium replacement chips to any user requesting one.

This incident demonstrates the growing power of online services and the Internet as tools of customer dissent. Connected customers feel free to express their opinions and attitudes in online forums and, beyond that, to align with other consumers and organize ongoing protests.

What's the lesson? A knee-jerk reaction might be to avoid

the volatile online medium entirely. But that simply isn't an option. If your customers use online services or the Internet, you're indirectly affected by it, like it or not. The lesson, rather, is to adapt by realizing that connected consumers have a new voice and a new power in the marketplace. One voice can reach many, and quickly swell to a chorus. To avoid public relations fiascos, proactively monitor the concerns of your customers that use online services and quickly respond to their needs.

Public Relations via Bulletin Boards

How about starting your own bulletin board system as a way of attracting press attention and building positive word of mouth with prospects and customers?

Household products marketer Owens-Corning of Toledo, Ohio, did just that. It started the HouseNet BBS where online users tap into home improvement data and advice. It's also a place for home improvement enthusiasts to share tips and experiences.

AT&T is taking a different approach with its AT&T News Online bulletin board. The board features news about corporate activities, new product announcements, and the text of selected speeches by AT&T executives. The service, created for journalists who cover AT&T, also maintains a library of 2,000 press releases, going back five years, and AT&T annual reports for the past three years. One of the more popular features on the board is the AT&T Fact Book, which is a summary of information on AT&T's businesses, revenues, industry alliances, joint ventures, personnel, and assets. There's no charge for accessing the system, and anyone with a modem can dial in.

Does your company generate enough press inquiries to justify creating this kind of online information center? Get a first-hand look at how AT&T's bulletin board works by dialing 908-221-8088. (Modify the settings on your communications software to 7 data bits, 1 stop bit, and even parity. When you're connected, type GO NEWS and hit ENTER.)

How to Be a Good Corporate Citizen of the Net

Good news travels extremely fast on the net. Unfortunately, so does bad. You've heard the old adage about one dissatisfied customer telling three, or five, or even ten other people about their negative experience with a company. If that angry customer is an active user of online services—well, it's almost too painful to contemplate. You can easily multiply the number of people an unhappy customer will gripe to in person by a factor of ten, or a hundred, or even a thousand other online users—you get the idea. In the online age, it's more important than ever to guard your company's good name and take good care of your customers. In short, it's important to be a good citizen of the net.

There will be more about "netiquette" in the chapter on advertising (Chapter 13), but here are a few suggestions to help you get started:

- *Become an online user before you become an online marketer.* When you use the services of the net, you'll begin to develop an appreciation for those resources that will make you think twice before abusing them in any way.
- *Go where you're wanted.* When posting information about your company on bulletin boards, in online forums, and with Internet newsgroups, focus on finding a fit between your product or service and the target audience. You'll only irritate people who see your message in inappropriate cyber areas. Familiarize yourself with what's acceptable for each medium in terms of messages, postings, and articles.
- *Give something back.* Always try to find ways to give back some value in the form of information or assistance, even as you're promoting your own business interests.

If you follow these simple rules, you'll make the online world a more pleasant place for everyone, as well as easing the way for future commercial users of the net.

Summary

This chapter explored a number of avenues for obtaining publicity online. It looked at a few organizations that have created a largely non-commercial presence online in order to interact with current and potential users. It considered the concept of hosting online events. It surveyed the relative advantages of using online wire services to distribute information to the press. The chapter covered some ways of sharing information and expertise online and examined the primary methods for spreading your message on the Internet and other online services. Finally, it revealed a short, flexible set of rules for being a good corporate citizen of the net.

The next chapter dives into the expanding (maybe exploding is a better word) world of online advertising.

Chapter 12 Connection Section

Contact information for organizations and resources mentioned in or related to this chapter:

> Business Wire, business newswire service, 415-986-4422
>
> CompuServe, online service hosting "X-Men: Generation X" comics forum, 614-457-0802
>
> Delphi Internet, online service hosting "The X-Files" television series forum, 800-695-4005
>
> Niehaus Ryan Haller, high-tech public relations firm with NRH Mailbot service, 415-615-7900 or *chip@nrh.com*
>
> Newsbytes, daily news service with high-tech focus, 612-430-1100
>
> PR Newswire, business newswire service, 800-832-5522
>
> Prodigy, online service hosting entertainment celebrities, 800-776-3449 or 914-448-8000

13

How to Create Dynamic Online Advertising

An entrepreneur who grows and sells organic vegetables from a tiny plot in small town near Blacksburg, Virginia, is setting up an ad on a local community network linked to the Internet. He's hoping that natural food lovers in his area will send him electronic orders for the appetizing asparagus or succulent squash featured in his Internet ad. When he receives their e-mail orders, he'll rush to the field, pick the produce, jump in his van, and deliver it, fresh, to the customer's door.

If a small-town organic farmer believes in the power of online advertising, shouldn't you start thinking about it too?

Advertising Turned Upside Down

Advertising is a $300 billion worldwide industry that, until now, has been mainly a one-way street, with consumers passively absorbing advertising messages. Advertisers hoped that potential buyers would remember their slogan or jingle long enough to make a trip to the store and purchase the product.

That is changing with the advent of interactivity. Interactivity turns the traditional concept of advertising upside down by putting the buyer in the driver's seat. Interactivity allows consumers to increase their control over the buying process. We're all deluged with data. We long for a sense of mastery over the information that washes over us. (Maybe that's the reason we fight for ownership of the TV remote control unit.) Given the opportunity, we'll be more selective about the kind of information we choose to receive. Interactivity gives us that option.

What does this mean for advertisers, ad agencies, and developers of new media? Simply this: The audience isn't captive anymore, and marketers are going to have to work harder to entice them. Your marketing efforts will have to be information rich and user friendly: It must be easy for prospects to find and select the information that appeals to them.

HOT TIP: Tap Into Advertising Insights Online

Busy marketing professionals will find many sources of advertising-related information carried online. You can perform quick text searches of these publications to key in on your market, your competitor's plans, or other topics of interest.

Advertising Age Online, the digital version of the weekly ad industry newspaper, is carried on the Prodigy online service.

Ad Age/Creativity is carried on Apple Computer's eWorld online service. In addition to industry news and marketing information, this online publication features ad reviews and ads that subscribers can retrieve and view on their computer screens.

Dow Jones/News Retrieval has over twenty marketing-related publications available online, including *Adweek, Business Marketing, Direct Marketing,* and *MediaWeek.*

Cyberbuyers, Cyberconsumers, and Cybersurfers

A major retail company with an online catalog reports that over 60 percent of their online orders come from people who have the printed version of the company's catalog in front of them as they're ordering online. Why don't these buyers just pick up the telephone? Maybe it's because they gain a sense of control over the buying process by ordering online.

Different people like doing business in different ways. Some folks would rather use an ATM, for example, than walk into a bank and go up to the teller window. And some people are bound to prefer purchasing products and services online. As the Nintendo generation—a demographic group highly acclimated to interacting with electronic devices—grows up, this trend is likely to accelerate.

As consumers with favorable demographic qualities spend more and more time online, you can bet that ad dollars will shift right along with them. As a friend of mine in the advertising business puts it, "Demos drive ad dollars."

It's time to recognize three new market segments:

1. Cyberbuyers
2. Cyberconsumers
3. Cybersurfers

Cyberbuyers are professionals who spend a good deal of time online, mainly at their places of business. They are most often engineers, technicians, and researchers, but more and more often there are also managers and executives right alongside them in cyberspace. This group hasn't been given nearly as much notice as consumers in the ongoing discussion of electronic commerce. Nevertheless, they probably represent, initially at least, a more important and lucrative market segment. These professionals often have to make complex purchasing decisions that require reams of data and difficult-to-locate sources of supply, all within a tight time frame. That's a perfect fit with the capabilities of online technology. And, on the marketing side, one major business deal generated from new media visibility can make an initial investment look very worthwhile.

Cyberconsumers are the home computer users wired up to commercial online services and the Internet. This group represents the pot of gold at the end of the digital rainbow that the retail and entertainment industry hopes to cash in on. Marketers and online service providers simply need to find ways to make it easier and more attractive to shop and buy online than to go to the local mall.

Cybersurfers use online technology to expand their horizons, challenge their abilities, and, because, well, because it's fun. This market segment is typically younger, hipper, and possess shorter attention spans. If something looks interesting to them, great, if not, they're off to the next place in cyberspace. This is a difficult demographic to appeal to, but they're attractive to marketers because they're influential and impulsive. If they like it, they'll buy it, and buying it right off the net is no sweat, same as walking into a 7-11 and paying cash.

Here are some characteristics that pertain to all three segments:

• *They are proactive.* Cyberconsumers are definitely not couch potatoes. They are online, plugged in, and aggressively hungry for the data that will help them make informed buying decisions. They don't particularly want to see a commercial for a refrigerator, even if they're in the market for one. They would rather go online, dial up an interactive demonstration of the product, check out its energy efficiency ratings, and download a chart comparing its features with other brands.

• *They are demographically attractive.* The demographics of this consumer group (like the demographics of computer users in general) is very attractive. They're affluent, they're intelligent, and they're technology-literate. Best of all, they enjoy interacting with information. If we present information to them in an interesting way—even if it's advertising information—they will respond to it.

• *They prefer information in a digital format.* The main reason marketers have to start considering how to create an advertising presence online is simply that there's a growing market that prefers to receive information in a digital, interactive format. In fact, a recent study noted that children nine years old and younger would rather receive information from a computer monitor than from a print source.

As a marketing consultant, I've consistently emphasized to my clients that it doesn't make sense to put all of your marketing budget "eggs" in one media "basket." Marketers are now going to have to add online advertising to a media mix that may include TV, radio, print, direct mail, and other traditional forms of advertising.

Five Advantages of Online Advertising

1. *Rapid presentation.* The lead time to run an ad in a business trade journal or consumer magazine can often be weeks or, in some cases, a month or more. That's definitely not the case with

an online ad. You can have an ad up on a bulletin board server or in an Internet cybermall the same day you create it. If you have an important message that can't wait, the online medium can't be beat for speed.

2. *Easy modifications.* When you need to make changes on a four-color ad or direct-mail piece, it can be very expensive and time-consuming. Making changes to an online ad, on the other hand, is often a snap. There usually isn't much more involved than typing in some new copy or uploading and positioning a new graphic image on the digital page.

3. *Low cost.* The cost to reach a given number of readers using an ad in a print publication, such as newspapers and magazines, is often measured with a formula known as CPM or cost per thousand, meaning the cost to reach a thousand readers. The viewership, or readership, of online advertising can in some cases be a little more difficult to measure. If you create your own BBS and place ads for your products on it, you can amortize the initial cost of the system. That means that your advertising is essentially free. Some Internet cybermall advertisers charge as little as fifty dollars per month for advertising, and your presentation on their pages may be hit (visited) hundreds of times a day. The bottom line is simply that online advertising can be a very inexpensive way to reach thousands of users.

4. *Buyer involvement.* Print and direct mail ads can include involvement devices like coupons and toll-free numbers that prospects can use to obtain more information. But an online ad can offer so much more to involve the prospect in the presentation. Online ads typically offer several levels of information, sometimes presented in a menu format. Prospects use the menu to select the information that's of interest to them, and they're able to retrieve it immediately, instead of waiting for it in the mail. You can also use reply forms that prospects fill out while they're online, either surveys that they can complete or messages asking specific questions.

5. *No limits on space and time.* Online advertising doesn't have the same time and space limitations as radio, TV, or print publications. In other words, you don't necessarily pay more for more space online. While a cybermall may charge by the megabyte, or according to how many pages are in your presentation, if you

Figure 13-1. A Merrill Lynch ad, featured in the online version of *Time* Magazine, carried on America Online.

create your own Internet server, you can stock it with as much information as its hard drive will hold. As far as the time limitation, I don't think online advertising services will charge for customers spending a lot of time reading your ad. Unlike TV or radio advertising, where you pay more for a sixty-second spot than you do for a thirty-second spot, the online relationship between a prospect and your ad can develop at whatever pace works for that prospect.

QUICK LOOK: Will Digital Publications Convince Advertisers to Switch From Paper to Cyberspace?

Many magazine, newspaper, and directory publishers are racing to develop some sort of presence for their publications in cyberspace. Other publishers are going further, creating experimental, digital versions of their publications (see Figure 13-1). Is this a prelude to full-fledged publishing in cyberspace? If so, most publishers have yet to determine if revenues will be generated primarily by subscriptions, by advertising, or by some combination of the two. Another question is whether readers of digital publications will remember to seek out each new issue online, or whether digital publications must somehow be delivered to the reader to be successful. The most important question, however, is whether enough advertisers who buy space in the print versions of these publications will be willing to devote some percentage of their ad budgets to cyberspace advertising. The jury's still out on that question. Meanwhile, here's a peek behind the scenes.

One publisher of high-tech trade magazines and newspapers, Manhasset, New York-based CMP Publications, is putting all seventeen of its business-to-business and consumer publications (including *Electronic Engineering Times, Computer Reseller News, Information Week, Interactive Age, NetGuide,* and others) on the World Wide Web. CMP expects that the site, called Tech-Web, will become a focal point for readers of its publications as well as a source of advertising revenue. Each CMP publication and business unit (the company also produces trade shows, newsletters, and other information products) has its own home page on the Web. Visitors to the site can read news items, correspond with editors, subscribe to publications, request advertising information, and search through publication archives. Advertisers can place "billboard" ads on a publication's home page, which can in turn be linked to fact sheets, news releases, or product spec sheets. Visit TechWeb at *http://techweb.cmp.com/ techweb.*

Time Warner has a site on the Web, Pathfinder, that spotlights three of the publisher's magazines, *Time, Entertainment Weekly,* and *Vibe.* At this point, the site focuses on descriptions of the magazines and carries no other merchant advertising, but with the marketing resources of Time Warner behind it, a "heavy traffic" site like this could probably attract major advertisers. Visit Pathfinder at *http://www.timeinc.com.*

The popular publication for the digital age, *Wired,* has a Web-based magazine called *HotWired.* Advertisers such as AT&T, MCI, and Volvo quickly signed on for the early issues of

HotWired, and many are watching to see if the cyber version of the publication will be as popular as its print sibling. Visit at *http://www.hotwired.com.*

Mecklermedia's Mecklerweb site was conceived as a place for Fortune 500 companies to be seen on the Web. When potential advertisers balked at the $25,000 per year price tag, Mecklerweb's mission quickly shifted to being a site to display the company's publications, including *Internet World.* Advertisers are still being solicited, but they will more likely come from the magazine's current advertiser base. Visit at *www.meckler web.com.*

Newspapers aren't about to be left out. A half dozen major dailies are testing online and Web-based versions of their publications, including *The Los Angeles Times* and *The San Jose Mercury News.* Several major yellow page directory publishers are involved in experiments as well, including the yellow page publishing division of Nynex. Radio and TV stations are also starting to pop up on the Web.

Five Rules for Online Advertising Success

Are you sold on the concept of online advertising yet? If so, here are some steps that will help make your online advertising experience a beneficial one.

Get Comfortable With the Online Culture

Doing business in cyberspace is somewhat like doing business in a strange country. The people are a little different and the customs and the culture are new. It's a good idea to take a little time to find out about the people, experience the customs, and acclimate yourself to the culture before you open up your sales kit and start pitching your wares.

This goes back to the suggestions in Chapter 12 on how to be a good citizen of the net. If you become an online user before you try to do business online, you'll instinctively know how to be a good online businessperson.

Play It Straight

Create your advertising message carefully. Try to stick to the facts and avoid exaggeration and hype. Keep it honest and accurate, and focus as much on providing good information as on making the sale.

The online world isn't the free-for-all that some would have you believe. The U.S. Federal Trade Commission recently charged a Sacramento man with making false advertising claims and providing bogus information on a $99 dollar "Guaranteed Credit Repair Kit" that he was promoting on America Online and the Internet.

The authorities are out there, lurking in the wires. If they don't catch the bad guys, well, the net has its ways of taking care of transgressors, as you'll see below.

Brush Up on Your "Netiquette"

A small law firm in Arizona decided to promote immigration litigation on the net. They created an e-mail ad advertising their ability to help individuals obtain green cards for U.S. citizenship. They sent out this mass mailing to anyone who subscribed to an Internet mailing list. The resulting uproar temporarily shut down the law firm's poor Internet service provider. The system was swamped with electronic hate mail from outraged Internet users, righteously indignant that someone would have the temerity to breach the Internet's set of unwritten rules, or netiquette, about sending unsolicited e-mail messages.

Advertising online is, in at least one way, more of a challenge than advertising on TV or radio. Advertising is an accepted presence on most traditional forms of media, but the reality of a commercial presence in cyberspace still upsets some long-time denizens of the net. Their lingering animosity toward the concept of online advertising revolves around a fear of seeing their online world "cluttered" with commercial messages. Online service providers are reasonably concerned that if they offer advertising, a portion of their membership might revolt.

So it's best to stick with established advertising outlets, like the ones we'll cover in this chapter. Don't advertise on Usenet, and don't send intrusive messages. Companies like Apple, Novell, and Microsoft encourage employees to monitor newsgroups that relate to their product areas and to respond to people with problems and questions. Follow newsgroups that relate to your area of interest and respond when appropriate. Release genuine news if allowed and when appropriate. But don't advertise there. It's not good business.

Remember, You're Not an Intruder

Back to the concept of online advertising as an intrusion for a moment. Is it an intrusion? In a sense, yes. But ALL advertising—online or not—is an intrusion, unless one or more of the following factors are present:

- The advertising is captivating in some way—it is funny, creative, interesting, unique.
- The consumer is in the market for the product—then the advertising message becomes, potentially, a source of valuable information.
- The consumer actually requests the advertising information.

The best way to overcome consumer resistance to online advertising is to offer the something extra in the way of information, interactivity, or benefits that will pay the online user back for the time they invest in your message.

Use Time-Tested Advertising Methods

Cybermarketing is about using new media. Sometimes new media demand to be used in new ways. But there are also valuable lessons to be learned from the past. It doesn't make sense to disregard everything you know about advertising, public relations, or customer service just because you are trying a new environment. Many traditional rules of advertising also apply to cybermarketing.

1. *Set your objectives.* Just as with any other type of advertising, you need to formulate a plan and some goals before launching a program of online advertising. Clear objectives will help

you decide on the best type of new media for your message and give you a target to measure yourself against.

2. *Give readers reasons to buy.* Writing good copy is just as important for online ads as it is for a print or radio advertisement. You still need to organize the presentation of features and benefits in a logical, persuasive way. The headline or opening screen of your ad is critical. You have to attract casual browsers immediately, and give them good reasons to spend some time with your message. And by the way, don't forget to ask for the order.

3. *Use testimonials.* Positive statements on the part of current users of your product or service are as effective in online advertising as they are in any other medium. They may even be more important. Many new online users may still be a little bit wary of the companies they see advertising online. They'll be looking for reassurance that others have done business with you and have been happy they did.

4. *Stick with it.* Consistency has always been one of the keys to an effective advertising plan, and this holds true for online advertising as well. Don't think that you can place a few ads, wait an hour or two, and expect the phone to start ringing off the hook.

5. *Keep testing.* Never stop testing. It will take time for your

---

HOT TIP: Avoid the Dark Side of Advertising on the Internet

Here are a few terms from the Internet lexicon with which online advertisers should be familiar:

flaming   aggressive, hateful, abusive, and/or libelous messages, sometimes targeted at business users who are perceived to have violated standards of netiquette.

mail-bombing   retaliatory mass mailings, which can flood the mail center or a mailbox of an individual or organization perceived to have been acting outside the bounds of Internet propriety.

spamming   posting advertising messages to many specialized discussion lists (Internet newsgroups) with no regard to the subject matter in which participants are interested.

company to develop just the right kind of presence online. In the meantime, evaluate and experiment. Spend some time researching what other companies are doing. What do you like about the best approaches to online advertising? Is there anything you can incorporate into your presentation?

Our advice: If you don't want to be the subject of flaming or mail-bombing, avoid spamming and other breaches of netiquette.

Text-Based Advertising Online

On Bulletin Board Systems

There are hundreds of privately run bulletin boards around the country that accept text-based, classified-type advertising from members or from local businesses. The best way to find these boards is to pick up a copy of your local computing magazine, the kind that is distributed free at computer stores in most major cities. These magazines usually list modem numbers for area BBSs, along with a brief description of the board. *ComputerEdge* is one of the local computer publications available near my office in the San Diego area. *ComputerEdge* has a list of local bulletin boards that accept advertising, including boards with the names Ads On-line, Online Business Network, and Online Advertisers. Ads On-Line promotes the fact that searches on its system are free to users and that its online ads run longer time periods than newspaper classifieds—and cost less. It allows advertisers to place their ads by modem. If your market is primarily local, a board like this may be for you.

In evaluating a local BBS as a possible advertising medium, you'll need to weigh the ad rates against the number of subscribers or frequent users of the board. Talk to the BBS's sysop about the kinds of people who use the BBS, their interests, where they live, and how frequently they use the system.

On Consumer Online Services

Classified advertising on consumer-focused online services is generally a bargain. All the major players, including America Online,

Figure 13-2. Home page from CompuServe's classified ad listing service, showing the various business categories available to users.

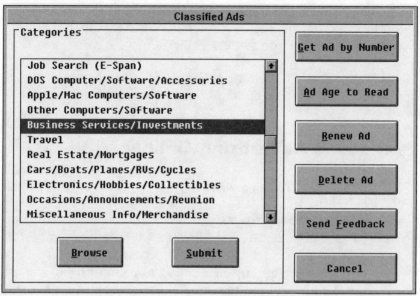

CompuServe, and Prodigy, offer some form of online classified advertising. The classified sections on these services offer the usual single-party buy-and-sell advertising, but CompuServe, for one, also offers a number of business categories for classified ad listings. All kinds of businesses, from consultants to entrepreneurs to desktop publishing services, advertise on CompuServe (see Figure 13-2). A subject heading (up to forty characters) acts as a headline for your ad. Rates run about a dollar for one line (up to seventy characters) for one week. You can arrange for interested parties to automatically send a reply to your e-mail box on CompuServe. Each advertiser is responsible for setting up and renewing his or her own ad.

Classified advertising on the Prodigy service is available only to Prodigy subscribers. The investment is about $75 for two weeks worth of advertising. Prodigy has agreements with three newspapers, *The Atlanta Journal and Constitution, The Los Angeles Times,* and a Tampa, Florida, daily to deliver local news—and local classified advertising—in special areas on the service. *The*

Atlanta Journal's Access Atlanta has been online with its own At-lanta-area classified section for some time.

On the Internet

E-Mail Advertising

Start by including your Internet e-mail address on your business cards, letterhead, and sales materials. Begin asking your customers if they have e-mail, and start collecting those addresses. Develop some ASCII text marketing information that you can send via e-mail. Then talk to your Internet service provider about setting up multiple e-mail addresses for various items in your product line. (But make sure you regularly check each of the mailboxes and follow up quickly to any inquiries that arrive there.)

Customers are now using e-mail to shop at the department store retailer Nordstrom's. Nordstrom's e-mail shopping service, called Personal Touch America, will match customers with a Nordstrom's shopping assistant, who will provide a variety of services, from filling specific orders to making wardrobe decisions. All e-mail requests will be routed to a Nordstrom's store in downtown Seattle. The retailer is also selling a customized e-mail package called Nordstrom Connection to computer users who don't have e-mail software. The service is free and doesn't require a minimum purchase. Are you a retailer who would like to try this approach? Check out Nordstrom's service first. Here's the e-mail address: *nordstrom-pt-america@mcimail.com.*

If you'd prefer to have an automatic response to e-mail inquires, you can set up an automatic e-mail response system, known as a "mailbot" or "mail reflector," that will allow Internet users to quickly and easily access information on your products and services. In the time it takes for you to check your company's mailbox and respond to inquiries, they can already have the information they need in their e-mail box.

It's a simple process. Your potential customers e-mail a message to a special address you've set up, typically something like *info@companyname.com* (or you can get creative with *i-want-it@* or *free-info@*). Immediately after the mail enters the mailbot, it automatically sends a prepared message back to the customer.

You can often set up your mailbot through your Internet service provider. Some include the service at no charge, others charge a small fee per message. Or, you can set up a mailbot on your own Internet server, if you have a dedicated, full-time Internet connection. A shareware mailbot, Major Domo, is available via anonymous ftp (file transfer protocol) at many file transfer sites on the Internet, including *ftp.greatcircle.com.* (Look in the directory: **pub/majordomo.**)

E-Mail Sig Files

Many e-mail software programs allow you to automatically include a brief, business-card-like tag at the top or bottom of all your messages. You can use this area (known as the signature file or "sig file") as a small "billboard" that describes who you are or what you do. Shown below is a good example of a professional, informative use of a sig file by an attorney specializing in communications law.

Neal J. Friedman njf@commlaw.com Telecommunications & Information Law	Pepper & Corazzini, LLP 1776 K Street, N.W. Suite 200 Washington, D.C. 20006	Voice: 202-296-0600 Fax: 202-296-5572

Web Server:　*http://www.commlaw.com/pepper*
Anonymous FTP:　*ftp.commlaw.com/companies/pepper*
Gopher:　*gopher.commlaw.com/11/pepper*

Some marketers even use their sig file area to announce special sales or new products. Some personalize their sig files by selecting and including a "quote of the day" or inspirational message.

FTP Advertising

Thousands of companies have made information files available to the Internet community by setting up "anonymous" ftp (file transfer protocol, a standard tool for moving files around on the Internet) sites. Anonymous ftp means any user can log on to the site by entering "anonymous" when the computer prompt

Figure 13-3. Screen from gopher site hosted by NetManage, a California-based provider of inter-networking software.

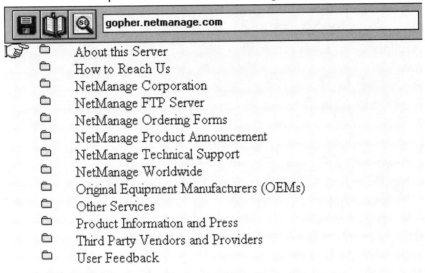

asks for the user name and then giving their e-mail address as the password.

Ask your Internet service provider if they can set up an ftp file "drop box" so that you can store marketing-related files in your personal ftp directory for public access. This will also allow customers and suppliers, with your permission, to deposit files into your ftp directory as well.

Gopher Advertising

Gopher servers allow users to access information files from simple menu systems (see Figure 13-3). Selecting a menu item may lead a user to a text file, another menu, or even another Gopher server.

Many Internet access providers allow corporate clients to rent space on their Gopher servers, so that Internet users throughout the world can have access to the information you have available.

You can also set up a Gopher through your own Internet

connection. Gopher server software is available for practically any hardware platform. For more information, visit the Library of Congress Gopher home page at *gopher.marvel.loc.gov*. Select "Gopher Software Servers and Clients" from the first menu, then "Guides to Building and Maintaining a Gopher."

On Bulletin Board Systems

Many bulletin board systems are now offering graphics capabilities on their systems. A technology called Raster Imaging Protocol (RIP) is finding its way onto many bulletin boards. RIP allows BBS sysops to offer colorful graphics, high-resolution photographic images, and even sound on their bulletin boards.

TeleGrafix Communications, the company behind the RIPscrip product for BBSs, recently signed an agreement with fourteen of the largest bulletin boards in America to create an advertising media network based on the technology. They're also developing an ad tracking system that will inform individual advertisers of exactly how many users saw their ad on a BBS.

If you'd like to add graphics and photos to your in-house BBS, look into a product called DC Genesys from Durand Communications. DC Genesys allows a BBS operator to mount full-color, searchable photo databases on their boards.

Graphics-Based Advertising

On Consumer Online Services

The consumer-oriented online service providers have been reluctant to allow graphics-based advertising (known in the print publishing business as display advertising) onto their systems for fear of alienating users.

Prodigy is still the only consumer-focused service to allow graphics-based display advertising in the main section of its service. Potential advertisers should be prepared to spend a minimum of $25,000 on a display advertising campaign on Prodigy. Prodigy's new Windows interface, scheduled to be released to service subscribers in early 1995, places ads in a small "billboard" space at the bottom of the user's screen. Actual company logos are displayed, and the ads are cycled through one at a time, starting over again when all of the ads have been viewed.

At the urging of several major publishing companies (including Time, Inc.) that would like to offer advertising in the online versions of their publications, America Online began allowing some display advertising in late 1994 on a test basis.

A number of details related to advertising on online services have yet to be worked out, including how to audit (independently verify) the membership numbers of online services.

America Online is attempting to address this problem by providing weekly usage reports that detail total "readership." For example, they report that *Time* magazine's online version, Time Online, is typically seen by 60,000 users per week.

On CompuServe, ads with limited graphics have started to appear within Time Warner's magazine section, which features *Time, Fortune, People,* and *Sports Illustrated* magazines.

Microsoft has recently asked at least four ad agencies (including McCann-Erickson, Saatchi & Saatchi, Bozell, and Modem Media) to develop a strategy to make interactive advertising acceptable to consumers as part of its plan to launch an online service entirely supported by advertising. Advertising income may allow Microsoft to offer the Microsoft Network online service without requiring any sign-up or monthly usage fees. But Microsoft will have to find a way to make advertising acceptable to users of the service—perhaps even making the advertising an integral part of the online product.

On the Internet

Because the Internet's World Wide Web is a multimedia medium, it opens up possibilities that go far beyond the text-based alternatives offered by other Internet formats. Web-based advertising presentations can include a variety of fonts, graphics, photos, sounds, and even video material.

You'll find a variety of businesses with informative advertising sites on the Web, from telecommunications to electronics to financial services (see Figures 13-4, 13-5, and 13-6).

Figure 13-4. Home page for the Bell Atlantic World Wide Web server.

Between one and two million Internet users now have access to the right kind of software and Internet connections (see Chapter 10) needed to cruise the Web in its multimedia format. That number will grow as more Internet users get their hands on Mosaic and as consumer-oriented service providers like CompuServe and America Online offer their members access to the Web. Even now, over half of all new Internet accounts include Web access, and every month thousands of new users experiment with the Web for the first time.

If there's one downside to the Web, it's this: With a normal 14.4 kbps (kilobits per second) modem, selecting a website address and then waiting for its graphics to appear on your monitor (sometimes known as "screen painting") can be frustratingly slow. New versions of Web software programs that are able to retrieve Web files more quickly will help to alleviate this problem. So will faster modems, and so will more Internet service providers offering (and users choosing) 56 kbps (four times faster) ISDN connections to the Internet.

You have two basic options when it comes to advertising on the Web: Rent space in a cybermall or set up your own dedicated

Figure 13-5. Home page for the GE World Wide Web server.

GE WWW Server

General Electric Company is a diversified technology, manufacturing and services company operating on a worldwide basis

- What's New
- GE Company Highlights
- General Electric Company 1993 Annual Report

Web server. Because the trend is for companies to use their website not just to advertise, but to try to move the buying process toward the completion of an online sales transaction, we cover Web servers in the next chapter, which focuses on selling online.

Figure 13-6. Home page for the First Union Bank World Wide Web server.

Welcome to
First Union Corporation

MEMBER FDIC

FIRSTACCESS
N E T W O R K

Where Cyberbanking(sm) begins...

First Union Corporation, with headquarters in Charlotte, North Carolina, is a bank holding company made up of eight financial institutions that is seriously interested in contributing to the free flow of information on the Internet. These pages provide information on First Union and its services, useful references of interest to any consumer, special services for small businesses wishing to use credit cards, and community information

QUICK LOOK: New Uses for Mosaic Will Make Internet Marketing Even Easier

Mosaic browsers will soon be available that can automatically open and read Adobe Acrobat portable document files (PDFs) that are posted on the World Wide Web. Marketers will be able to create marketing materials or ads in practically any word processing or graphics software, and then save them as PDF format files. Those files can then be placed on the Internet for Web users to retrieve and view through their Mosaic software.

Meanwhile, Macromedia (the company behind the popular multimedia development program Director) has inked an agreement with the cybermall moguls at the Internet Shopping Network. The partners are developing a run time (used only to view a particular file) version of Director that will "play" multimedia demonstrations within Mosaic browsers. Here's how it will work: First, a Web user clicks on a Director-created file that's been posted on a website. Next, the visitor's Mosaic software retrieves that file. Then the run time version of Director will launch itself to "play" the multimedia presentation contained in the file, complete with animation, sound, and perhaps even video. Macromedia hopes to make Director the front-runner as development format of choice for multimedia online ads.

How Digital Media Is Changing the Advertising Profession

The digital media phenomenon is starting to gain momentum, and many traditional advertising agencies are still struggling to come to terms with it. Some try to adapt by forming partnerships with marketing firms that are already exploring interactivity. Others have rushed to form new media divisions. Most agencies realize that they have to confront this new challenge of two-way media. If they don't, they may be pushed aside.

In fact, Lockheed Corporation admitted recently that one of the reasons it switched from McCann-Erickson, its agency of almost 30 years, to D'Arcy Masius Benton & Bowles, was that

D'Arcy seemed to have a more creative and aggressive approach to new media opportunities. News like that sends shivers up the spines of agencies who don't have a grip on new media marketing possibilities.

To other agencies, digital media just seems to come naturally. One firm, TBWA Advertising, created a "virtual museum" of vodka ads for their client, Absolut. TBWA introduced a highly visible and successful campaign for Absolut several years ago that featured paintings, photos, and graphic images of the Absolut logo. Agency creatives mused, "Why not computerize the campaign?," and so they did. The result is a computer-graphics generated Louvre-like museum, complete with 216 Absolut Vodka paintings. As users push their computer mouse forward, they have the sensation of moving through the museum. The environment seems three-dimensional, allowing viewers to wander down corridors, enter rooms, and zoom in on the images, which are accompanied by music, sound, and text. The enabling technology behind this interactive ad is provided by Knowledge Adventure (see profile in Chapter 18). If you'd like to see the Absolut Museum for yourself, you can download it to your computer from CompuServe (GO ABSOLUT) or order it for $29.95 from 800-94-ABSOLUT.

A computer specialist by training, Justine Correa left a position at the San Diego Supercomputing Center to start Online Press, a consulting firm that assists companies in putting business information online. Justine says she doesn't regret starting her consulting company. "I really don't have to sell the concept at all. I just talk to people about what I do and they say, 'I need you— I've been looking for somebody like you!' There's a tremendous interest out there right now. Organizations want to get their information on the Internet and to be seen online. I just give them a little help."

Some agencies are skeptical that online advertising projects will pay off. They don't believe consumers will undertake the extra effort that interactivity demands. But they don't understand that many of us are getting tired of traditional advertising.

A colleague of mine, John Houston, is director of strategic consulting at Modem Media. Modem Media is an ad agency developed specifically to address new media marketing challenges. John doesn't even use the same vocabulary as the traditional ad agency executive. He thinks in terms of creating marketing messages that subsidize whatever content the consumer is interested in viewing. He talks about "smart commercials" that morph (adapt) themselves based on the demographics of the customer requesting the content—commercials that actually interact with their environment.

Perhaps the successful ad agencies and marketing firms of tomorrow will be a new breed, comfortable with computers and confident in their multimedia skills. They will have a knack for building interactivity into marketing messages and will find ways to leverage new technologies to help customers understand the products and services their clients are selling.

Summary

This chapter examined the transformation that advertising is currently going through and one of the key reasons behind that transformation: the rise of the cyberconsumer. It looked at the advantages of online advertising and explored a number of challenges that online advertisers need to face to achieve success. The chapter also looked into advertising on bulletin boards systems, consumer-oriented online services, and on the Internet, including both text-based and graphics-based advertising opportunities. It finally looked at the changes driving the advertising and marketing services profession.

If you want to do more than just announce your electronic existence, and if, in fact, you want to actually set up shop and conduct sales transactions on the net, read on.

Chapter 13 Connection Section

Contact information for organizations and resources mentioned in or related to this chapter:

Adobe, Acrobat portable document software, 415-961-4400
Adweek's Directory of Interactive Marketing, profiles of interactive service providers, 800-468-2395
Ameritech, Net Publisher software, 708-866-0150

Durand Communications Network, DC Genesys multimedia database software for bulletin board systems, 805-961-8700

Electronic Book Technologies, DynaWeb software, 401-421-9550

Exoterica, OmniMark software, 613-722-1700

Illustra Information Technologies, Web DataBlade software, the "database for cyberspace," 510-652-8000

Information Dimensions, BASIS WEBserver software, 614-761-8083

Inside Media, media journal with "Interactive Ad Review" column, 212-683-3540

The Interactive Advertising Council, organization dedicated to interactive advertising and other applications of interactive media, 202-624-7372

Interleaf, Cyberleaf software, 617-290-0710

MacroMedia, Director multimedia software, 415-252-2000

MediaShare, PB.web software, 619-931-7171

NetScape Communications Corp., NetSite software, 415-254-1900

Online Press, digital publishing and advertising consultants, 619-488-5165

Open Market, Inc., StoreBuilder software, 617-621-9500

Oracle Corp., Oracle Media Server software, 415-506-7000

Personal Library Software, PLServer software, 301-990-1155

Process Software Corp., Process Web Server for Windows NT software, 508-879-6994

Prostar Interactive MediaWorks, MiniCat Builder and CommCat Internet software, 604-273-4099

Silicon Graphics, WebMagic HTML authoring software, 800-800-7441

SoftQuad, HoTMetaL PRO software, 416-239-4801

TeleGrafix, technology for creating multimedia on bulletin board systems, 714-379-2131

Ubique, Ltd., Virtual Places, Doors and Sesame, 415-896-2434

Verity, TOPIC text retrieval engine software, 415-960-7600

WAIS Inc., WAISserver database indexing software, 415-614-0444 or *info@wais.com*

14

How to Develop Effective Channels for Online Sales

Sure you can close sales online. Not only that, you can seal deals that are airtight. Just ask the folks at TuppNet. They hold "live" Tupperware parties every Wednesday night, using a text-based conferencing system known as Internet Relay Chat. The TuppNet merchants provide a Tupperware catalog that potential buyers browse during this online get-together. Participants are able to ask questions and even place orders online.

This chapter takes the topics covered in the last chapter one step further. It defines selling online, and then looks at some of the many options now available to marketers who want to open the online sales channel. It explores the requirements for setting up a sales platform on the Internet's World Wide Web (including the elements that can lead to profits or disappointments on a Web-based cybermall site) and examines the progress on efforts to achieve safe and easy electronic sales transactions.

Time to Start Selling Online

What do we mean by selling online? For the purposes of this chapter, selling online is defined as an actual sales transaction taking place—a buyer filling out some sort of an online order form and agreeing to price and payment terms.

Online advertising and online sales are closely entwined. One parallel is mail order advertising in which a consumer responds to advertising and then may place an order using a reply form or coupon. In the same way, online advertising can act as a kind of doorway leading to an electronic order form where a purchase takes place.

It's no secret that a growing number of marketers are looking for the right way to use new media to buy and sell goods and services. There's no single "right way" to approach the question of selling online. The primary consideration is finding a sales format that fits your product and your company's approach to the marketplace. Let's look at some of the options available today.

Create a CD-ROM Sales Catalog

Torrance, California-based Curtis Software Corp. has a product called Catalog On Disk that you can use to put your catalog on CD-ROM disc or computer floppy disk. If you choose, you can also transmit your catalog to customers online. Curtis Software's president, Jim Curtis, says that the typical catalog requires approximately one megabyte of disk space and takes about ten minutes for a customer to download.

When a buyer receives a catalog you've created with Catalog On Disk, it's a simple, one-step process to install it. They can begin using it almost immediately. The first screen includes your company's name and logo, and other pages include your product shots and product numbers, your order forms or credit application forms, and information about your company. The buyer doesn't have to understand database technology to be able to search through the program. Product information can be displayed in a columnar format (like a spreadsheet) or in a format similar to the page of a catalog.

So CD-ROM discs allow marketers to package complete marketing presentations on a small silver platter (see Figure 14-1), and finish the presentation by placing an order form in front of the customer (see Figure 14-2).

An add-on module to the system allows for on-screen ordering. Buyers simply click on the Order menu, and product information automatically transfers to the electronic order form. The software automatically computes the price, tax, and shipping charges and prints out the completed order form.

Here are some of the advantages of CD-ROM catalogs:

Figure 14-1. Screen from CD-ROM disc presenting Microsoft's PowerPoint program to potential customers.

- Your customers can browse through the database at their leisure or search out a specific item for which they may have an immediate need.
- The complexities of the database containing your product information is hidden from customers. All they see are simple search menus.
- Distribution is almost free by modem, CD-ROM disc, or computer diskette.
- The information in the digital catalog can be quickly updated and reissued.

To create a disc-based catalog, all you need is a computer, Microsoft Windows, a scanner (to convert your product photos into a digital format), and the Catalog On Disk software. A Canadian company, Prostar Interactive Media Works, has a similar product called Minicat, which can make your catalog data available either on disk or on the Internet.

Figure 14-2. An on-screen order form from a CD-ROM disc for Microsoft.

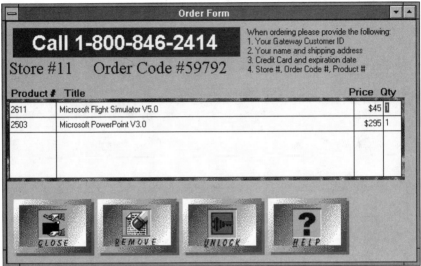

Use a Bulletin Board to Take Orders or Distribute Product

Computer retailer CompUSA has introduced an interactive electronic ordering system for federal government buyers. The system, based on BBS technology, enables holders of the federal government's International Purchase Authorization Card to dial up and review CompUSA's government price schedule, search through an electronic catalog of hardware and software products, and order products online.

Open Shop in an Online Service Shopping Mall

Many online users enjoy shopping directly from their computers, and they've been doing so for years. On CompuServe's Electronic Mall, over 130 companies sell products and services direct to online users (see Figure 14-3).

Keith Arnold, the general manager for the mall, says that his staff carefully controls the number and type of merchants who become part of the system. "We're looking for the right balance

Figure 14-3. A Pontiac ad on CompuServe's Electronic Mall.

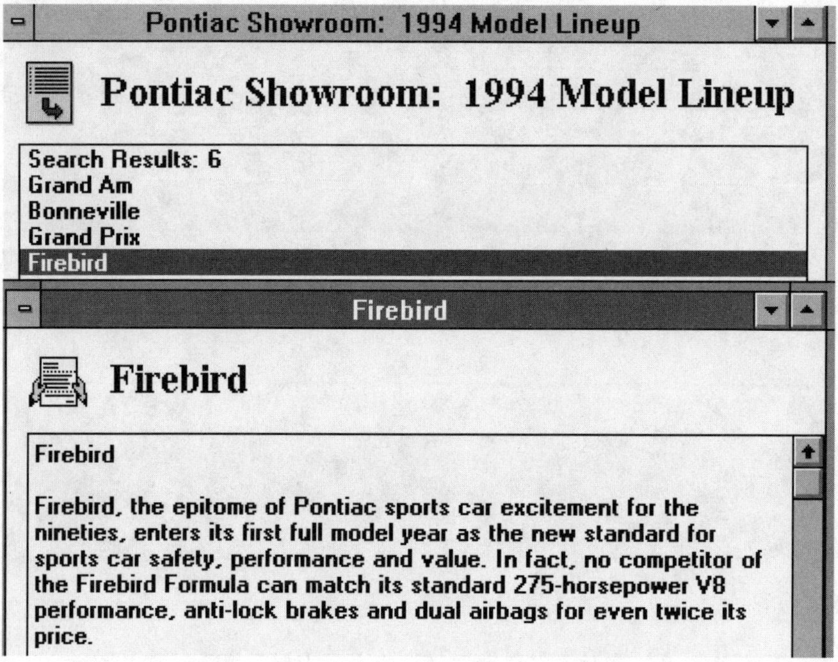

of products and services, and we try to choose vendors who we think will have the best chance of success. Brand name products seem to have an advantage over lesser-known companies, and we try to avoid over-saturation in any one area. We have companies calling us every day who want to sell flowers online. But we already have FTP and 1-800-Flowers."

Many smaller companies call CompuServe with expectations of opening an online shop and waiting for the money to roll in. But it takes a significant initial investment (approximately $25,000 on CompuServe—plus 2 percent of sales), as well as a long-term commitment. As an online merchant, you have to keep your site information up-to-date and you have to give online users reasons to visit and then return to your store—for example, promotions, advertising, special sales, etc.

I asked Keith if there are any underrepresented categories, offering pockets of opportunity within his mall. "Although the demographics indicate that more men than women use online services, there's still room for women's clothing and women's catalog companies in our mall. I think we need to give female consumers—female computer users—more reasons to go online to do their shopping."

CompuServe's mall has the potential to reach over 2.3 million subscribers. At the time of my conversation with Keith, CompuServe was adding 80,000 new members each month.

A wide variety of products and services are available, from contact lenses to clothing to gourmet coffee. Here's a representative sampling of some of the merchants in the CompuServe Electronic Mall:

- Express America Mortgage Corp., allows consumers to apply for a mortgage online.
- IAMs sells upscale pet food online.
- Lens Express allows consumers to order prescription glasses online.
- Quick & Reilly offers online trading via Quick Way and access to quotes on any listed stock, option, or market index.
- The University of Phoenix offers online college degrees and uses the slogan: "Online. The Intelligent Way to Get to Class."

CompuServe, of course, isn't the only service provider that offers its members online shopping. Prodigy features online catalogs of goods and services, and America Online is also building an electronic mall.

Norwalk, Connecticut-based advertising and research agency Modem Media indicates that the top ten of the 150 merchants selling on consumer-oriented online services in 1993 generated 80 percent of the $50 million in sales made by vendors on the major online shopping malls. About 90 percent of all sales came from Prodigy and CompuServe. Larger merchants generate an average of $3 million annually from online sales, while medium-size merchants earn about $500,000, and small merchants around $83,000.

Sell It on the Internet

The Internet Mall: Shopping on the Information Highway is a list and description of companies that sell products on the Internet.

Figure 14-4. Home page for FAST.

This is the home page for the FAST Electronic Broker, a prototype automated procurement
service being developed by the FAST Project at the University of Southern California's
Information Sciences Institute, under the sponsorship of the Advanced Research Projects Agency.

- Introduction to the FAST Broker
- The FAST Service Charge
- Requesting Quotes
- Ordering from FAST
- Combined Quote-and-Order Service
- Vendors Accessible through FAST
- The FAST Line Card

Dave Taylor, who manages the list, arranges companies into departments and floors, based on what they sell. You can obtain the list to see who else is selling online by sending an e-mail addressed to *taylor@netcom.com* with the subject "send mail." To be included on the list, just send another message describing what you're selling and your company's Internet address. The list is also available on the Web at *http://www.mecklerweb.com.*

FAST is an Internet-based purchasing service sponsored by the University of Southern California's Information Sciences Institute (see Figure 14-4). The FAST service, which started in 1987, is used by over 120 government agencies and major corporations to specify, locate, order, and pay for products from over 2,000 vendors online. FAST has provided well over 30,000 price quotes to buyers who have purchased over 10,000 products for a sales volume exceeding $5 million.

Here's how it works: First, the buyer opens a FAST customer account. The buyer then sends a request for a price quote on a particular product—pencils, floppy disks, etc. FAST locates sources of supply and provides a list of those sources to the buyer. The buyer places an order (or the product is automatically ordered based on prespecified specs, e.g., lowest cost quote), and FAST transmits the order to the selected vendor. To conclude the transaction, FAST bills the buyer and pays the vendor, adding in an 8 percent transaction fee, which is charged back to the buyer.

Like to be listed as a vendor on the FAST system? Visit FAST's Web site for more information *http://info.broker.isi.edu/1/ fast*, or see the Connection Section at the end of this chapter for a phone number. (Incidentally, an online catalog system somewhat like FAST's is under development at the University of Utah. It's called PartNet.)

QUICK LOOK: The Corner Drugstore Goes Online

Shopper's Express on America Online is an interactive home delivery service offering consumer goods from local supermarkets and drugstores nationwide. Called Shoppers Express Online, the service allows subscribers to choose from over 10,000 products available from local supermarkets and drug stores nationwide, including perishables, health and beauty supplies, and other items. Payments are made by personal check, credit card, or selected insurance plans for prescription orders. Participating retailers include Safeway, Inc., The Kroger Company, Winn Dixie Stores, The Vons Company, Eckerd Drug Comapny, and others.

Renting Space in a Web Cybermall

A cybermall is an online shopping site in which a group of marketers or merchants showcase their goods and services on a common server. The site is usually developed, managed, and maintained by a group of entrepreneurs who have the technical skills needed to help participating vendors create either simple Web-based home pages or more elaborate marketing presentations.

Some cybermalls on the Web receive thousands of visitors every day. The cybermall's server software usually has the capability to track the number of visitors to the site (a visit is often known as a "hit"), so that the mall's management can tell merchants at their site how many hits each presentation received and even which pages or documents within the presentation were viewed.

Making the Decision to Rent or Build

Here are the factors you need to weigh before you select the cybermall option:

• You should consider renting cybermall space for your website if you don't have the in-house technical expertise to evaluate, procure, and set up the necessary hardware and software; if you don't have the time to design and create an effective Web presentation; or if you don't have the money to buy a work station or set up a dedicated line (a full-time connection to the Internet).

• You should consider building your own website if you have the in-house technical expertise to work on setting up your website or you're willing to pay consultants to do the work; if you've allocated the funds to have a full-time connection to the Internet, along with a hardware platform (typically a Unix workstation) dedicated as a server to that connection; or if you anticipate that your website will be a primary marketing communications vehicle for your company.

There is also a third option that lies somewhere between the above two. Some organizations are having cybermall service providers "host" their website. The fact that the site is maintained on a server at the cybermall service provider's location is invisible to Web visitors. The merchant has his or her own Internet domain name, and the site appears separate from the cybermall (visitors don't use the cybermall's home page as a doorway to the merchant's site), although it may reside on the same server. The costs for this option would fall somewhere between the other two.

If you determine that renting space is the best course of action, you'll next need to evaluate potential commercial sites for your Web storefront.

How to Select the Right Cybermall

There are plenty of cybermalls that will be more than happy to help you create a sales site for your company or product on the Internet. As a marketer, you'll probably get a kick out of visiting Web mall sites and seeing how they display information and the different kinds of merchants selling goods at the various sites. But how do you know which site will be the best place to position your product? Here's a list of tough questions you can ask that will help to narrow the field.

• *How many hits/visits?* Ask about the number of hits the site's server receives on a daily/weekly/monthly basis. Are the numbers documented in any way? Can they fax you a computer printout of site activity over a recent period?

• *What's selling at this site?* Ask probing questions about the kinds of products or services that are selling at the site. That will give you some idea of the kinds of customers who are visiting the site, and whether or not your product will be a success at this location.

• *What do current tenants say?* Get the names, phone numbers, and e-mail addresses of a few of the vendors with presentations at this site. Contact them and ask if they're happy with the service they've received. How do they feel about the response the site has generated? Has it been worth their investment?

• *How is the site promoted?* Are there hypertext links to and from other sites? Does the site manager send out news announcements or press releases when a new merchant opens shop at the site? Is the site actively seeking publicity and news coverage to attract more visitors?

• *Is there any other content online?* Some cybermalls have electronic publications online as well as vendor presentations. These information "extras" can add value to the site and help attract visitors, not just once, but on an ongoing basis as visitors return to view the next issue of an electronic magazine, journal, or newsletter.

• *Who manages the presentation?* Is the vendor responsible for keeping their own documents up-to-date, or does the site manager handle that? (If you need to make some quick changes to the information on your pages, can you count on someone being there to make that change for you?)

• *How does the actual sales transaction take place?* Is the site authorized to accept credit card orders? Which cards? Is any sort of encryption technique employed? How does it work? How are orders forwarded to vendors?

Cybermalls With Space to Rent

Since there are no physical limitations on the "space" available on the Web, and since the barriers to developing a Web shopping site are relatively low, it's likely that new cybermalls will be springing up for some time. The next phase this new industry will go through (which is already under way) is for larger companies to get involved, either in purchasing an existing cybermall, or starting their own site. There may also be a trend toward cybermalls that are more specialized, focusing on a particular product category. It will be interesting to see which cybermalls succeed and thrive over the long run.

The following list is a sampling of some high-profile, well-designed Web cybermalls.

• *Branch Mall at http://branch.com*. The Branch Mall is one of the original Web cybermalls, with a long list of active merchants at its site (see Figure 14-5). 313-741-4442.

• *CommerceNet at http://www.commerce.net*. CommerceNet is supported by a nonprofit consortium of major high-tech companies committed to the concept of electronic commerce. 415-617-8790.

Figure 14-5. Home page for the Branch Mall site on the Web.

Welcome [voice] to the Branch Mall, exit 1, just off the information superhighway. We encourage you to add this page to your hotlist or to make a link to it. Jump to bottom.

Quick Reference

Flowers, Gifts, Foods | Miscellaneous Gifts, Toys, Decorations | Art/Jewelry | Clothing | Books, Music and Videos | Computer Related Products & Services | Electronics and Electrical | Communications | Business/Legal/Financial | Catalogs | Safety/Security | Health Products & Cosmetics | Education | Travel and Vacations | Information Resources/Help/Non-Profit Organizations | Real Estate, Home Improvements | Government | Other Malls |

• *CTS Net at http://www.cts.com.* CTS Net is the Web mall of a San Diego-based Internet service provider. 619-637-3637 or *webmaster@cts.com*

• *Downtown Anywhere at http://www.awa.com.* This is a friendly-looking, well-organized, community-like commercial site. 617-522-8102 or *downtown@awa.com*

• *First Virtual Holdings, Inc., at http://www.fv.com.* First Virtual's site demonstrates the company's unique approach to electronic commerce. 307-638-3688.

• *Global Network Navigator at http://gnn.com.* GNN is a high-traffic commercial site that also includes pointers to a wide variety of resources on the Internet. 707-829-0515.

• *Goldsite Europe at http://www.cityscape.co.uk.* Goldsite is Europe's busiest commercial Web server. 0223-566950 (UK).

• *IndustryNET at http://www.industry.net.* IndustryNET is, as the name implies, a site that puts a focus on creating an Internet presence for industrial companies. It features an extensive directory of industrial information and resources. 412-967-3500.

• *Internet Distribution Services at http://www.service.com.* The operators of this site have helped to design some of the most attractive and effective commercial sites on the Web. 415-856-8265.

• *Internet Shopping Network at http://www.internet.net.* Cable TV's Home Shopping Network (HSN) purchased the Internet Shopping Network in the Summer of 1994. ISN was one of the first to sell merchandise on the Internet, and they offer over 20,000 computer-related products from nearly 1,000 companies. The backing of HSN should help turn the Internet Shopping Network into a full-fledged shopping center, broadening their product line to include a wider variety of products. 415-617-0595.

• *marketplaceMCI.* This Web site, tied to the internetMCI Internet access service, has been announced, but was not yet open to public access as this book went to press. It's included in this list because of the likelihood that MCI's marketing expertise will make it a very attractive and busy site on the Web. 404-668-6000.

Figure 14-6. Home page for Shopping2000 listing the site's merchants.

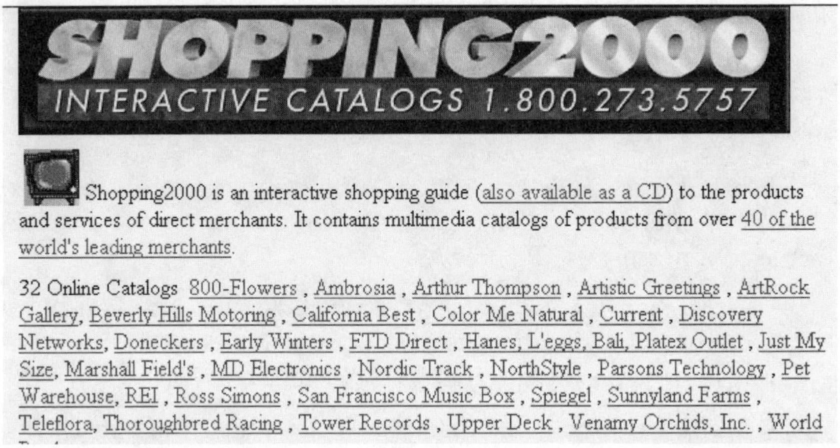

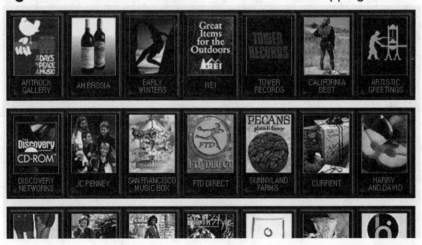

SHOPPING2000
INTERACTIVE CATALOGS 1.800.273.5757
Shopping2000 is an interactive shopping guide (also available as a CD) to the products and services of direct merchants. It contains multimedia catalogs of products from over 40 of the world's leading merchants.
32 Online Catalogs 800-Flowers , Ambrosia , Arthur Thompson , Artistic Greetings , ArtRock Gallery, Beverly Hills Motoring , California Best , Color Me Natural , Current , Discovery Networks, Doneckers , Early Winters , FTD Direct , Hanes, L'eggs, Bali, Platex Outlet , Just My Size, Marshall Field's , MD Electronics , Nordic Track , NorthStyle , Parsons Technology , Pet Warehouse, REI , Ross Simons , San Francisco Music Box , Spiegel , Sunnyland Farms , Teleflora, Thoroughbred Racing , Tower Records , Upper Deck , Venamy Orchids, Inc. , World

• *MecklerWeb at http://www.mecklerweb.com.* MecklerWeb is the Web site of Mecklermedia, publishers of *Internet World* magazine. 203-226-6967.

• *NetMarket Company at http://netmarket.com.* NetMarket, recently purchased by a large direct marketing firm, was one of the

Figure 14-7. Icons for access to merchants on Shopping2000.

ARTROCK GALLERY
AMBROSIA
EARLY WINTERS
Great Items for the Outdoors
REI
REI
TOWER RECORDS
CALIFORNIA BEST
ARTISTIC GREETINGS
Discovery CD-ROM
DISCOVERY NETWORKS
JC PENNEY
SAN FRANCISCO MUSIC BOX
FTD
FTD DIRECT
FTD DIRECT
PECANS
SUNNYLAND FARMS
CURRENT
HARRY AND DAVID

Figure 14-8. A page from the Tower Records site on Shopping2000 as a result of selecting the Tower Records icon shown on screen in Figure 14-7.

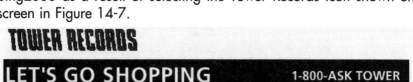

TOWER RECORDS

LET'S GO SHOPPING   1-800-ASK TOWER

When you shop at Tower Records, your selection of records is huge. Make your choices from the following index of music categories. Press the icon next to your selection and begin your shopping fun.

 (1.3Mb)

When you shop at Tower Records, 1-800-ASK-TOWER, your selection of records is huge. Make your choice from the following index of Music Catagories.

- Boxed Sets
- Children's
- Classical/Opera
- Comedy
- Country

first sites to conduct secure electronic transactions on the Internet. 617-441-5050.

• *The New York Web at http://nyweb.com.* This site has a hip, urban flavor. 212-921-5000.

• *Online Computer Marketplace at http://www.ocm.com.* This site features merchants who sell computer products and computer services. 508-480-0577.

• *OnRamp at http://www.onramp.net.* This is another hot-looking commercial Web site. 214-746-4710 or *info@onramp.net.*

• *Open Market, Inc. at http://www.openmarket.com.* Merchants at OpenMarket's site include Mead Data Central, Time Warner, Harcourt Brace Jovanovich, and others. Their approach is to help companies easily set up a storefront in cyberspace, using their StoreBuilder system. 617-621-9500 or *info@openmarket.com.*

• *Shopping2000 at http://www.shopping2000.com.* Shopping2000 features over forty major retailers and direct mail catalog merchants—be sure to visit this site (see Figures 14-6, 14-7, and 14-8). 212-447-9494.

QUICK LOOK: Views of a Merchandising Expert

Barry Diller, the Chairman and CEO of home shopping giant QVC, Inc., thinks shopping by computer will eventually be bigger than shopping by phone, but that the impulse buying of the TV shopper will be replaced by more "considered" purchasing.

In remarks made at a recent cable industry convention, Mr. Diller explained that when computers are connected to vast stores of data on products and services, consumers will be better able to research and consider purchases for as long as they like before clicking the mouse to consummate a transaction.

He was blunt in his opinion, however, that the current approach to guiding customers through online "malls" and "shopping centers" is the wrong one. He believes the new digital medium needs a new model for navigation. QVC's online shopping service, Q Online (which will be online sometime in 1995), will use some form of "smart agents" that perform tasks on behalf of users.

Creating Your Own Website

Evaluate and Compare Other Websites

Your first step, before you even consider setting up your own website, is to act like a digital private eye, cruising the Web for

HOT TIP: A Hyperlink Directory of Commercial Sites
on the Web

OpenMarket (the commercial website cybermall listed earlier in this chapter) sponsors DirectoryNet, a Web-based listing of commercial sites on the Web. The alphabetically arranged listing offers hypertext links to the hundreds of listed sites: Simply click your mouse on the name of the site, and the directory takes you there. This is the best place to find out which of your customers, competitors, and suppliers are doing business on the Web, as well as to see how other companies are presenting themselves in cyberspace. Visit Directory Net at *http://directory.net*.

clues to indicate what other successful companies are doing with their websites. For starters, visit the three business-oriented and three consumer-oriented websites listed in the "Quick Looks" in this chapter. (And if you still don't have your Web browser software and Web access yet, do not pass "go"—head straight back to Chapter 10 and follow the directions there.)

Set Up Your Web Server's Network Connection

A commercial website should be available to visitors around the clock, twenty four hours a day, 365 days a year. Having your Internet connection "down" would be a little like unplugging your company's telephone. To publish information on the Internet, you need a full-time, dedicated Internet connection.

QUICK LOOK: Three of the Best Consumer-Oriented "Showrooms" on the Web

Dealer Internet Services Corp., an online service developed by the owner of a car dealership in Lynwood, Washington, showcases car dealerships, automotive parts, and automotive information in a slick-looking site called DealerNet. Visit DealerNet at *http://www.dealernet.com.*

Shopping IN is a retail site that brings to mind the experience of shopping in a department store. There are "departments" for men's, women's, and children's clothing, plus jewelry and accessories. The copy describing items for sale is well written, and photos of clothing items look quite professional (see Figures 14-9 and 14-10). Visit ShoppingIN at *http://www.onramp.net/shopping_in.*

Ventana Media, a publisher of computer books, has developed a site that is one of the most attractive on the Web, with a wonderful full-page graphic for a home page, online order forms, and interesting, detailed descriptions of every book featured at the site. Visit the Ventana site at *http://www.vmedia.com.*

Figure 14-9. Home page for the Shopping IN retail site on the Web.

Departments *(High Resolution),* click here
Departments *(Speedier Version),* click here
First Time Shoppers, click here
About This Production, click here

Figure 14-10. Department selection page from Shopping IN.

Select Your Web Server Hardware Platform

Although Web server software programs have been written for most types of computers, the most commonly used Web server platforms are Unix workstations from manufacturers like DEC, Hewlett-Packard, and Sun Microsystems. That could be because the Internet relies heavily on Unix software tools and commands, because Unix workstations are more powerful than most personal computers, or because the technical folks who have often had the responsibility of setting up websites are familiar and comfortable with Unix. (Before long, there will probably be many computer vendors selling Internet "information servers" that will include Web server software along with the computer on which it runs.)

QUICK LOOK: Four of the Best Business-to-Business "Catalogs" on the Web

When you visit these Websites, you'll see how companies can create interactive catalogs to showcase all of their products and services using the Web.

• *Digital Equipment Corp.,* a major provider of computer systems and services, hosts the DECdirect Interactive website to showcase their broad line of computer systems and supplies. Visit DECdirect Interactive at *http://www.service.digital.com/ddi/html.*

• *GTSI,* a computer distributor with a focus on government markets, hosts the GTSI Online website, a hypertext catalog featuring tens of thousands of hardware, software, and networking products (see Figure 14-11). Visit GTSI Online at *http://www.gtsi.com.*

• *Marshall Industries,* a distributor of electronic components, tools, and accessories, hosts the Marshall on the Internet website to help users quickly and easily locate specialized electronic products and components from their desktop (see Figure 14-12). The site includes a Products section that users can search by manufacturer, by type of product, or by part number, a Technical publications section, and a Quick Quote option for visitors who just want a quick price check on a particular item. Visit Marshall on the Internet at *http://www.marshall.com.*

• *Electronic parts distributor AMP* has created a Web-based catalog that's being used to locate parts by electronic product engineers who incorporate AMP's components into their product designs. AMP marketers say that the engineers who use the e-catalog love it because they don't have to search through a huge manual to find the right part. Although corporate buying departments don't always have Internet access, many engineers do, and engineers are often the key contact when it comes to specifying parts and components. Visit Amp at *http://www.amp.com.*

Obtain and Install Your Web Server Software

What does Web server software do? It sends files (Web "pages") to the browser program of visitors to your site. It also runs prescripted programs. (A script, for instance, might tell the computer to take information that a visitor enters on an online form and automatically save it in a database.) Some sophisticated scripts can search a large database and present specific information

Figure 14-11. Home page for GTSI site on the Web.

Welcome to GTSI's Electronic Catalog and Ordering System

ONLINE CATALOG

Press here to shop and order from over 40,000 multiplatform hardware, software, and networking solutions on selected government schedules and contracts.

Figure 14-12. Home page for Marshall Industries site on the Internet.

 Entrance

 Feedback

 Help

 What's New / What's Hot

based on input from a visitor. For example, your server might list thousands of different kinds of office chairs. An online form would allow visitors to select certain preferences from a list, such as "leather upholstery," and the server would respond with all chairs that match that description.

HOT TIP: Free Web Server and Web Authoring Software

A surprising number of Web-related software programs are available as freeware on the Internet, including Web server software (which provides a kind of software platform or operating system for a website by interacting with the client browser software used by Web visitors) and Web authoring programs (which assist website designers in creating pages and files for a website).

Freeware is software that is distributed at no charge to users. Freeware programs are typically developed at universities or (as in the case of Microsoft, below) by software publishers who want to add additional value and utility to popular commercial programs.

You can access information on retrieving the freeware Web-master Starter Kit (for Unix systems) from Enterprise Integration Technology's website. Visit *http://www.eit.com* and select the "EIT Web Resources" heading from the home page.

You'll find the Unix version of the National Center for Super-computing Applications' NCSA httpd Web server software at *ftp://ftp.ncsa.uiuc.edu/Web/ncsa_httpd* and the Win-dows version at *ftp://ftp.ncsa.uiuc.edu/Web/ncsa_httpd/con-trib/whtp11ab6.zip*.

You can access information on retrieving the freeware In-ternet Assistant for MS Word 6.0 from Microsoft's website. In-ternet Assistant features HTML authoring tools for creating web documents using Word. Visit *http:www.microsoft.com* and select the "What's New" heading from the home page.

Design Your Website

Once your server is up and running, you need to start preparing the presentation visitors will see when they access your site. Web documents are formatted using HTML (Hypertext Markup Language). HTML is not as difficult to use as the name might suggest, and software publishers are now creating tools that will make it faster and easier to create Web-ready documents from your favorite word processor or database program. (See the "Quick Look.") If you're concerned about the visual appearance of your site (which you should be), you'll either need a good computer illustration package to create images, or a computer-savvy graphic artist to produce digital images for you.

Put special care into your "home page," because it's the first page vistors will see when they access your site. It should include brief descriptions of each option for additional documents that can be accessed from that page.

Keep in mind as you design your website that large, dense graphic images may transmit very slowly to the computer screen of someone visiting your site. This depends on a number of factors, including the speed of their computer, their modem, or their browser software. If possible, keep graphics small, and limit the number of images per page. Consider giving users the option of "turning off" the graphics and viewing only the text of your site.

QUICK LOOK: Commercial Website Software

The World Wide Web is emerging as an important means for sharing information either broadly across the Internet or more locally through corporate networks. Information on the Web is made available as pages on web servers, which are typically accessed using browser software like Mosaic. The pages are written in HTML (Hypertext Markup Language) and may contain text with embedded icons, graphics, sound, video, and hyperlinks to other pages.

The software products listed below are being developed by companies that specialize in database management programs, search and retrieval software, and electronic cataloging or documentation tools. In many cases, they've modified existing technologies so that company databases can be made accessible to the Web.

Commercial products can offer some advantages over either freeware Web server software or Web authoring software, including documentation, support, and features which are not available on the freeware programs.

> BASIS WEBserve from Information Dimensions
> Cyberleaf from Interleaf Software
> DynaWeb from Electronic Book Technologies
> HoTMetal PRO, the "word processor for the Web" from SoftQuad
> MMB TEAMate software from MMB Development Corp.
> NetPublisher from Ameritech
> NetSite Web server software from NetScape Communications
> Omnimax from Exoterica
> Oracle Media Server from Oracle
> PB.web electronic Web catalog software from MediaShare
> PLServer software from Personal Library Software
> Process Web Server for Windows NT from Process Software
> StoreBuilder electronic commerce software from Open Market
> TOPIC text retrieval engine from Verity

> Virtual Places software for creating "Web environments" from Ubique
>
> WAISserver Internet database indexer with search and retrieval capability from WAIS, Inc.
>
> Web Datablade software, the "database for cyberspace" from Illustra Information Technologies
>
> WebMagic authoring system, part of the WebFORCE hardware/software package, from Silicon Graphics

Post Information on Your Website

Here are some of the kinds of information other companies have posted on their websites. Scan this list and check off the items that you would most like to see available on your website.

- [ ] Descriptions of organizational business units, joint ventures, and marketing partners
- [ ] News announcements and press releases
- [ ] Your company's newsletter
- [ ] Text and charts from annual reports
- [ ] Historical information about the organization
- [ ] Contact data for departments, divisions, sales offices, and distributor offices
- [ ] Information on your organization's research and development efforts
- [ ] An overview of your market or of technology issues related to your product line
- [ ] Simple product and service descriptions
- [ ] Complete online catalogs of products and services
- [ ] Technical data and specifications on your products, including comparisons to competitive products
- [ ] Forms for ordering products and services online
- [ ] Online product registration forms
- [ ] Short video product demonstrations
- [ ] Brief audio clips from company executives
- [ ] Pointers or links to related information resources on the Internet
- [ ] Lists of questions frequently asked by customers—and their answers

☐ A calendar listing industry conferences, training seminars, or events
☐ A feedback or suggestion form for visitor input

Danger! Robots Invade the Web!

I've visited and reviewed many World Wide Web sites, and there seems to be a common thread that runs through those that work best—the sites that Internet visitors tend to visit and then visit again. (Because, after all, what good is a site that no one sees?) The best Web pages seem to intelligently integrate many different kinds of information, and they don't drag the viewer through the site—they let the user control the action and make the choices.

To design a great Web site, you need to take off your linear thinking cap and put on your "hyper-hat." Think in terms of information links instead of traditional information structure. And try to use the full range of multimedia available to you on the Web. Remember the famous command of the movie director in all those Hollywood movies? "Lights! Sound! Action!" You have a number of tools at your disposal—including text, graphics, sound files, video, and user interaction—why not use them all?

Let's visit a make-believe website. Say this site is operated by a U.S. company that distributes high-tech industrial products from around the world. This particular website features a new industrial robot, Mr. Roboto, imported from Japan.

On the home page, we see a photo of Mr. Roboto in action, along with the headline:

Welcome to the
Mr. Roboto Interactive Customer Center
Please make your selection from the following menu:
Mr. Roboto's Handsome Features
Mr. Roboto's Resume and Background
What People Are Saying About Mr. Roboto
More Information on Robotics
Schedule an On-Site Demonstration of Mr. Roboto

If we select the page "Mr. Roboto's Handsome Features," we see a brief description of the robot's finer points, using bulleted, hyperlinked text:

- Designed using advanced composite materials
- Retractable arm has grasping fingers
- Fuzzy logic sensors detect slightest motion
- Emits pleasant whistling tone while it works
- Each line of text is linked, when selected, to a more detailed description of that particular feature

Then we select "Mr. Roboto's Resume and Background," which presents the credentials of the design team who created Mr. Roboto, and the ability to access brief case histories of how Mr. Roboto cut costs and saved time in various manufacturing situations.

When we select the page "What People Are Saying About Mr. Roboto," we see hypertext references to product reviews of Mr. Roboto in several industrial trade journals, as well as testimonial letters from several happy customers. With a click of the mouse—voila!—the complete text of each selected review or letter appears on our screen.

To obtain a better insight into robots in general, we next select the item "More Information on Robotics." This page gives the contact information for the International Robotics Association, a list of conferences involving robotics, and the e-mail addresses to subscribe to Internet mailing lists focused on robots and robotics. Click on an icon at the bottom of the page and up pops a glossary of terms for anyone who may be unfamiliar with the robotic lexicon.

Finally, we select "Schedule an On-Site Demonstration of Mr. Roboto." This takes us to a page that includes a multipurpose electronic form. The form gives us the option of:

- Requesting to be placed on a mailing list for future announcements regarding Mr. Roboto
- Asking for a sales rep to contact us to schedule a live demonstration
- Obtaining a brief survey indicating how we use automation at our company

Promote Your Website

Once you have your new website set up, post an announcement on the Web's popular "What's New" page at *whats-new@ncsa.ui uc.edu*. Put some free, useful information on the server and then announce it in a few selected Internet newsgroups that are relevant to your business. If your customers, suppliers, or business associations have their own websites, ask them if they'll include links to yours. And be sure to put your Web address (along with your e-mail address) on your business cards, press releases, and collateral materials.

Making Online Sales Transactions Simple and Secure

How secure are sales transactions that take place online? Is it OK for a consumer to type in her credit card number on an online order form? When will we be able to use "digital cash" to buy and sell goods on the net?

These are some of the questions currently being debated by Internet marketers. Opinions vary widely. Some observers say that completing credit card sales transactions on the Internet shouldn't be a subject of concern. They cite the fact that many people write their credit card numbers on magazine subscription cards and then send them through the mail without a thought—so why should buyers worry about entering a credit card number on an online order form? Others point out that most of us don't

Figure 14-13. Home page for First Virtual.

First Virtual -- Bringing the World of Electronic Commerce to Your Computer -- TODAY!
If you can read this, you can buy and sell information over the Internet right now!

Figure 14-14. Home page for Open Market.

use voice scramblers when we conduct sales negotiations or discuss market strategies over the telephone, so why all the fuss about transferring sensitive business information via the Internet? Others note the fact that there are plenty of hackers willing to invest significant time, effort, and resources in order to steal information—especially financial information—that's being transmitted over public networks.

First Virtual (see detailed discussion later in this chapter) and Open Market are two companies promoting formulas for electroniccommerce using the Internet (see Figures 14-13 and 14-14).

Whoever ends up winning the argument, it's clear that many companies want a reasonable level of security before making major commitments to electronic commerce. They want to make sure their transactions are immune to wiretaps, electronic eavesdropping, and theft.

How Should Buyers Pay Sellers Online?

The marketplace, as usual, is responding quickly to this concern. In fact, loads of research, lots of test projects, and plenty of secure sales transactions are taking place as you're reading this. Secure approaches to commerce already exist. But no clear standard has emerged, and the tools to conduct these transactions are not yet widely available.

Nevertheless, a few basic models or approaches to net-based sales transactions are beginning to come into focus.

• The consumer, responding to a net-based marketing presentation, sends in a check or calls and verbally transmits a credit card number over the merchant's telephone. This is a fairly traditional approach, and no financial transaction takes place on the net.

• The consumer (1) sets up an account with a merchant or third party organization, (2) leaves his or her credit card number by means other than the net, and (3) gives the merchant the authorization to bill the account whenever the consumer chooses to buy something.

• The consumer leaves his or her credit card number on an unsecure online order form. With this approach, the consumer is put at some risk that the credit card number will be compromised, but the risk is perhaps not much greater than giving it out over the phone.

• The consumer uses a secure (encrypting) client software program to transfer his or her encrypted credit card number to a secure (decrypting) merchant server.

• The consumer exchanges traditional currency (cash, check, credit card authorization) for some form of digital currency, and then "spends" units of that currency whenever and wherever he or she likes. This approach requires some type of software-based

---

QUICK LOOK: Selling Pizza on the Internet

Pizza Hut is selling pizzas on the Internet in a pilot project called PizzaNet. Residents in Santa Cruz, California, use their Internet connections and Web browser software to access the PizzaNet server at Pizza Hut headquarters in Wichita, Kansas. Customers see a menu of available pizza options and fill out an online order form. The order is sent by modem to the nearest franchise in Santa Cruz. The local restaurant calls the customer to verify the order, and money changes hands at the point of delivery. *http://pizzanet.net.*

"electronic wallet" to hold the currency and an account set up between the currency provider and participating merchants.

Which approach do you think buyers will be most likely to accept and use? And will consumers favor one model and business buyers another? The winning system will probably be the one that makes it easiest for both buyers and sellers to conduct transactions under a reasonable standard of security.

The Strange Language of Network Security

Digital security is a somewhat mysterious and arcane science, but the basic premise is a simple one: Deny unauthorized individuals access to sensitive information. If you get involved with digital sales transactions, you may find yourself dealing with security-related issues. It would help to have a basic understanding of the following terms. (P.S. Sprinkle a few of these into a cocktail party conversation, and people will suspect you're with the CIA.)

authentication   verifying a party's identity through the use of a digital certificate or digital signature.

certificate authority   a trusted third party that signs and issues digital certificates.

cipher   a code used to encrypt (scramble) and decrypt (unscramble) messages.

DES or data encryption standard   a U.S. government standard for encrypting data.

digital certificate   an electronic document that includes the name of a digital key holder, his or her public key, the certificate's validity dates, the name of the certificate's issuer, and the digital signature of the Certificate Authority.

digital signature   a unique binary code identifying a single party.

encryption/decryption   ensures the in-transit privacy of a message between two parties by encrypting (scrambling) the message upon transmission and decrypting (unscrambling) the message on receipt

firewall   a device that blocks unauthorized access into a computer system or network.

public/private key cryptography   a method of encrypting data so that only the sender and intended receiver can read it. The user creates a pair of keys—one public and the other private. Any message encrypted with the public key can only be decrypted with the private key—and vice versa.

sniffer   a device that can be used to illicitly intercept and capture data transmissions (like credit card numbers) crossing public networks like the Internet.

Profiles of Pioneers in Electronic Sales Transactions

If you have any doubts about the future of electronic commerce on the Internet, take a look at this list of organizations involved in the effort. In particular, note the combined financial, organizational, and technical expertise of some of the major players.

The projects, products, and services profiled here run the gamut from digital cash systems to encrypted credit card transactions to traditional payment mechanisms that have been adapted to the needs of electronic commerce. If the level of interest and effort is any indication, the digital marketplace may just turn out to be the biggest growth industry since the PC.

BankAmerica Corp.

Merchants holding accounts with BankAmerica will soon be able to securely process credit card orders in real-time over the Internet. About a dozen merchants are expected to participate in the first phase of BankAmerica's electronic payment project. Merchants participating in the new payment service will be able to accept Visa, MasterCard, Discover, Diners Club, Carte Blanche, JCB Cards, and American Express. The service will be based on Netscape Communications' Netsite Commerce Server software, with additional transaction processing capabilities to handle payment processing.

BankAmerica's business customers will create their own Internet presence or virtual storefronts using the Netsite Commerce Server, and then enroll in the service through BankAmerica. Consumers using Netscape Communications' Netscape Navigator can then access and establish a secure link with the server, enabling credit card information to be sent securely over the net.

CheckFree

CheckFree has been providing electronic payment processing services for years. All CheckFree users need is a computer, a modem, and a CheckFree account to pay virtually any bill to anyone, regardless of where they bank. All payments are itemized on the user's bank statement. CheckFree subscribers often use CheckFree in unison with electronic checkbook software programs like Quicken.

CommerceNet, EIT, RSA, and Terisa

The companies that make up this partnership are hard at work establishing standards for commercial transactions on the Internet and other networks. CommerceNet's encryption systems are based on mathematical formulas developed by RSA Data Security, a leader in encryption technology. RSA and CommerceNet's parent company, Enterprise Integration Technologies (EIT), have joined together to form a new company, Terisa Systems, which is providing SecureWeb Toolkit software for Web transaction security, and consulting for Internet software developers.

The partners feel that the key to secure online commerce is user authentication, access authorization, and bullet-proof encryption. RSA's industry standard public key cryptography technology provides privacy through encryption and authentication through digital signatures that are unique for each user. Applications based on this technology will permit the transmission of digital contracts that are legally binding and allow credit card numbers and bid amounts to be encrypted and safely transmitted on the net. You can visit the CommerceNet website at *http:// www.commerce.net*, EIT at *http://www.eit.com*, RSA at *http:// www.rsa.com*, and Terisa at *http://www.terisa.com*.

CyberCash

CyberCash is a trial payment system that will offer two services: (1) secure credit/debit card transactions and (2) electronic money transfers for the Internet, online services, and private networks.

Here's how it works:

1. For credit card transactions, the card holder runs a small, free program on his or her PC that encrypts their personal credit

card data using a special method that allows only CyberCash to decrypt it. This encrypted data is included with the ordering data that is sent to the merchant. When the merchant is ready to authorize, charge, or debit the card, they send the still-encrypted info to the bank via CyberCash. CyberCash decrypts the info before forwarding it to the bank.

2. The electronic cash system enables funds to be transferred between individuals or to small businesses that aren't qualified credit card merchants.

CyberCash's partners include Enterprise Integration Technology, RSA Data Security, Trusted Information Systems, and Wells Fargo Bank. You can visit the CyberCash website at *http:// www.cybercash.com.*

DigiCash

DigiCash is a Netherlands-based company that's developing a digital cash system using public key cryptography. Its project is currently in the pilot stage, with several hundred users and over fifty vendors participating in buying and selling products using what the company calls "cyber bucks."

DigiCash's goal is to provide a currency that has the privacy of paper cash, while achieving the high security required for electronic network environments. The company hopes that buyers will be able to "click and pay"—in other words, to touch an on-screen button with their computer mouse using cyber bucks to pay for something. You can visit the DigiCash website at *http:// www.digicash.com.*

First Virtual

A company called First Virtual Holdings, Inc., is promoting a system based on what it calls InfoCommerce. Using this system, consumers interact with merchants using First Virtual's server, which it calls the InfoHaus (information warehouse) or the vendor's own Internet server. Several of First Virtual's founders were originators of e-mail technology, and their partners include a number of major technology and financial service companies, including Electronic Data Systems (EDS).

First Virtual's system, which is up and running today, requires only that users have e-mail access and a First Virtual account to purchase information from a participating vendor. First Virtual's system is limited to the sale of digital products. But for vendors of information and other digital goods (books, newsletters, software, video or audio products), the system offers a number of advantages. They don't need to worry about printing, packaging, postage, shipping, or warehousing.

No cryptography is needed because no financial data moves over a public network. Buyers and sellers register for a very low fee with FV. (You can open a buyer or seller account by sending e-mail to *apply@card.com*) Under First Virtual's rules, buyers retain the right to examine goods and decide whether they want to buy. If a buyer retrieves goods on a frequent basis without agreeing to pay, First Virtual will review and cancel the account. The seller assumes the risk, but it's a relatively small risk. If the buyer agrees to purchase the product, a charge is registered to the user's card. First Virtual makes twenty-nine cents plus two percent on each transaction, and then forwards payment to the vendor. You can visit the First Virtual website at *http://www.fv.com*.

Mastercard International

Mastercard announced recently that it would develop standards enabling its over 360 million card holders to use their cards for purchases on the Internet. The company, which hopes to have the system operational by the Fall of 1995, will use Netscape Communications' encryption technology (see below) to scramble account numbers and other data, and then forward the information to MasterCard computers connected to the Internet.

According to MasterCard, merchants won't require the dedicated phone lines or card authorization terminals needed today to process transactions because customer data will be sent directly to MasterCard's computers for processing.

Microsoft and Quicken

Microsoft's recent acquisition of Quicken (the hugely popular computer checkbook program) has led many in the computer industry to speculate that Microsoft will move rapidly to combine Quicken in some way with Microsoft's new online service, placing the software giant squarely in the arena of electronic commerce and digital transactions. (See below for info on Microsoft's partnership with Visa.)

NetBill

A number of universities also have projects in the works, including a project under development at Carnegie Mellon University called NetBill. Using NetBill, both buyers and sellers establish an account with a central exchange. Once digital goods are delivered over the network (and the digital bits arrive successfully), the user is billed.

NetCheque and NetCash

Similar programs (dubbed "NetCheque" and "NetCash") are under development by the University of Southern California's Information Sciences Institute (also developers of the FAST system covered earlier in this chapter). Users registered with NetCheque accounting servers are able to write checks to other users. When deposited, the checks authorize the transfer of account balances from the account against which the check was drawn to the account in which the check was deposited.

NetMarket and Pretty Good Privacy

A company called NetMarket Company in Nashua, New Hampshire, is using encryption software called Pretty Good Privacy (PGP) to encrypt sales transactions on the net. In one of the first trials of its type, NetMarket sold a fellow named Phil in Philadelphia (doesn't that have a nice ring to it?) a copy of rock artist Sting's collection of songs called "Ten Summoner's Tales" for $12. Phil's Visa card number was encrypted using PGP and then sent over the Internet to NetMarket, who processed the order. PGP is a shareware program available today on numerous software sites on the Internet.

NetScape Communications

The NetScape Communications Corp., headquartered in Northern California, is populated by many of the original developers of the World Wide Web's hugely popular Mosaic software interface. While providing a new commercial version of the Mosaic browser program (Mosaic NetScape as freeware), the company is also selling Web server software configured to manage commercial transactions. This product, called NetSite Secure Server, uses digital key cryptography to enable businesses to initiate secure transactions on the Internet.

BankAmerica Corp., First Data Corp., and MasterCard are all utilizing the NetScape system to some degree in their own electronic commerce projects.

Visa International

Visa has signed a letter of intent with Microsoft to provide a standard, secure method of electronic commerce on public and private networks. This method is expected to consist of software that will support both the merchant and card holder sides of net transactions. The already-existing VisaNet payment system will be used to authenticate buyers and sellers, secure the transactions, and manage the clearing and settlement process. The agreement with Microsoft is not exclusive, and Visa indicates that they will be reviewing other options for electronic commerce as well.

HOT TIP: Where to Get More Background Info on Data Encryption

If you'd like to know more about data encryption, PGP software, or secure messaging, contact SLED Corp. (a digital certificate authority and publisher of an online Internet "white pages") at 415-323-2508 or send an e-mail message to: *info@four11.com* for a mailbot-delivered document on the subject.

RSA Data Security, a leader in encryption technology, has a Frequently Asked Questions (FAQ) file on their Web home page that covers encryption and authentication technology. Visit at *http://www.rsa.com*.

Finally, you can pick up a copy of the book *PGP: Pretty Good Privacy* by Simson Garfinkel, published by O'Reilly & Associates (1994).

Summary

This chapter considered the differences between online advertising and sales, evaluated the online marketplace as a medium to reach prospects and customers, and analyzed current efforts to create a secure environment for online transactions. It also looked at the wide variety of options for selling online and offered an overview of some of the companies that are using the Web as an effective medium for online sales.

Finally, it armed you with a list of hardball questions with which to grill the proprietors of Web cybermalls.

The next chapter examines how you're going to take care of all the new customers you'll win with your online sales efforts. If your customer support operation needs a little support of its own, read on for information about how you can manage customer service online.

Chapter 14 Connection Section

Contact information for organizations and resources mentioned in or related to this chapter:

Ameritech, Net Publisher software, 708-866-0150

Amp, an electronic parts distributor with a Web-based electronic catalog, 717-780-7450

CheckFree, electronic payment processing system, 800-882-5280

CommerceNet, solutions for electronic commerce, 415-617-8790

CompUSA, computer retailer with interactive electronic ordering system for federal government buyers, BBS: 214-888-5406, 800-468-4682

CompuServe, provider of The Electronic Mall online shopping center, 614-457-8600

Curtis Software Corp., publishes Catalog on Disk software for creating CD-ROM based catalogs, 310-320-2451

DigiCash, company working on the development of electronic currency systems, + 31(20)665-2611 or *info@digi cash.nl*

Electronic Book Technologies, DynaWeb software, 401-421-9550

Exoterica, OmniMark software, 613-722-1700

EIT, 415-617-8000 or *info@eit.com*

FAST, an online purchasing service, 310-822-1511 or *info@i si.edu*

First Virtual Holdings, Inc., solutions for electronic commerce, 800-570-0003 or *info@fv.com*

Illustra Information Technologies, Web DataBlade software, the "database for cyberspace," 510-652-8000

Information Dimensions, BASIS WEBserver software, 614-761-8083

Interleaf, Cyberleaf software, 617-290-0710

MediaShare, PB.web software, 619-931-7171

MMB Development Corporation, MMB TEAMate software, 800-832-6022 or 310-318-1322

NetScape Communications Corp., publishes NetSite software for creating Web servers (offers a version of NetSite for secure Internet transactions), 415-254-1900 or 800-NET-SITE

Net Market Company, an Internet marketing company using PGP software to encrypt sales transactions on the net, 603-881-3777

Open Market, Inc., StoreBuilder software, 617-621-9500

Oracle Corp., Oracle Media Server software, 415-506-7000

Personal Library Software, PLServer software, 301-990-1155

Process Software Corp., Process Web Server for Windows NT software, 508-879-6994

Prostar Interactive Media Works, MiniCat, CommCat, and MaxiCat catalog software, 604-273-4099

RSA, 415-595-8782 or *info@rsa.com*

Silicon Graphics, WebMagic authoring system, 415-390-3900 or 800-800-7441

SoftQuad, HoTMetal PRO software, 416-239-4801

Terisa Systems, SecureWeb Toolkits software for Web transaction security, 415-617-1836 or *info@terisa.com*

Ubique, Ltd., Virtual Places, Doors, and Sesame, 415-896-2434

Verity, TOPIC text retrieval engine software, 415-960-7600

WAIS Inc., WAISserver database indexing software, 415-614-0444 or *info@wais.com*

15

Help Your Customers Help Themselves With Online Service and Support

Boeing Aircraft in Seattle, Washington, is one of the world's largest aircraft manufacturers. When Boeing ships out a new jet to one of its airline customers, the package includes a great deal of technical support documentation. So much, in fact, that if the information were delivered in a hard copy paper format, the buyer would get a stack of documents longer, wider, taller, and heavier than the jet itself. Because of that, as well as the fact that electronic documentation is easier to update, search, and distribute, Boeing delivers technical support documentation to new buyers in a variety of digital formats.

Whether or not your product needs as much support documentation as a 747, there are many advantages to using new media technologies to better serve, support, and simply stay in touch with your customers. In fact, customer support shouldn't be defined merely as fixing something that's broken. The concept of customer support should be expanded to include your efforts to help your customers receive as much value as possible from the products they purchase from you. With that in mind, there are more customer support applications for new media technology than you might have expected.

This chapter examines the advantages of online customer support and points out the various options available, including electronic documentation, bulletin board systems, and the Internet. You'll find profiles of companies that are successfully engaged in online support and some worthwhile tips and techniques for setting up your own online support systems.

Seven Reasons to Switch to Online Customer Support

Customer service and support is becoming an ever more critical piece of the marketing puzzle. Marketers now know that it typically costs a great deal more to find new customers than to keep the customers they already have. The quality of the service after the sale is a critical component in the customer's decision to buy from that company again. Therefore, marketers must continually explore new ways to serve, support, and satisfy their customers.

The term *customer service* means different things in different industries. When you consider the idea of online customer support, you may automatically think it only applies to companies that sell complex products (e.g., computer systems) that have extensive maintenance requirements. But there's another way to look at online customer support. Online connectivity can be used as a way to put your company in closer touch with current and potential customers. In this chapter you'll see examples of retail, shipping, and real estate companies that are making use of digital technology to satisfy real customer needs.

What do customers want out of your service department? It's simple: They want information and support that will help them make the most out of their purchase. Remember, your customers don't care if online support saves *you* time or money. They want to know how *they're* going to save time and money by using *your* new system. It's your job to sell them on the concept. Your customers have to feel confident that if they address a service question or problem to an automated online service site, their problem or question will be promptly addressed. They want to know that if they leave a suggestion on an online customer feedback form, your company will take that suggestion seriously and will acknowledge it.

If these issues are taken into consideration, online customer support applications can be designed that will both satisfy customer service managers and their customers. Here's how.

1. *Automate routine service procedures.* Online customer support can help to relieve the technical support staff from answering the same questions over and over and over again. Instead, the staff can gather the answers to frequently asked questions and post them for customers to review at an online support site.

2. *Offer support around the clock.* When customers need help, they want it immediately. They don't want to call a support number and get an answering machine or voice mail. This issue is even more important for customers who do business on an international basis. Customers in foreign countries may be starting their day just as your service reps are getting ready to go home. One of the great aspects of online customer support is that it can be available twenty-four hours a day, seven days a week, 365 days a year. It's there whenever the customer needs it.

3. *Keep technical information accurate and up to date.* When customers look for critical support information, they expect it to be accurate and up to date. Online customer support documentation can be more up to date and accurate than printed manuals. You can input changes and corrections into technical support material on an electronic bulletin board or Internet support site in minutes and have it available to a worldwide customer base almost instantaneously.

4. *Slash hard copy distribution costs.* Online customer support documentation can dramatically cut the costs of printing and shipping paper-based technical support materials. For most companies, support is still considered a cost center, not a profit center. To these companies, any suggestion that can reduce the expense of support is a welcome one. Even organizations that make money on service are always looking for new and more efficient ways to deliver that service. Examine the costs involved in printing and mailing customer support information in your organization, and imagine the savings if you could distribute even a small percentage of that information electronically.

5. *Give your customers more control.* Online customer support options allow customers to help themselves to the information they need when they need it. Many customers like to be able to access customer support information for themselves rather than wait on hold for the next customer service representative or wait even longer for a repair technician to show up at their site. In a

do-it-yourself culture, many customers like to be able to take the reins of the support process into their own hands.

6. *Stay in closer touch with customers.* Companies in virtually any industry can benefit from online technology by starting from the premise of building closer connections with customers. A book club can set up a Gopher server to present book buyers with background information or even a sample chapter from a particular book. A health food manufacturer can create a website where visitors find recipes that include the company's products. Another company may post an online suggestion form or questionnaire to gather customer opinions or ideas. Online applications like these help to build relationships that translate into customer satisfaction, customer loyalty, and products that meet the real needs of the marketplace.

7. *Position your company for the future.* You may protest that only a moderate percentage of your customers have access to CD-ROM drives, online service accounts, or links to the Internet today. That percentage will likely be significantly higher by late 1995 or mid 1996. More and more computers are being shipped with CD-ROM capability. The number of users connecting to on-line services and the Internet is growing quite rapidly. When Windows 95 begins to replace the current version of Windows operating system software, millions of new users will have access to online service and the Internet from their desktops. If all the customer has to do is tap an icon on his or her computer screen

---

QUICK LOOK: FedEx and UPS Set Up Online Links for Electronic Interaction With Customers

Package shippers FedEx and United Parcel Service of America, Inc. (UPS) have both decided that they can serve customers better online. Both companies will allow customers to order package pick-ups, track deliveries, and view billing information from their computer desktops. FedEx is giving away free software called FedEx Ship, which quickly links individual customers to the company's huge delivery database. FedEx has an ambitious goal: *to conduct 100 percent of all customer transactions online by having 100 percent of customers online before the year 2000.*

to get in contact with your company, that can open up many new options for customer service, support, and interaction. Will you be ready?

Turn Paper Manuals Into Digital Documents

Digitizing technical support documents offers many of the same advantages as digital versions of any marketing support materials. Printing, mailing, and distribution costs can be cut significantly. Digital documents are easier to keep up to date. Electronic indexing permits users to search through documents to quickly and easily locate the information they need.

HOT TIP: Online Support Applications Can Do Double-Duty

It's possible to integrate digital documentation with other online technologies to accomplish multiple marketing objectives. Remember the Powercom 2000 project described in the chapter on electronic data interchange? This project was initiated to address a technical support problem, but the solution ended up also enabling online ordering through EDI.

Service managers may find it easier to get approval for digital customer support projects if they team up with marketing and sales managers to address their needs as well. A CD-ROM-based technical support manual, for instance, might be funded more quickly if the disc also included the capability for current customers to purchase upgrades, add-ons, and new products directly from the disc.

Set Up an Online Customer Forum or BBS Support Site

We've covered the basics of bulletin board system (BBS) technology in Chapter 6. A BBS is a computer equipped with a modem and special bulletin board system software. Users dial in to the system from their computers and use simple text-based or graphi-

Figure 15-1. Opening menu from AST Computer's AST On-Line!

```
Main Menu                                            AST On-Line!

This is the Main Menu for the AST On-Line! Technical Information Network.

For help on using the system, select System Information below.

  A --=> AST Techlines           HP --=> AST Press Releases
  F --=> Files Section           HI --=> AST Product Information
  H --=> Headline Bulletins Section   HF --=> Products and Services For Sale
  E --=> Electronic Mail
  S --=> System News and Information
  U --=> User Account Display/Edit   X  --=> Logoff (hang-up)

TOP
Options: A F H E S U HP HI HF   X to exit   ENTER for menu
Select: █
```

cal menu systems to locate information and communicate with other users online. Now it's time to focus on using a BBS as a customer support option. It's an option that more and more companies are taking advantage of.

A BBS can let customers check on the status of an order or on the progress of a product being repaired. A BBS can let customers exchange information and share ideas with the company and with other customers. A BBS can also give customers access to libraries of technical support information. A BBS can even distribute software patches and upgrades for high-tech systems (see Figure 15-1).

Before you start thinking about setting up your own bulletin board, it's a good idea to go online and see what other companies are doing in this area. A significant number of computer hardware and software companies have set up customer-support boards, where users can dial in to get answers to frequently asked questions, obtain support online, and download patches and fixes to repair software glitches. Here's a sample:

AST Computers (modem: 714-727-4723)
AT&T (modem: 612-638-2854)
Boca Research (modem: 407-241-1601)
Borland (modem: 408-431-5250)
Central Point Software (modem: 714-727-4723)
Dell Computer (modem: 512-728-8528)

Figure 15-2. Digital Equipment Corp.'s Electronic Connection BBS menu.

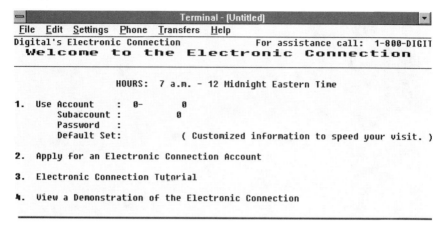

Digital Equipment Corp. (modem: 800-234-1998)
Hewlett-Packard (modem: 916-785-8275)
Intel (modem: 503-645-6275)
Quarterdeck (modem: 310-314-3227)
Seagate Technology (modem: 408-438-8771)
WordPerfect (modem: 801-225-4414)

Digital Equipment Corp.'s Electronic Connection opening menu can be seen in Figure 15-2.

Client/server software developer Software AG has started a BBS-based service for its customers called SAGnet. Customers gain access to online databases with product fixes, release notes, tips, and documentation. There's even an online forum where customers can request enhancements to the product.

High-tech marketers are very familiar with BBS technology, and it fits in well with their particular customer support needs, but any manufacturer with a product that requires significant customer support can benefit from a bulletin board.

The BBS phenomenon is also starting to spread to media-related companies, like magazine publishers and radio stations. Many of them see starting a BBS as a way to develop a stronger relationship with a core segment of customers who are avid information seekers.

Figure 15-3. Gateway 2000's customer support forum on CompuServe.

Gateway 2000 + Forum

You don't necessarily have to start your own bulletin board to take advantage of the benefits of a BBS. You can also set up a service site through an online service provider like CompuServe.

CompuServe is noted for the large number of technical support forums it hosts on its online service. Although other consumer-oriented online services also carry support forums, CompuServe has well over 500 software and hardware companies represented in its support area (see Figure 15-3).

Users can leave a message with a vendor in one of these forums and typically receive a reply, either from the vendor's technical support personnel or from other online users—within twenty-four hours. Some of the forums provide direct links into the vendor's technical support departments. Most companies also provide libraries of online information, with tips and techniques users can apply to get more value out of the vendor's product.

Some of CompuServe's best technology forums bring together suppliers from a particular product category such as the Multimedia Vendor Forum. Users can browse through information from a number of vendors, ask questions, and decide which combinations of products will best meet their needs.

QUICK LOOK: Real Estate Agents Host Virtual Open Houses to Save Homebuyers' Time and Trouble

In California's San Fernando Valley, realtors can show over 32,000 homes online, helping potential buyers to screen properties without having to drive from house to house.

The area's realtor association has developed a database of every home listed in the areas' computerized multiple listing service. Using an ISDN telephone line from Pacific Bell and a Wave-Runner ISDN modem from IBM, realtors can download up to ten color photos of each home in the database within seconds. (It takes a little longer using a regular modem.) Realtors can also create a home shopping list customized to meet the buyer's wishes (e.g., "We're looking for a three-bedroom, two-bath home with a pool in the Woodland Hills area. . . ."). Realtors can also create computer-generated maps of the area showing local schools, shopping centers, and churches. Soon, the association expects to have software that will allow realtors to electronically transmit loan applications and documents, which is expected to trim ten days off the average sixty-day escrow.

US West and Edina Realty of Minneapolis are making use of a similar system called AgentEdge. AgentEdge will first be tested in a few local sales offices before rolling the system out to all Edina Realty offices by late 1995. US West wants to license the service to real estate agencies around the country. (It may also become part of interactive TV systems US West is building. Viewers will be able to review listings of homes that match their specifications and then view images of those homes on their TV screens.)

Here's how the AgentEdge works now: An Edina real estate agent visits the home or office of a prospective home buyer. The agent carries a laptop computer equipped with a wireless cellular modem. As the agent's laptop dials up the AgentEdge server, the buyer gives the agent a profile of the type of home they desire. This profile is used to search an extensive database, which provides a list of homes on the market that match the buyer's needs.

Harness the Internet for Customer Support

The Internet is, in many ways, the ultimate customer service platform. The user doesn't have to have a subscription to a particular online service to use the Internet, and, if the customer has a fast dedicated connection through their office network, accessing the Internet for support can be faster than dialing in and logging onto an online service forum or BBS. In addition, the Internet provides a standard set of user interfaces like e-mail, Gopher, and the Web that are widely used, and very adaptable to the needs of customer support. As a final bonus, the Internet is a great way to communicate with customers located around the world.

Software publisher Borland International, for example, has recently arranged for their customers to access technical bulletins, programming tips, and bug-fixing techniques from the Internet. Customers in the U.S. already have access to technical support through Borland's presence on America Online, CompuServe, and other bulletin boards. So why Internet access as well? Many of Borland's international customers, particularly in Russia and other Eastern European countries, don't have access to commercial online services, but they do have access to the Internet. The Internet provides a quick and easy way for Borland's overseas customers to receive updates on Borland technical information.

Take Care of Your Customers With Internet E-Mail

I ordered some computer software recently, and when I received it, several items were missing from the package. I called to get it straightened out and immediately got into a telephone tag situation with the customer service representative. When I called, it seemed I could only reach his voice mail, and when he called, I was always out of the office. After several days, my patience was wearing thin. He called to ask what my order number was. I called back and left it on his voice mail. He left a message that he wanted me to give him a list of missing items that should have been included with my order. I called and left that information on his voice mail. It took a full two weeks and at least eight telephone calls to get it straightened out.

When I finally had the chance to speak to the customer service representative on the phone, I discovered that he had access to e-mail. Using e-mail, we probably could have solved the whole problem in about fifteen minutes, for about twenty-five cents in transmission fees. Instead, his long-distance charges calling me, and my long-distance charges calling him back, probably added up to $25 or more, not including the value of his time and mine.

E-mail is a viable, cost-effective, easy to use, and often overlooked customer support option, and companies are finding ways to make good use of it.

Lufthansa Airlines, for example, uses an Internet-based e-mail center to answer travel-related questions from customers around the globe. One visitor may leave a question in the e-mailbox about schedules and itineraries related to a flight from Sydney, Australia, to Tokyo, Japan. Lufthansa staffs its e-mailbox with knowledgeable customer service agents who can quickly provide answers, satisfy potential customers, and, they hope, fill seats on airplanes.

The uses for Internet e-mail for customer support are many and varied. Have you ever wanted to send out a newsletter to your customers, but put it off because of the expense of printing and postage? Why not collect your customer's e-mail addresses and send out the newsletter on the Internet? It's fast, cheap, and there won't be any stamps to lick.

Here's an idea for any company that has to maintain a large customer list: Consider accepting address changes or other information updates via Internet e-mail. Receiving address changes in a digital format will eliminate the repetitive re-keying of information into your database. Using the right software, clerical workers can simply "cut and paste" the new information into the appropriate customer file.

We mentioned the automation of routine service procedures as a reason to switch to online customer support. E-mail can fulfill this function as well. You can set up a mail server, such as those described in earlier chapters, to deliver specific support documents. A user could, for instance, send an e-mail message to an address like *help!@yourcompany.com* and receive back a document outlining typical customer support problems and their solutions. This type of document is often known as a Frequently Asked Questions (FAQ) file.

Just the FAQs, Please

FAQs are a common feature on the Internet. FAQ lists compile the questions users most commonly ask about a particular topic, paired with (usually) easy-to-understand answers. FAQ lists save time because users don't have to post the questions and wait for a reply, and those who are responsible for answering those questions don't have to respond repeatedly to the same questions.

Strictly speaking, FAQs address questions that are frequently asked within the context of a particular Internet discussion group, and they are posted for easy access by members of that group. In the looser sense, a FAQ includes the answers to any frequently asked group of questions. You can create a FAQ about your industry or about some process in which people are interested. You can create a FAQ about what your company does or what services it provides. You can create a FAQ about problems encountered in using your product. If your FAQ is in any way self-serving, then it should be posted in your own commercial space.

The concept of FAQ lists apply to online customer service. Service providers can post FAQ lists on an e-mail server, on a Gophersite or website, or on any online medium customers use to seek support.

Create a Customer Information Site With Gopher

Support-focused websites give you a sense of the multi-level nature and interactive possibilities of online service. The customer is able to guide himself through the process of finding the information that will best solve his problem.

The main opening menu of software publisher Microsoft's Gophersite offers the following choices:

- Welcome to Microsoft Gopher Server
- Information on *gopher.microsoft.com*
- Access to Microsoft Knowledge Base
- Microsoft Developer Network Library files
- Shareholder and Financial Information
- Information on Microsoft Support Network
- Access the Microsoft Software Library

The first two selections introduce the site to the first-time visitor. Selecting the Knowledge Base menu leads visitors toward search fields for various Microsoft product categories, including business systems and desktop applications. These categories are further subdivided into specific products, leading to an empty field labeled "Text to find." The user types in something related to the problem here, and then selects a search button. (I typed in "install" and retrieved a list of thirty-nine articles related to problems with installation.)

If you go back to the main menu and select "Information on Microsoft Support Network," you'll access a file that details all of the various service and support plans Microsoft offers. If you select "Access the Microsoft Software Library" from the main menu, you gain access to over 1,500 software fixes, patches, and drivers that can be used to fix common software problems.

You can visit and explore this support site at *gopher.microsoft.com*.

Build a Total Customer Support Center on the Web

Support-focused websites give you a sense of the multi-level nature and interactive possibilities of online service. The customer is able to guide himself through the process of finding the information that will best solve his problem.

Novell, a leading networking software developer, uses a bookshelf metaphor to give visitors a familiar point of reference when they access the Novell website. The home (main or opening) page features a graphic of seven bright red manuals, each linking the visitor to different kinds of support-related information (see Figure 15-4). The following titles appear on the covers of these manuals:

- What's New
- Service & Support
- File Updates
- Product Manuals
- Sales & Marketing
- Novell Programs
- New User Info

Figure 15-4. Novell's Web-based support site.

Please take a moment to fill out our OnLine Services Survey.

Welcome to Novell's Online Services!

Let's take a quick look at the type of information displayed when different menu options are selected.

Clicking on the What's New manual brings up information on product updates, press releases, and other announcements.

Selecting the Service & Support manual brings up a page with several more options, including archives of Novell-related Internet newsgroup postings and a searchable technical support information database. You search this database by entering a "search query" in a box right on the Web page. Site visitors could type in the word *memory* and retrieve technical support articles related to how Novell's software is affected by a computer's memory settings.

The File Updates manual takes visitors to a page that lets them download software patches to fix bugs in a program or extend the capabilities of their software.

Selecting Product Manuals switches the visitor from a Web page to a Gopher page, which has a menu of technical support manuals that can be accessed in five languages: German, English, Spanish, French, and Italian.

The Novell Programs manual has information on how to take part in various Novell training programs and professional associations.

Figure 15-5. Home page for Cisco Information Online.

Welcome Aboard Cisco Information Online (CIO)!

CIO is your online destination for a wide range of Cisco Systems product information and interactive support services. General company and product information is publicly available. Access to technical support databases, software updates, product documentation and interactive support tools are available only to registered users with Cisco maintenance or partner service agreements.

To take full advantage of CIO's features, your browser must support forms capabilities. If you are entering as a registered user, your browser must also support user authentication.

You can visit and explore this support site at *http://www. novell.com.*

Cisco Systems Inc, a Silicon Valley network products provider, has created a Web version of its formerly character-based Cisco Information Online (CIO) support site (see Figure 15-5). The previous version of CIO was quite popular with users—in fact it had over 5,000 users who, in total, logged on to the system as many as 3,000 times a week. Now that Cisco has a means of presenting support information using the Web's graphic, visually exciting format, CIO will probably attract even more customers seeking support.

Cisco uses the metaphor of "boarding" their website, as if the visitor was boarding a train. You can board the site as a guest or as a registered user. Boarding as a registered user requires a maintenance contract number. The site features technical assistance, training and seminar schedules, and information on installation, warranties, and support contracts.

You can visit Cisco's CIO website at *http://www.cisco.com.*

In designing your support website, keep in mind that graphic images tend to slow navigation performance for visitors with average speed modems. You may want to include a "text only" option for users who want to avoid the graphics altogether.

In touring the Internet, I'm surprised at how many companies are using it for publicity, advertising, and sales, and how few (at least at this point) are using it for support. The Internet is a natural medium for technical support. Monthly access fees are relatively low, it provides a standard for the presentation of information, and the Web, in particular, is a snap to learn for customers. That's why it's likely we'll soon see more companies using the Internet for customer support, especially companies with significant support requirements, such as manufacturers of heavy equipment, medical technology, industrial automation equipment, and aviation, space, or defense-related products.

Diagnose and Repair, Even When You Aren't Really There

If service technicians could routinely diagnose problems and fix a customer's system without visiting the customer's worksite, that would be a major revolution for the service industry. Not only would customers be happier with faster response time and systems that are up and running in minutes instead of hours, but service companies would save huge amounts on support calls made to customers who have service contracts.

Service companies have been using remote control software programs to dial in and take control of user systems for some time. But these programs, including Carbon Copy for Windows, Close-Up, Norton pcAnywhere, and ReachOut Remote Control, have limited capabilities and weren't designed for the Internet.

Systems that are attached to the Internet can also be configured so that vendors can access them from a remote site. This would let the vendor diagnose a problem, change settings, and install upgrades more quickly than trying to do all that over the phone. IBM is testing a program that allows remote technical personnel to look into the user's system and even fix problems via the Internet.

In the future, homes will be more "intelligent" than they are today, with some type of a personal computer acting as a central brain for a network nervous system that will run throughout the house. Plugged into this network system will be just about anything that uses electricity. Perhaps technicians will be able to use the Internet to diagnose problems with your TV, stereo, refrigerator, or other products. Products may even be designed so that they can be accessed and diagnosed over the Internet.

HOT TIP: The Fastest Way to Start Serving Customers Online

If your company now takes orders over the phone, why not also take orders via modem? Kinko's Copies (a fast-growing California-based supplier of self-service and high-speed copies, desktop publishing, binding, and other office support services) is making arrangements at several of their locations so that computer users can order copies and other services via modem.

Why not give your customers another convenient way to communicate with your company? All you need to put this simple customer service option into action is a spare computer equipped with a modem, a phone line, and some simple bulletin board software.

What are you waiting for?

Summary

This chapter discussed the advantages of using online technology for customer support, as well as the options available: digital documentation, electronic bulletin board support, and the Internet.

At this point, each of the five primary marketing tasks you can automate online (research, publicity, advertising, sales, and customer support) have been reviewed. It's time to move on to the next level. Part III explores various methods for incorporating cybermarketing techniques into your business and marketing plans.

Chapter 15 Connection Section

Contact information for organizations and resources mentioned in or related to this chapter:

> *The BBS Construction Kit,* by David Wolfe, John Wiley & Sons, 1994
>
> Borland International, Inc., software publisher using the In-

ternet to distribute support information to international customers, 408-431-1000

Bulletin Board Systems for Business, by Lamont Wood and Dana Blankenhorn, John Wiley & Sons, 1992

Electronic Book Technologies, software for electronic publication of online information and documentation, 401-421-9550

eSoft, TBBS bulletin board system software, 303-699-6565

Galacticomm, The Major BBS bulletin board system software, 800-328-1128

GW Associates, BBS consultants, 508-429-6227 or *pwwhite@tbbs.com*

MMB Development Corp., TEAMate bulletin board system software, 800-832-6022 or 310-318-1322

Mustang Software Inc., Wildcat! bulletin board system software, 805-873-2500

NovX Systems Integration, online services provider and bulletin board system consultant, 206-447-0800

Silicon Central, Bay Area, California-based bulletin board system consultant

Software AG, offers the SAGnet BBS as a service for its customers, 703-860-5050

Telescan Inc., online service provider and bulletin board system consultant, 713-952-1060

Part III

Integrate Digital Media Into Your Marketing Strategy

It's time to combine all the cybermarketing tools, technologies, and tasks and see how they relate to your long-term marketing objectives.

The new, digital media of cybermarketing—CD-ROMs, multimedia technology, online services, electronic bulletin boards, the Internet—present opportunities to grow your business and tap new markets, but only if you begin to integrate them into your day-to-day operations, marketing plans, and long-term business strategies. Here are three reasons this section of the book may be the most important to your business and your marketing career:

1. Integrating digital media into your marketing mix can enhance and expand the impact of the traditional marketing media you're already using.
2. Integrating digital media into your marketing plan can open new markets for your products and services that weren't being reached by your traditional marketing campaign.
3. Integrating digital media into your marketing strategy can lead to breakthroughs in other areas of your business by exposing you to new technologies and their applications.

The first chapter in this section takes a look at some of the challenges you'll encounter as you begin to put the lessons of this book into practice. The second chapter explores the potential to locate international business intelligence and develop worldwide business contacts on the net. The final chapter profiles companies that have not only woven various aspects of cybermarketing into the fabric of their business process, but have actually structured their companies around the opportunities and capabilities presented by these new media technologies.

16

Introduce Your Organization to the Interactive Marketplace

"I don't think the boss will like all this digital media stuff."

"Things are just fine the way they are."

"Isn't this Internet project overly ambitious?"

"We've never done *that* before."

"We tried an online ad once, but it didn't seem to work."

"It just isn't in the budget."

"We'll need to take this whole World Wide Web thing up with the financial committee."

"Have you run this by management?"

"What's a 'seedy romm'?"

"But we've *always* done it this way."

Before you're through reading this chapter, you're going to be prepared to deal with objections, obfuscation, and lame excuses like these. You'll find out what it takes to be an effective digital marketer, and you'll be presented with a short-term action plan that includes rapid ramp-up to total online connectivity. You'll also get a chance to explore how to blend digital media smoothly into your current marketing mix.

Lay the Foundation for a Digital Media Campaign

If your company is going to be an active participant in the digital media marketing revolution, someone is going to have to be committed to the battle, to getting the troops in order, and to taking a stand. Since you're the one reading this book, I guess you're elected.

I'm not saying you'll have to do it all alone. If you can enlist support, so much the better, particularly if you can find someone in top management who believes in new media as much as you do.

But you'll have to be the digital media teacher, coach, and maybe even evangelist within your organization. You have to be the one to stay on top of new developments in hardware, software, services, and applications. You have to deal with the messy process of competing standards, limited budgets, and an ever-changing array of technology options. There will be frustrations, disappointments, and missed opportunities along the way. You have to be willing to stick with it long enough to get results.

How do you light a fire under the troops (and yourself) when things aren't progressing as smoothly as you would have liked? Here are a few suggestions:

• Keep everyone informed about what other companies in your field are doing, especially your company's business partners and competitors.

• Emphasize that the companies who learn how to use digital media today will enjoy the greatest benefits tomorrow. Remind skeptics that there's a small window of opportunity for companies that work through the experimentation phase now so that they can be the first to apply the technology for competitive advantage.

• Demonstrate how the technology of connectivity presents ways to perform marketing tasks faster, giving the company the opportunity to rocket ahead of slower competitors. Everyone can understand and appreciate the opportunity to reach more prospects, stay in touch with more customers, and close more sales.

The reward will finally come one day when all the time you've spent with technical manuals and computer journals pays off. You'll be able to put it all into focus and realize that your efforts resulted in the real goal: finding, winning, and keeping customers.

But first, you'll need to begin by chipping away at the huge mental block that some of those around you may have toward the concept of digital media and digital marketing options.

Overcome Resistance to Using Digital Media

As a confirmed digital marketer, you're somewhat of a pioneer. In fact, you're pushing the cultural and technological envelope. You will almost certainly encounter at least a little resistance, indifference, and even outright hostility in your attempts to reengineer your company's marketing process. That's only natural. If you're well prepared, you'll be ready to take on the challenges that lie ahead.

Traditional Mindsets

First of all, you're likely to encounter resistance from those in your own company who don't understand, who are intimidated by technology, and who want to keep doing things the way they've always been done. You need to slowly introduce them to new media options like CD-ROM and online services.

You're also going to upset the traditional media sources who have always counted on receiving a lion's share of your marketing dollars—the magazines, the newspapers, the TV networks, the radio stations, the cable stations, etc. Don't be surprised if one of your biggest challenges is simply creating a new line item in the media plan that says "electronic media."

But you have to fight for the right to experiment. Any media plan worth its salt assigns some portion of the total budget to experimentation. And real experimentation doesn't just mean more of the same (another magazine, another radio station buy) with a different vendor.

You'll probably catch some flak from your traditional vendors and suppliers, too. Your ad agency and public relations agencies may not like the sound of it. They may not be ready to start playing in the digital world. (They're also worried that they won't be able to earn the big commissions they're accustomed to receiving through the placement of traditional media buys.) But they've got to adapt and grow if they're to stay on your team.

You need creative consultants and marketing services suppliers who will be partners in the learning process, not mouthpieces for doing things the way they've always been done.

And your printer? The mere mention of the phrase "digital media" is horrifying. To your printer it means less ink applied to less paper. That's heresy!

Cost Justifications

Be ready to quantify your decisions: if not in dollars and cents, at least in terms of the kinds of audiences you will reach when you begin to develop a presence online. Talk about the cyberconsumer and the quality of demographics of the typical online user.

Use this book and other resources to make the case for digital media to higher levels in your company. Let management know that it's time to develop a comfort level with new forms of media now—because later may be too late. Point out that it was the smart marketers back in the early days of radio, TV, and cable who saw the opportunity to develop brand awareness on what were, at that time, "new media."

Some, in their eagerness to quantify actual sales results from new media marketing, forget that billions of dollars are spent annually on advertising and PR that have no direct correlation to sales. They also forget that prospects are often not ready to buy from a company the first time they become aware of it. These prospective buyers want to know more about the company and become familiar with it. It takes a while to build a comfort level, and digital media can help with that process.

Skeptics should be reminded to compare new media marketing costs with the costs of printing and distributing full color direct mail pieces, or buying ads on TV or radio. Remind them that a website on the Internet can handle so many marketing functions at once, acting like a kind of total information center for company promotions, product demonstrations and samples, product reviews and endorsements, upgrades, manuals, licensing agreements, service contracts, and customer service and support.

Don't forget to point out that many Internet users are accessing the Internet from work, and that these individuals often have significant purchasing authority, buying everything from oscilloscopes to office furniture, from CAT scanners to cranes.

Managing Expectations

Finally, keep your expectations—and those of your supervisor—reasonably low. Some marketing tests using new media won't work out—just like not all tests using traditional media end up being successful. The important thing is to keep testing and trying new approaches. You should eventually find the right fit and the right niche.

Don't worry too much about naysayers. Time, trends, and technology are all on your side.

Sell the Benefits of Digital Connectivity

Part of your challenge in promoting the use of new communications technologies like the Internet is in pushing your organization in the direction of corporate interconnectivity. Computer usage in business environments tends to be intra-corporate, connecting members of the same enterprise or business group. As intra-company networks develop the ability to connect to others through the Internet and other online networks, business-to-business and business-to-consumer communications via network connections will increase. The shift from "closed loop" local area networks to "open loop" organizations connected to public networks is one of the most profound business trends of this decade.

The rise of this "connected enterprise" coincides with the evolution of business organizations from a headquarters staff with a few satellite offices, to organizations with many offices, mobile workers, and information-hungry customers. Ideas and information flow in and out of the connected enterprise, because it isn't as insulated as a traditional organization.

Here's why it makes sense to connect your organization's computers to online networks:

• *Extends the reach of the organization.* The connected enterprise is better able to tap contacts and information sources outside the corporation, so that managers and employees are better equipped to make informed decisions. Because of this, the connected enterprise actually competes with more "information ammunition" in its marketing arsenal. The company has the ability to get important instructions out into the field faster, as well as enabling representatives in the field to feed information from the marketplace back into the company.

• *Moves the company closer to the customer.* The connected enterprise conveys the image—and the reality—of being in closer touch with customers. Truly connected companies even go so far as to allow customers to obtain information about the company for themselves (e.g., annual reports, research and development in progress, and corporate press releases).

The connected enterprise has its "ear to the ground" and is able to pick up signals that identify changing trends in customer tastes, enthusiasms, and opinions.

By the end of this century (a few years from now) being close to the customer will absolutely mean giving customers online access to the company. Online services will undergo a major shift in 1995. The profile of today's online user reflects highly proficient computer users, but it will rapidly extend (due to a number of factors covered earlier in the book) to practically anyone with a PC in their home or office. This is a customer communications trend that simply cannot be ignored.

• *Keeps a finger on the pulse of the marketplace.* The connected enterprise is more accessible to learning about new business opportunities, and is faster on its feet so that it can respond more quickly as those opportunities arise. The connected enterprise is fully plugged into the real world where it can operate on the basis of current data instead of the theories, assumptions, and whims of the home office. In short, the connected enterprise is fully in tune with its environment.

Select the Right Digital Media for Your Marketing Message

Which digital medium or media will best deliver your marketing message? Should you run advertising on an online service? Produce a CD-ROM? Create a customer service bulletin board system? The answer to this question is so complex and individualized that the answer can only be obtained through the process of analyzing your marketplace, your company, and your customers.

Explore and Evaluate

Begin the process by conducting an informal survey of your marketplace, your industry, or your field. In particular, observe what the most forward-thinking companies are doing. Are they involved in any digital media projects that you can adapt to your situation? Are there any companies you can engage in partnerships with to share costs? Next, look outside your field. What are other companies doing that you can adapt to your marketplace?

Compare and Contrast

Next, survey the digital technology resources you already have available. Do you have a connection to the Internet? A work station that can be configured as an information server? To what kind of technology do your customers have access? Do they have modems? CD-ROM drives? What about your service representatives? Your suppliers?

What will the elements be for your winning digital marketing platform? Here are three key questions to keep in mind:

1. Does it makes it easy for customers to get their hands on the information they want and need to make buying decisions?
2. Is it easy for you to change your marketing message as needed?
3. Is it compatible with your customers' ability to retrieve information?

Acknowledge and Deliver

Finally, what do you feel comfortable with? What kind of technology do you think best fits your personal style and your company's corporate culture? What about the other players on your marketing team? Are they quick to adapt or will a slow learning curve hamper your campaign's chances for success?

This may be the most important question of all: What fits your message best? What do you want to communicate to your target audience, and which medium will deliver that message most clearly? The bottom line is still the message you want to deliver to customers.

Blend Digital Media Into Your Marketing Mix

Now that you've beaten back the bullies who want to keep your company's marketing strategy stuck in the 1960s. Try to insert at least one form of new media into each new marketing campaign you plan. Better yet, dedicate a fixed percentage of your annual marketing budget for digital media marketing tests. Mail order flower specialist 1-800-Flowers devotes a full 10 percent of its total marketing budget every year to new-media marketing experiments.

But don't proceed without a plan of action. Below are some steps you can follow as you develop your strategy.

Identify Challenges

What are your primary marketing challenges this year? If you have a complex or innovative product that your customers don't understand, you may need to start with a CD-ROM-based solution. If your customer service representatives complain about answering the same questions over and over, you can address that problem with a bulletin board system. If your company is drowning in paper-based forms, perhaps you should implement EDI. Let the problem lead you to the solution.

Set Objectives

What kind of results do you want to achieve with your digital marketing campaign? When you've selected the digital platform you'd like to use, determine what you want to accomplish from your marketing efforts. Be specific. At the end of your campaign, what quantifiable results do you want to be able to report? Setting objectives will help to clarify and define your approach.

For Internet-related projects, keep in mind that it isn't how many prospects you reach, it's how many relevant prospects you reach. With business-to-business applications in particular, it's more important to reach a selected target audience than a mass of Internet surfers. If your company makes petroleum drilling equipment, you want to see hits from *texaco.com* and *exxon.com*, but you probably don't care much about hits from *harvard.edu* or *kmart.com*.

Allocate Resources

What's your budget for the project?

Don't launch into a program that you'll only be able to take halfway to completion. Wouldn't it be better to start with a modest success rather than a spectacular failure?

Execute the Plan

What are you waiting for? It's time to take your campaign from theory to practice. Start production on your CD-ROM. Get your Web server software and design your website. Create a digital ad for that online service or bulletin board.

Examine the Results

What were the results of your campaign? After you've put your plan to the test, it's time to step back and evaluate how close you came to meeting your objectives. Where did you hit the mark? What did you learn in the process? How can you improve next time? Use the feedback to continually improve your digital marketing campaign.

Summary

This chapter presented an action plan for overcoming internal and external resistance to cybermarketing, getting connected, and adding digital media into your marketing mix.

The next chapter reviews the potential for your company to develop an international presence online and to interact with a global population of customers and prospects using digital networks.

Chapter 16 Connection Section

Following is a list of publications that will help you stay on top of news and developments related to the digital media marketplace and information superhighway.

Business Marketing, 312-649-5260
Communications Week, 516-562-5000
Interactive Age, 516-562-5000
Inter@ctiveWeek, 516-229-3700
Internet Business Advantage, 502-493-3200
Internet World, 203-226-6967
Marketing Computers, 212-536-6585
Marketing Tools, 800-828-1133
Network World, 508-875-5000
NewMedia, 415-573-5170
Upside, 415-377-0950
Washington Technology, 703-848-2800
Wired, 415-904-0660

17

Expand Into International Markets on the Worldwide Net

It's happening from Indiana to Istanbul, from Sioux City to Singapore. Major corporations, growing businesses, and solo entrepreneurs are using the Internet and other online networks to help dismantle the barriers that hold back companies who want to buy, sell, and trade on an international scale. Some have access to well-developed computer and telecommunications resources. Others do not. But in this new virtual marketplace, perhaps it won't matter how large your business is or what country you're communicating from. The only thing that will matter is the power of what you have to say and the quality of what you have to sell.

Networked enterprises will be able to draw on talent and technology from within and outside the borders of their country: software development from India, technical support from Ireland, manufacturing from Malaysia. Growing companies will be able to more easily locate and forge alliances with distributors in other countries. Entrepreneurs will find that having a presence on the Internet means having a presence throughout the world.

Even if you're at the stage where you're just looking into the possibilities of international trade, by far the best place to find the information you need is by going online. Whether it's export counseling, international market research, foreign trade leads, calendars of overseas and domestic trade events, export financing, or advice on export licenses and controls, you'll find it all online.

This, perhaps, is the birth of a new global society where all participants can come together to create, to share, to interact, and to profit. You should be a part of it.

This chapter is for readers who hope to use online resources to expand their businesses beyond local, regional, or national horizons and reach out to new markets and new buyers in foreign lands. It looks at the ways that new communications technologies are lowering the barriers to doing business outside the borders of this country and also reviews the amazing increase in online activity around the world. There are listings of some specific sources you can use to expand your company's international reach, including online information and trade exchanges.

Using New Media Technologies to Boost International Trade

There are three ways that the technologies of cybermarketing can support companies of all sizes in developing and maintaining international business contacts.

Access to Information

Information provides a basis for international business relationships. You need information about cultures and customs of countries that you want to do business in. You need information about business practices in those countries, and you need to understand the size of the market. You need to know who the key contacts are in your industry—key buyers, distributors, and sales agents. You need to know if agencies exist that can assist you in making those contacts. You need specific information on bids and contracts on current projects you can get involved in as a vendor. You can find all this information online.

Dissemination of Information

Breaking into a foreign market typically isn't an easy process. Buyers in new foreign markets aren't familiar with your company. They don't know what you do, how long you've been doing it, who've you've done it for or how reliable you've been at doing it. You've got to spread the word. You can do that very effectively online. You've got to show what you have to offer. Again, online marketing resources offer some wonderful opportunities to do so. But, most importantly, you've got to reach that international audience. The internetworked, online world offers you the opportunity to do so at a low cost.

Ease of Communication

Once you've established relationships with foreign contacts, you have to nurture and support them as they grow into profitable business opportunities. Establishing and maintaining relationships requires communication. Online resources provide the ability to conduct international communications at low cost through electronic messaging. Online communication isn't hampered by differences in time zones. E-mail doesn't watch a clock to see if the customer has left the office or is sound asleep in bed. And online technology has an immediacy that exceeds anything else in the context of international communications.

There's even a service now on the Internet that will help you translate documents into several other languages. Globalink, a software company specializing in foreign language applications, has launched the Foreign Language Message Translation Service.

QUICK LOOK: The World Goes Online

The burst of online activity we've recently seen in the United States is mirrored in many countries around the world.

- *Germany.* Germany's nationwide online service, Bildshirmtext, launched in 1990, had some 500,000 members by early 1994. It's growing so fast that it's expected to double its membership base, with nearly a million subscribers, by the end of 1994.
- *The Philippines.* If Filipino-Americans have their way, the Philippines will soon be linked to the Internet. The Science and Technology Advisory Council (STAC), which is composed of Filipino-American scientists and businessmen based in the United States, plans to set up an Internet link as part of a new science and technology park under construction in what was formerly the Subic Bay U.S. Naval Base.

- *Canada.* Over the next ten years, Canada's Stentor consortium (composed of nine Canadian telecommunications companies) plans to upgrade local telephone networks in every province in Canada. The consortium will lay optical fiber in every neighborhood serviced, and develop a seamless nationwide network connecting Canadian businesses, universities, and government agencies. There's so much interest in the Internet in Canada that Rick Broadhead's book, *The Canadian Internet Handbook,* was recently the number one nonfiction paperback in Canada. Apple Computer recently brought their e-World online service to Canada, and they expect to have French, German, and Japanese Kanji versions by early 1995.

- *Russia.* The United States and Russian Ministry of Posts and Telecommunications signed an agreement to cooperate on the development of a global information infrastructure. The two countries will work on a pilot project that will show how this network infrastructure can be used to promote health care, education, and electronic commerce.

- *Mexico.* Although Mexico universities have been part of the Internet for years, two companies, InRed and Pixel Internacional, now offer Internet connections to the public. CompuServe access became available to Mexican computer users in May 1994, and 1,600 businesses and individuals signed up in the first ninety days. There's also a new public access BBS called Mexico Online where travelers can post questions and get free tourist info on transportation, hotels, and restaurants.

- *Planet Internet.* In 1994, new Internet connections were established in Algeria, Antigua, the Bahamas, Jordan, Lebanon, Mongolia, and many other countries. Before long, it will be hard to find a country that isn't linked to the Internet.

You don't have to be a genius to figure out that one of the fastest ways to locate and set up relationships with international trading partners will be to use online services and the Internet.

The service allows registered users to send messages and text files over the Internet and receive rapid software-generated draft translations of their documents from English into Spanish, French, or German for as little as five cents a word.

Finding International Market Data on CD-ROM

CD-ROM discs can offer users one of the fastest and easiest ways to develop background information on foreign companies and foreign markets. Some discs can also help you familiarize yourself with the culture and business practices of foreign countries. Others can assist you in preparing a business trip to a foreign country, and even help you learn the language.

China

China Books sells the China Investment Guide, a disc for companies doing business in The People's Republic of China, or hoping to open doors there. The disc includes all published foreign-related laws of China, lists of government agencies, data on leading organizations, information on Special Economic Zones, a detailed atlas, and background on China's telecommunications infrastructure.

Europe

EuroPAGES lists phone numbers and addresses for thousands of European manufacturers and distributors. You can order it from TigerSoftware. Eastern European Business Database includes over 30,000 pages of information on 100,000 Eastern European companies. Thousands of pages of text cover trade, tax, and legal topics. The disc is available from the U.S. Department of Commerce. Best of all, it's updated monthly.

Japan

Japan Business Travel Guide includes information on appropriate etiquette and ethics for business situations you may encounter in

Japan. The disc includes recommendations on establishing lines of communication and initiating contact with Japanese corporations. Bayware's Power Japanese is an award-winning disc-based Japanese language instruction program, with interactive drills and a database of audio recordings.

This is only a small sampling of the hundreds of CD-ROM products that can help you prepare for and conduct international trade. For a complete listing, see *Business & Legal CD-ROMs in Print*, which is a comprehensive annual review of thousands of CD-ROM titles.

Scanning International News and Intelligence Online

Business-oriented database services provide a fantastic range of sources focusing on international news and information. You'll find international news wires that focus on a particular country, such as Japan Economic Newswire or Australian Associated Press Online. You'll find directories of foreign companies, such as the Kompass directories available on Dialog. You'll also find specialized newsletters and reports that provide in-depth news about a particular industry in a foreign country, for example, the AsiaPacific Space Report. If you're looking for inside information about doing business in another country, going online is almost as good as being there. (In some cases, it's probably better!) Here's a sampling of the international news sources carried by selected online service providers. (Providers frequently add to or modify their online offerings, so check with the service before going online.)

CompuServe

International news, periodicals, and databases carried on CompuServe include Australian Associated Press Online for news from Australia (GO AAPONLINE); Australian/New Zealand Company Library (GO ANZCOLIB); Associated Press France en Ligne for French news and information (GO APFRANCE); British Trade Marks (GO UKTRADEMARK); Duns International Market Identifiers (GO DBINT); German Company Library (GO GERLIB) and Press Association Online, for news with a U.K. focus (GO PAO).

Data-Star

International news, periodicals, and databases carried on Data-Star include: Canadian Trademarks, Derwent World Patents Index, Fairbase, German Buyer's Guide, and the Japanese Corporate Directory.

DataTimes

International news, periodicals, and databases carried on Data-Times include: Africa Intelligence Report, Asian Economic News, China Intelligence Report, East Europe Intelligence Report, Global Telecom Report, Japan Computer Industry Scan, Japan Consumer Electronics Scan, Japan Economic Newswire, Kyodo News Service, Latin American Intelligence Report, Middle East Intelligence Report, Pac Rim Intelligence Report, Russia/CIS Intelligence Report, Russia Express Contracts, West Europe Intelligence Report, Worldscope, and Worldwide Energy.

Dialog

International news, periodicals and databases carried on Dialog include: International Trade Daily from BNA Daily News, Canadian Business & Current Affairs, FBR Asian Company Profiles, ICC British Company Directory, the Kompass group of international company directories, Teikoku Databank of Japanese Companies, and Textline Global News.

Dow Jones News/Retrieval

International news, periodicals and databases carried on Dow Jones News/Retrieval include: Africa Intelligence Report, Asian Economic News, China Intelligence Report, East Europe Intelligence Report, Global Telecom Report, Japan Computer Industry Scan, Japan Consumer Electronics Scan, Japan Economic Newswire, Kyodo News Service, Latin American Intelligence Report, Middle East Intelligence Report, Pac Rim Intelligence Report,

Russia/CIS Intelligence Report, Russia Express Contracts, West Europe Intelligence Report, and Worldwide Energy.

NewsNet

International news, periodicals, and databases carried on News-Net include: AsiaPacific Space Report, Brazil Watch, Inter Press Service International News, Mexico Trade & Law Reporter, and Political Risk Services. It also features Africa Intelligence Report, Asian Economic News, China Intelligence Report, East Europe Intelligence Report, Global Telecom Report, Japan Computer Industry Scan, Japan Consumer Electronics Scan, Japan Economic Newswire, Kyodo News Service, Latin American Intelligence Report, Middle East Intelligence Report, Pac Rim Intelligence Report, Russia/CIS Intelligence Report, Russia Express Contracts, West Europe Intelligence Report, and Worldwide Energy.

HOT TIP: An Internet Discussion List on International Trade

INTLTRADE is the name of an Internet discussion list in which members share ideas and information on developing trading partners in other countries. To subscribe, send an e-mail message addressed to *majordomo@world.std.com* with the following command in the body of the message: subscribe intltrade *your e-mail address*.

Exploring International Trade Databases and Periodicals Online

The resources listed below go one step beyond the reports and news wires listed in the previous section. They offer an insight into actual trade transactions and business opportunities that your company can participate in. If you need information that goes beyond basic international market research—if you need to know who's buying and who's selling—here's where you'll find it.

• *Euro-Select.* Euro-Select is a database of business opportunities in Europe and includes offers of preferred tax rates from municipal European governments. The database also highlights special grants and low-interest loans tied to business projects and investments in the European Community. Euro-Select is available on Data-Star.

• *International Trade Leads Database.* Entrepreneurs Online features the International Trade Leads Database. This database includes information on companies seeking trade partners worldwide.

• *Journal of Commerce Online.* The Journal of Commerce compiles a daily record covering all aspects of imports, exports, shipping, trucking, rail, and air cargo. You can access the online version of the Journal on Dialog and NewsNet.

• *Port Import Export Reporting Service (PIERS).* PIERS compiles manifests of vessels loading or unloading at sixty-two U.S. continental seaports. You can access PIERS to identify new sources of supply, monitor exports, and locate potential trade partners. You can access PIERS Imports and Exports Online from CompuServe.

• *Scan-a-Bid.* Tap into Scan-a-Bid through research database provider Data-Star. Scan-a-Bid is the online version of the publication *Development Business,* which provides information on project opportunities, primarily in the third world. The database includes procurement notices, announcements of approved projects, and World Bank Contract Awards for products, goods, and services.

• *Tenderlink.* Tenderlink includes information on requests for proposals, new tenders, development projects, and equipment for sale or hire around the world. It's available on CompuServe.

• *Tenders Electronic Daily.* Dialog carries Tenders Electronic Daily, which provides information on the public sector markets in over eighty countries, including details on invitations to bid on public supply and public works contracts.

• *Washington Trade Daily (WTD).* WTD is a daily report on world trade policy from a Washington perspective. You'll find coverage of GATT, NAFTA, and import cases currently pending before the International Trade Commission and the Commerce Department. WTD is available on NewsNet.

QUICK LOOK: Japanese Book Lovers Love This Bookstore on the Internet

The University of Irvine in California set up a space for the University bookstore on the campus Web server so that students could order books and supplies online without having to wait in long lines (see Figure 17-1). Little did they guess that the bookstore's special line of Japanese anime (animation) materials would attract an active group of buyers from Japan. So much mail order business is coming from Japan, in fact, that the bookstore's associate director is taking a class to learn the basics of the Japanese language in order to help process the orders. Visit at *http://www.uci.edu* and select "bookstore" from the home page.

Figure 17-1.   Opening page for the UCI Bookstore web server.

UCI Bookstore, University of California, Irvine

Thank you for taking our exit off the World Wide Web data highway. We are located an hour south of Los Angeles and a few miles inland from the coast at Newport Beach. Of course, on the Web, we are just a few seconds away from anywhere in the world. Welcome.

UCI is the ninth campus in the University of California system. The UCI Bookstore is an institutionally owned academic bookstore open to the public -- both local and worldwide on the Web. We invite you to explore further, selecting areas of interest to you.

UCI Bookstore WWW Server (CWIS)

Gathering Trade Data From Government BBSs, Gophers, and Websites

The government has a natural interest in fostering trade. Various government agencies supply information that can help U.S. companies in their efforts to research foreign markets and develop trade contacts overseas. Much of that information is available in the form of online databases.

• *Bureau of Export Administration.* The Bureau of Export Administration (BEA) is responsible for controlling technology exports. The Bureau's two main agencies are the Export Administration, which overseas the licensing of U.S. technology for export, and Export Enforcement, which investigates breaches of export control laws. This website explains the Bureau's STELA system, which is used to track the status of export license applications, and the ELAIN system, which accepts export license applications electronically. The site also offers details about the Bureau's export counseling and seminar programs. To visit the BEA website, go the Department of Commerce home page (see below) and select the menu item U.S. Department of Commerce Agencies, and then Bureau of Export Administration.

• *Customs Department BBS.* This bulletin board system has two lines. The first line features international trade information. The second line has information on international currency conversion rates. Voice: 202-343-7715. Modem 1: 202-376-7100. Modem 2: 202-535-5069.

• *Department of Commerce.* The Department of Commerce (DoC) website hosts information valuable to exporters, and also is a doorway into other agencies that provide trade-related information (the Bureau of Export Administration, above, and the International Trade Administration, below). The department's Commerce Information Locator Service is an information search tool that will help you find information filed on DoC servers. Visit the DoC's home page at *http://www.doc.gov*.

• *The Economic Bulletin Board.* This board, sponsored by the U.S. Department of Commerce, includes statistics on foreign trade for every major business category. Voice: 202-377-2949. Modem: 202-377-1423.

• *Export-Import Bank/EXIMBank BBS.* This bulletin board supplies information on seminar and training programs that the bank sponsors for companies interested in international trade. Voice: 202-566-4490. Modem: 202-566-4699.

• *International Trade Administration.* The International Trade Administration (ITA) is an agency whose primary responsibility is the promotion of non-agricultural exports. The agency provides a wide variety of trade information services in its export centers and overseas offices. You can obtain a listing of these offices at this website, which also includes a Frequently Asked Questions (FAQ) file covering trade issues. To visit the ITA website, go to the Department of Commerce home page (see below) and select the menu item U.S. Department of Commerce Agencies, and then International Trade Administration.

• *Small Business Administration.* The U.S. Small Business Association (SBA) has an extensive website, which includes information on trade financing. To access this data, go to the SBA's home page on the Web and select the menu item Financing Your Business. This will lead you to a page from which you can access information on International Trade Loan Guarantees, created to finance U.S.-based facilities or equipment that will be used for producing goods or services for export, or Export Revolving Lines of Credit, which are loan guarantees to help companies penetrate foreign markets. Visit the SBA's home page at *http://www.sbaon line.sba.gov.*

• *The Texas-One Gopher.* The Texas State Department of Commerce's Texas-One Gopher server is located at the following address: *gopher.texas-one.org.* Although some of the information contained at this site is specific to the needs of Texas companies, importers and exporters from all around the world will find a visit to this Gopher to be well worth the trip. Here's a quick tour of the site:

From the opening menu, select Information for Small Business and Manufacturing. That leads you to a menu that includes the following option: Export, Trade, NAFTA, and Country Info.

Selecting this directory leads you to a menu with specific information on many countries and regions of the world, including Asia, Canada, Europe, and Mexico. If you select the menu option that leads you to information on Asia, for example, here are a few of the information files available there:

• Asian Development Bank Business Opportunities
• China's Trade Fairs and Exhibitions
• International Business Practices: Asia & Pacific Rim

HOT TIP: National Trade Data Bank Is a
Gold Mine for Exporters

The National Trade Databank (NTDB) has an amazing wealth of
information for companies interested in expanding their markets
overseas, with over 200,000 trade-related documents, numerous
periodicals, and valuable directory listings, all available online.
The NTDB's databases and files are available through both a
Gopher server and a website on the Internet.

Following is a quick tour of the Gopher. From the opening
menu, select STAT-USA. From the next menu, choose National
Trade Data Bank. The menu that pops up next is rich with resources, including:

A Basic Guide to Exporting
American Chambers of Commerce Abroad
Asian Development Bank Business Opportunities
Bankable Deals: A Small Business Guide to Trade Finance
Breaking Into the Trade Game: Small Business Guide to
    Exporting
Back Issues of *Business America* (a government publication
    that includes export tips, trade leads, and trade outlooks
    by country, along with other export data)
Country Commercial Guides
Export Yellow Pages
Market Research Reports
Guide to Trade Opportunities in Mexico

And there's much, much more.

The information on the NTDB's Gopher server, at *go-
pher.stat-usa.gov*, is available at no charge to users. The Web
database, at *http://www.stat-usa.gov*, is available only on a
subscription basis. Subscribers can select from two options:
$24.95 per month for first three months and $8.95 for each
additional month, or a flat fee of $100 per year. To subscribe,
call 1-800-STAT-USA.

Go back to the previous menu and select the Export listing. This leads you to the following files:

- International Trade Leads from the Dept. of Commerce
- Circle International Inc. (data of international cargo and logistics)
- Foreign Exchange Rates
- International Trade Administration Country Desks Contacts
- International Trade Commission Industry Contacts

The Texas-One Gopher will soon include a new database called Texas Marketplace, where Texas-based companies will be able to list goods and services they want to buy or sell.

Buying and Selling in an Online International Trade Exchange

A number of online services assist marketers who want to buy and sell internationally. These bulletin boards do more than simply supply information. They help participating companies contact potential trading partners and forge business relationships.

BOSS

Business Opportunities Sourcing System (BOSS) is an online registry of over 25,000 Canadian companies, including manufacturers, consultants, customs brokers, and freight forwarders, that are interested in developing trade contacts in the United States and around the world. Users are able to retrieve information about these companies by industry sector, product line, size of company, location, interest in joint ventures, etc. BOSS will send businesses interested in accessing the system a software diskette customized for their PC.

Trade Point

Trade Point is a worldwide electronic commerce initiative sponsored by the United Nations Conference on Trade and Develop-

Figure 17-2. Screen showing part of the opening page for the North American Trade Point on the net.

THE N🌎RTH AMERICAN TRADE P🌎INT

The North American Trade Point Project

Columbus, Ohio, USA

In August 1992, as part of a global U.N. Trade Efficiency Initiative, the United Nations Conference on Trade and Development (UNCTAD) designated Columbus, Ohio, USA as The North American Trade Point, and one of a rapidly expanding network of Trade Points worldwide.

ment (UNCTAD), with backing from Digital Equipment Corp., and IBM. The idea for Trade Point came about three years ago when members of UNCTAD determined that by harnessing network technology it could help to foster relationships between new business partners throughout the world. Sixteen cities were originally designated as "Trade Points" for the electronic network, but it grew quickly and now includes over fifty cities. The North American Trade Point is located in Columbus, Ohio (see Figures 17-2 and 17-3).

The Trade Point can be accessed on the World Wide Web, and will feature a wide range of trade-related information and services, including an index of importers and exporters, international credit reports, and a listing of financial institutions willing to lend money to overseas ventures.

Eventually the Trade Point system will allow participants to conduct commerce using electronic data interchange (EDI), the standardized system for transmitting transaction information, covered in Chapter 5. Using it, companies will be able to make purchases, sign contracts, and make shipping arrangements—all online. The goal is to cut down on the steps necessary to complete an international business deal while saving time and money in the process.

To visit the Trade Point, use the following Web address:

Figure 17-3. Another screen from the North American Trade Point on the net.

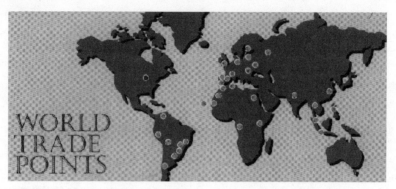

Click on a Trade Point location to view the city name...

Trade Points -- The Gateway to Global Trading

http://www.commerce.digital.com and select Ohio Online Export Directory from the home page, and then select North American Trade Point from the next screen.

World Trade Center Network

The World Trade Center Network is an online service provided by the World Trade Centers Association, an organization that

---

HOT TIP: Japanese Megafirm Opens Door to Foreign
Suppliers via the Internet

Japan's Nippon Telephone and Telegraph (NTT) purchased over $1 billion worth of products from over 1,000 non-Japanese companies in 1994. This website, hosted by NTT, explains exactly what the company purchases, how their procurement process works, and how to get on their vendor list. (What a progressive idea. Wouldn't it be nice if more major buyers did this?) You can visit NTT's vendor information website at *http://www. ipo.hqs.cae.ntt.jp/procumement.html.*

seeks to foster world trade. Their bulletin board system offers Wanted to Buy and Wanted to Sell sections where members place text-based listings. Users of the network have access to e-mail, to a daily listing of foreign currency exchange rates, and to over 150 business and trade-related news and information databases.

Creating Your Own Personal Global Village

You have a miraculous device sitting on your desk that can take you around the world in seconds. It's a PC with a modem linked to a phone line. Why not take advantage of it to do the following:

- Exchange e-mail instantly with customers in Brazil or New Zealand.
- Offer information about your company on the Internet where prospects from Antigua to Zambia can retrieve it.
- Identify sales representatives who can open new markets on your behalf.
- Access information on potential markets in South Africa or Russia.
- Locate trading partners in distant parts of the world.

In short, you can use your modem and computer and network connections to create your own personal "global village."

Summary

This chapter looked at how the availability of new digital technology is lowering the barriers to conducting business on worldwide basis. It examined the rise of online activity around the world and focused on how you can use CD-ROM discs and commercial and public online databases to learn about international markets. The chapter reviewed several online exchanges that specialize in trade-related services and covered the impact and potential that international connectivity holds for your business.

The final chapter explores the business and marketing opportunities uncovered by digital technology.

Chapter 17 Connection Section

Contact information for organizations and resources mentioned in or related to this chapter:

Bayware, Power Japanese on CD-ROM, 415-312-0980

Business & Legal CD-ROMs in Print, an annual review of CD-ROM titles, 203-226-6967

Business Opportunities Sourcing System (BOSS), online database of Canadian companies interested in international trade, 613-954-5031

China Books, the China Investment Guide CD-ROM disc, 415-282-2994

CompuServe, international news wires and databases online, 800-848-8990 or 614-457-0802

Data-Star, international news wires and databases online, 800-221-7754 or 215-687-6777

DataTimes, international news wires and databases online, 800-642-2525 or 405-751-6400

Dialog, international news wires and databases online, 800-334-2564 or 415-858-3785

Dow Jones News/Retrieval, international news wires and databases online, 609-452-1511

Entrepreneurs Online, a specialized online service carrying the International Trade Leads Database, 800-784-8822 or 713-784-8822

Globalink, Internet-based language translation service, *info@glnk.com*

Lexis/Nexis, international news wires and databases online, 800-227-4908

Mexico Online, BBS with tourist information, modem: 407-582-7801

NewsNet, international news wires and databases online, 800-952-0122 or 215-527-8030

The North American Trade Point, the U.S. site for an Internet-based worldwide trading network sponsored by the United Nations, 614-645-1700

World Trade Centers Association, the World Trade Center NETWORK bulletin board system and TradeLinks database, 800-937-8886 or 212-435-2552

18

Launch a New Business in Cyberspace

You've been reading this book hoping to get some clues on how to market your company's products and services using digital media and the information superhighway. But some of you might want to know not only how to use new media as a marketing platform, but how to actually exploit the new market openings presented by the net.

New fortunes will be made on the information superhighway. Will you be one of those who will reap the benefits?

In this chapter, we'll talk about the opportunities available to corporations or entrepreneurs who want to start a business on the information superhighway. We'll discuss the three main keys that will open the door to this world of opportunity. We'll zero in on some of the best market niches for doing business in the digital world, and provide some case histories of companies who are staking their claim on the digital frontier.

There's a window of opportunity that's open right now for companies with fresh ideas and big imaginations. But that window won't be open forever.

Mom and Pop Are Opening Shop on the Net

It isn't that difficult to set up a business in cyberspace. Many of the financial and logistical barriers that confront a traditional business in the "real world" are conspicuously absent in the digital world. In fact, there's a little cybermall, called "Gastown" *http://www.xmission.com/gastown,* that offers to set up digital entrepreneurs with their own Internet storefront for as little as $52.

But if anyone can start a business in cyberspace, and everyone decides to go ahead and do it, that's going to create a new set of very interesting challenges.

Sure, you can set up a shop without a physical storefront, an inventory, or even company letterhead, as many in this virtual boomtown are doing. But how will buyers find you? How are you going to distinguish yourself from all the other storefronts? And how are you going to convince potential customers that your business is legitimate? How can you even know ahead of time whether your business has any chance of success?

Here are a few general guidelines for the kinds of products most likely to achieve success on the net:

• The product is digitized (e.g., software, digital video, digital publication, etc.) and can be downloaded in a limited (lite) version, and later upgraded for an additional fee (see Id Software profile later in this chapter).

• The product is relatively unique, hard to find, or exclusively available on the net (see "Specialized Merchandizing" in this chapter).

• The product or service is targeted toward the kind of people who frequent the net: technically savvy, information-seeking individuals who are as often on the net for business as they are for fun (see "Hot Niches" in this chapter).

One of the ways that small businesses may cope with the wide open spaces of the electronic frontier is to band together in community-oriented sites on the net. Does it make sense for local retailers to team up in this way? If you ask Cortney Vargo at The Blacksburg Electronic Village in Virginia, she will answer "Yes!" Cortney is the Operations Manager for the Village, a pilot project developed by Virginia Tech, Bell Atlantic of Virginia, and the Town of Blacksburg. This network links local businesses, residents, and university students and staff into a digital community that can be accessed directly via modem, via the Internet using Gopher *gopher.bev.net*, or via the Web at *http://WWW.bev.net/* (see Figure 18-1).

Storefronts within the Village community include Backstreets, a pizza parlor that keeps their menu online (along with a

Figure 18-1. Home page for the Blacksburg Electronic Village.

Welcome!

Here in the rolling hills of Southwest Virginia between the Blue Ridge to the east and the Appalachians to the west is a community of people working together with diverse partners to develop a new idea--linking an entire town electronically, both to local resources and to the global resources comprising the much heralded "information superhighway."

coupon that consumers can print out and redeem for a discount on their pizza); King Video, a local video store that updates new releases and a weekly "critic's choice" list; and Wade's, a Blacksburg grocery store that includes weekly specials, an e-mail service, and photos of flower bouquets that you can order online. (There's even a form with pop-up menus that customers can fill out to indicate what they'd like to say on the card that accompanies the flowers.)

Blacksburg modem users can dial directly into a pool of forty-eight high-speed, in-bound modems at the Village. And there are 500 apartment units in various apartment complexes around town that are, courtesy of Bell Atlantic, wired with ethernet for direct Internet connections. A nearby technology office park, The Corporate Research Center, is also wired into the network.

Cortney believes there is definitely a future for local mom and pop marketers on online networks. She thinks the cyberconsumer of the not-too-distant future will be more likely to fire up a modem than to thumb through the yellow pages to find a dry cleaner that's open twenty-four hours a day or a pizza parlor that features Canadian bacon and mushroom thin-crust supremes.

Three Paths to Success on the Digital Frontier

Business opportunities abound on the information superhighway. Risks are present as well. As you explore the profit-generating potential of cyberspace, it is important to focus on these three areas: creation, conversion, and delivery.

Creation

In the television business, programming is the fuel for the fire that attracts viewers to a particular network. In the film industry, it's concepts or scripts that attract stars and funding to a project. In digital media the magic element is known as content. Content is one of the main ingredients that brings subscribers to an online service or attracts visitors to a website. The services of individuals and companies that can create compelling information or entertainment content will be in high demand.

Content can be as sophisticated as a database of information about nuclear technology projects or as simple as a guy who writes poetry and sells it on the Internet. Without entertainment and information content, the electronic superhighway is just a super e-mail system. Content provides a significant percentage of the value offered by the superhighway. Content is what will bring people online and keep them coming back for more.

Here's a prediction: Providing digital content for the information superhighway will not only be an important business opportunity in the near future, it will eventually become one of the world's biggest and most influential businesses.

Conversion

There's a huge mountain of non-digital format (paper, audiotape, videotape, etc.) information and entertainment content that can be digitized for consumption on the information superhighway.

Some of that content is currently owned by book and magazine publishers, and some of it by movie and television studios. Owners of consumer-oriented content (e.g., publishers of children's books) will need conversion assistance, as well as owners of business-oriented content (such as marketing materials and business directories). Someone is going to have to convert all those paper- and analog-based information products into a digital format, and that presents a real business opportunity.

This process has already created a new category of companies that specialize in helping organizations establish themselves on the Internet. Companies like Free Range Media, Network Publishing, and One World Interactive find ways to transform printed materials into interactive, digital presentations.

Digital conversion has the potential to be a lucrative business because this conversion process will take special skills. Significant value will be added as static, one-way media are transformed into interactive, two-way media. If you just take a magazine and put it on the Internet, it appears as though you just took a magazine and put it on the Internet. It's obvious when little thought or effort has gone into the process of making the content fit the medium. Conversion specialists will have to be aware of what kinds of materials are the best candidates for digital conversion and how that conversion can best be achieved. That's what conversion is all about and that's why the skills that provide the foundation for this type of service will be in high demand.

Delivery

Digitized content needs to be packaged for delivery to information consumers. America Online, CompuServe, Dow Jones News/Retrieval, and all the other online services you've read about in this book are essentially "content packagers" on the information superhighway. They put together combinations of information, entertainment, and services in such a way as to attract the greatest number of users and subscribers.

There is still plenty of room for specialized delivery options targeted to specific groups of users. Someone could design an online service, for example, that specializes in helping consumers quickly and easily get their hands on health care information, as well as allowing people with certain medical conditions to interact with each other in online support groups.

The concept of delivery also refers to the superhighway itself, which will always need additional bandwidth to handle the ever-increasing number of users, packets of data, and multimedia applications that will strain available resources. In short, the superhighway will consume bandwidth like a ravenous tiger. There will be a constant demand for tools that make it easier, faster, and cheaper for business users and consumers to access whatever content and services appeal to them. Companies that can provide these tools and technologies will be positioned to profit as the superhighway expands.

Red Hot Niches for the Supernetwork Marketplace

The digital revolution is shaking up traditional ways of doing business. There are unprecedented opportunities to use new media to reach into new markets and offer valuable online alternatives to both consumers and business users. This list is designed to stimulate your thinking as you explore or create a place for yourself and your company on the electronic highway.

Specialized Merchandising

Internet marketers constantly debate among themselves about the kinds of products that users are most likely to buy via online services and the Internet. The debate will undoubtedly continue to rage for some time, but a few reliable patterns are beginning to emerge.

Products that are sometimes difficult to buy through traditional sources are good candidates to be sold online. Unique musical instruments such as concertinas or zithers would immediately capture a music aficionado's interest. A bird breeder with rare birds and an Internet site would likely get Internet bird lovers talking. How about Peruvian textiles or other hand-made goods? Conversely, if you can pick up a product in your local convenience store, toothpaste for instance, there's no reason to believe it will sell online.

Digital storefronts that cater to people who are nuts about something, whether it be Star Trek memorabilia, baseball cards, or antique glass, will likely have a steady stream of fanatical customers.

Entrepreneurs who find a way to let customers get involved in the design of their own products should also be successful. Buyers, for example, could be encouraged to write their own copy for bumper stickers or T-shirts online. The owner of another site could allow her customers to create their own personalized stationery products. That's taking advantage of the power of online service to involve users in the purchase.

Other obvious products to sell online include anything that can be digitized (books, music, software, etc.), specialty food products (imagine how popular a "chocolate" site on the Internet would be), or hard-to-find foreign films.

Specialized Database Publishing

The online world is already such a fantastic source of information that it's hard to believe there would still be any subject that you couldn't find information about online. Still, there are opportunities for digital marketers to create specialized products that meet the needs of a particular market or special interest group.

How about designing a database directory of certain kinds of manufacturing sites located around the world and then offering access to the database for a "per-search" charge on the Internet? The basic model for databases of this type is one in which the user provides some input (e.g., a text query), and then, based on these variables, the pertinent information is presented.

Specialized databases already exist for the chemical industry, the telecommunications field, specialized manufacturing technologies, and financial data institutions. Many of these are available on CD-ROM or through private online business networks like Dialog and Lexis/Nexis. Aggressive marketers may be able to create new databases targeted to these markets that use a simpler interface a better search mechanism, or that enable the databases to be accessed via the Internet.

Specialized Periodical Publishing

Some publishing experts predict that there will soon be a major shift under way from paper-based publishing to digital publishing. Will this transformation kill books, newspapers, and magazines? That's not likely. Digital publishing, however, will open many new doors for savvy entrepreneurs.

It wasn't too long ago that if you wanted to publish something, your only option was paper. Now your choices are much broader. You can publish on CD-ROM. You can publish on the Internet. You can publish on a bulletin board. CD-ROM, in fact, is a very viable publishing medium. Many companies are making money publishing digital books and reference works. It's an inexpensive medium with standards and a growing base of play-back vehicles. You can capture massive amounts of information on disc, and access to that information is very quick.

On the net, the term "publishing" may take on new meanings. New hybrids are being created that combine news wire services with publishing. A service called EnviroKnow, for example, compiles environmental news and technical information for professionals in that industry. Instead of receiving a stack of magazines and newsletters, EnviroKnow culls information from selected industry periodicals, as well as government sources like the EPA, and then sends it via e-mail to subscribers, which include engineers, managers, laboratory technicians, scientists, and business owners in the environmental field.

The audiotex-based Minitel System in France (audiotex is a precursor to today's online systems) has over 15,000 merchants who sell information via the system. Why? Because it's a commonly accepted, easy-to-use information platform that's been in general use for many years. The Internet and other online services will soon produce the same level of information commerce.

Specialized Consumer Services

What are consumers looking for online? They're looking for fun, entertainment, education, information, and interaction. That's why AT&T recently purchased the ImagiNation online games network, and why ESPN is starting an online sports information service. Entrepreneurs who can make online users excited about going online will reap big rewards.

If I were starting a consumer-oriented online service, I would explore opportunities in interactive games, sports information, medical and health-related information, travel services, dating services, and financial information.

In the last category, for example, I could imagine a service that would help consumers prepare a will or trust online. An online financial information service could also include information and documents on insurance, investments, or retirement planning. It could even calculate the rate of return on certain investments, and give advice on buying a home or leasing a car.

Specialized Business Services

You already know that the Internet and online databases offer vast information resources. You probably also know that it isn't always easy to find what you need. Companies that can take the hassle out of finding information are well situated to score points with busy executives. In fact, there's a big demand for researchers who can find information on the net. Some make over $100 per hour.

Businesses that are using the net to open up new relationships with foreign customers could use help with online transla tion, or specialists who can smooth foreign currency transactions. These are perfect net-based businesses.

There will also be a big demand for people who can teach others how to use network resources. There's a crying need for people who can show business owners and managers how to unlock the value that resides in doing business online. I've attended standing-room-only seminars on the topic of how businesses can be more productive on the net.

Five Key Challenges for Digital Entrepreneurs

I would be leading you astray if I gave the impression that starting a business in cyberspace is a piece of cake. There are special problems unique to this type of business that you must address in order to be successful.

The Credibility Factor

A common challenge for companies doing business on the net is the problem of how to establish credibility. How do online users know you are who you say you are? This problem also exists in the world of retail merchandising, where the customer can see and touch the product, and in mail order, where the customer knows there's probably a significant investment involved in printing a nice four-color catalog. However, it is more acute in the world of electronic commerce, because there is little history to support this form of doing business; the buyer can't see the product, and he can't see how much of an investment you've made in your business.

Doing business on the net is a brand new form of business. Over time, customers will become accustomed to it, and will learn to appreciate the convenience. Plus, their positive experiences with online purchases will promote their confidence in doing business online.

Managing the Transaction

We covered online transactions in detail in the chapter on sales. This is an area that may be in ferment for some time. Selling digital products and services depends on secure information servers in which the server links up with the browser to complete a transaction and "unlock" the digital product for delivery or viewing.

Another issue for transactions is how to charge the customer, whether it's "time online" for entertainment or games or information searches, or "per record" charges for each record viewed from a specialized database.

Protecting Content You Own or Create

Unfortunately, it's all too easy for electronic pirates to illegally copy and redistribute digitized information. U.S. copyright law covers the copying and distribution of books, magazines, and software disks, but it is less clear on network piracy. The government has recently formed a panel to look into expanding copyright protection to publishers distributing information on the Internet, and researchers are working on a way to tag copyrighted information with hidden serial numbers so that publishers can detect unauthorized distribution of their materials. In the meantime, include a brief warning message in materials you don't want copied and redistributed. Identify yourself or your company as the copyright holder, and make clear your intention to enforce and protect that copyright.

Limiting Your Liability as an Information Provider

Are you responsible for whatever ends up on your server? Some feel that if service providers don't monitor their content, then Big

Brother will do it. Others feel that bookstore owners aren't held accountable for the contents of the books they sell, so information providers shouldn't be held accountable for information posted on their server. However, you should consider having your clients sign a waiver form that makes them responsible for whatever material they post on the system. After all, as sysop, you can't be expected to read every text file on your server, just as a telephone company can't be responsible for every conversation carried on their telephone lines.

Staying One Step Ahead of the Technology Curve

Once you begin to contemplate starting a business on the information superhighway, you become a part of the computer and communications networking industry—one of the fastest changing, most complex industries you're likely to encounter anywhere. It's not only a challenge to stay ahead of the technology curve in this business, it's hard to even stay in place. It's a world of constantly shifting standards and protocols, competing technologies, and ever-present uncertainty.

Business Success Stories Straight From Cyberspace

Now let's examine how companies have put cybermarketing principles into practice as they seek profits on the information superhighway.

Companies profiled in this section show that there are many different approaches to doing business on the net. Included are examples of music distribution (CDnow!), periodical distribution (The Electronic Newsstand), film and video stock distribution (Footage.net), entertainment industry promotions (Hollywood Online Network), entertainment software (Id Software and Knowledge Adventure Worlds), specialized book distribution (The Nautical Bookshelf), financial information (Quote.Com), software distribution (Soft.net), electronic publishing (Tabor/Griffin Communications), book promotion (Titlenet), and virtual education (Walden University).

For each business, we'll ask the following questions:

- What marketing problem or marketing opportunity was this business created to address?
- In what way does the use of digital media technology give the company an edge?
- What can this company teach us about starting a business in cyberspace?

Entrepreneurial energy is racing the length of the information superhighway. As fast as you can identify a new market, there's a new company there to capitalize on it. The great thing about this tremendous transition that society is going through is that there are so many markets and sub-markets, niches and micro-niches that there just may be room enough for everyone on this high-

---

HOT TIP: Naming Your Company for the Net

The profiles of net-based companies in this chapter reveal several companies that have selected names (e.g., Software.net, Quote.Com) that help to identify them as enterprises on the information superhighway.

Master-McNeil is a California firm that specializes in creating names for new companies, particularly high-tech companies. They recently announced that they will be routinely including a check of the availability of Internet domain names in its standard company name creation process.

Master-McNeil believes that Internet e-mail addresses are becoming an important part of a company's identity. After all, they appear on business cards, letterhead, and ads—right next to the company's logo. When they recommend potential names to a client, they want to make sure the corresponding InterNIC registry e-mail address is available, since there's only one possible owner of an Internet domain name.

If you're considering starting a company that involves the net, you should consider the Internet domain name question as well. How will your company name and Internet address look on your business card? Will it properly identify your company as a net-savvy enterprise?

---

way. Slide over into the driver's seat and we'll see who's out there.

This profile should give you an idea of what's possible, who's doing what, how they're going about it, and how business is being built on the net.

CDnow! Sells CDs on the Web

At CDnow!'s website you'll find you can order just about any kind of music including: Cajun, Zydeco, Bluegrass, Gospel, and even soundtracks and Christmas music (see Figure 18-2). The site's owners claim that they are selling more product than just about any other commercial site on the net.

Music lovers often have a hard time finding the music CDs they're looking for. CDnow! lets users browse through their site or enter search terms to find a particular artist or album title listed in the CDnow! database in mere seconds.

CDnow! specializes in giving CD buyers quick, easy access to a wide range of music titles without having to get in their car, drive into town, and find a parking space. CDnow! even has a stable of writers that creates short, informative reviews of selected CDnow! titles.

You can visit the CDnow! site at *http://cdnow.com*.

Figure 18-2. Home page for CDnow!

Color Monochrome Text mode (fast)

Selling over 140,000 CDs, cassettes and mini-discs, with over 100,000 different titles, CDnow! is the largest music store in the world.

CDnow! delivers most US orders in 3 to 6 business days, standard. US customers won't pay more than $4.94 for shipping and handling. And we deliver overseas via airmail to most countries. We accept Visa, MasterCard and American Express, as well as US checks and US$ denominated money orders. We accept PGP encrypted email for total credit card security. We do not charge your credit card until your order is in the box and ready to ship.

At CDnow!, we guarantee your satisfaction. You can return any disc for any reason.

The Electronic Newsstand Is a Marketplace for Magazines

The Electronic Newsstand was founded in July 1993 to give the Internet community easy access to general interest and special interest periodicals from major publishing companies and small presses.

Like traditional newsstands, The Electronic Newsstand allows visitors to browse—at no charge—through numerous publications, and have their interests stimulated by a variety of subjects. The publishers who buy space on The Electronic Newsstand server to promote their publications provide tables of contents and several articles from current issues. The Newsstand, which archives previously featured material, is also searchable by key word.

Visitors can order single copies and subscriptions to the printed versions of any of the publications found on The Newsstand using e-mail or an 800 number.

Here are some of the kinds of publications visitors will find at The Newsstand:

- Hip consumer magazines with names like *Buzz, Genre,* and *Pulse!*
- High-tech publications like *Multimedia Producer, Computer Design,* and *Dr. Dobb's Journal*
- Scientific publications like *The Neuroscientist* and *Applied Genetics News*
- Industrial publications like *International Product Safety News* and *Oil & Gas Journal*
- Specialized medical journals like *Medical & Surgical Dermatology* and *Chronic Immune Dysfunction Syndrome*
- Business magazines like *Export Today* and *The Far Eastern Economic Review*
- Financial newsletters like *Bull & Bear's Hot Stocks Review* and *Louis Rukeyser's Wall Street*
- Newspapers like *The Village Voice, Newsday,* and *The Sporting News*
- Mainstream periodicals like *Field & Stream, Smithsonian,* and *Mother Jones*

• Special interest publications like *Ski Magazine* and *Guitar Player*

The Electronic Newsstand has an advantage over a traditional newsstand in that it reaches an international market and offers browsers a readily available selection of publications accessible via computer.

Internet entrepreneurs can take a tip from The Electronic Newsstand in creating a business that incorporates many vendors who might not have created an Internet presence on their own, but who will gladly take part in a friendly, well designed, shared Internet site.

You can visit the Electronic Newsstand via Gopher at *enews. com* or Telnet *enews.com* and login as "enews."

Footage.net Gives Producers Access to Film and TV Stock via the Net

The demand for video and film is skyrocketing as new television networks and cable TV channels are being formed. Some of these outlets (the recently launched cable TV channel The History Channel, for example) have enormous need for vintage film and video footage. CD-ROM titles also require short video clips.

Footage.net rents server space to companies that have footage to sell. The company was designed to be a single source point of contact for companies looking for stock footage. The service has identified over 5,000 sources worldwide that have footage for rent, including TV stations, cinematographers, production companies, and companies that specialize in stock footage.

Before Footage.net, finding the right piece of footage was a time consuming, frustrating process. Producers, content developers, and ad agencies would have to call several different sources, hoping that someone would have the material they were seeking.

Now they can go online, visit Footage.net's Gopher server (the company will soon have a website as well), perform a keyword search, and pull up several references for the type of footage they're seeking, whether it is footage of soldiers in Vietnam or flappers dancing the Lindy.

The service is free to users. Companies that have footage to sell or rent pay to have a database describing their material online. Users can search individual company catalogs on an individual basis.

Soon Footage.net will be able to send a single frame of footage over the Internet for potential buyers to review, instead of the traditional, more lengthy process of waiting for a sample of the footage to be shipped through the mail.

John Tariot, the founder of Footage.net, has been in television production for over ten years. A recent project he was involved with involved co-producing a documentary for Turner Broadcasting.

Here's what we can learn from the Footage.net business model:

- It helps if you're familiar with the industry you're serving, just as when you're starting a traditional business.
- The Internet is an ideal medium for pulling together information from diverse sources and putting it in one easy-to-access site.
- It's probably a good idea to target an industry (in this case the entertainment/communications business) that is already relatively aware of the world of the Internet and online communications.

You can visit Footage.net via Gopher at *footage.net*.

Hollywood Online Network Uses New Media to Promote New Movies

A company called Hollywood Online has created Hollywood Online Network, carried on America Online, CompuServe, and eWorld. Hollywood Online Network recently created and distributed interactive promotional materials for the feature films "Forrest Gump," "The Mask," and "Wolf." Online subscribers can access not simply a media kit (which is standard operating procedure for movie releases), but what Hollywood Online calls an Interactive Multimedia Kit, combining animation, sound clips, pictures, text, and more. Their Addams Family Values Interactive Multimedia Kit was a recent winner of *Advertising Age* magazine's Interactive Advertising and Media Award.

The Hollywood Online Network gives its customers (television producers, and movie producers), a vehicle to reach an attractive market demographic in an exciting, unique way. If you can create a service that enables consumer marketers to reach their target audience online, you could have an attractive business on your hands.

You can visit the Hollywood Online Network on the America Online, CompuServe, or eWorld online services.

Id Software: "Doomed" to Success?

Id Software, a small company based in Mesquite, Texas, sells story-based interactive computer video games. Id offers a fully functional version of its software (but only a single episode of its multi-episode game) for free. Users download the software from online services like CompuServe or America Online, from the Internet, or from the company's own electronic bulletin board. Prospective buyers try the software, get hooked, and then call a toll-free number to order the full package. The software is so popular and so addictive that some have taken to calling it "heroin-ware."

So far, over a million computer users worldwide have downloaded the "try-before-you-buy" version of Id's first product, Wolfenstein 3-D, and 150,000 have paid for the full version. The company's newer product line, Doom and Doom II, are selling even better.

The critical point is that Id's early success relied almost entirely on an online approach to marketing. The company had no sales force, no advertising, and no four-color brochures. They simply made a sample of the product available online and bet that enough users would enjoy it to ensure future sales.

Does this marketing model only make sense for computer games? Of course not. All kinds of products and services can be "electronically sampled," from magazines to musical performances, from books to bookkeeping services.

Knowledge Adventure Worlds Knows the Virtues of Virtuality

Software visionary David Gobbel founded a company called Knowledge Adventure, a publisher of interactive educational software, with a couple of partners in 1991. He left recently to start an even more inventive enterprise, Knowledge Adventure Worlds, which he describes as "a developer of virtual distributed worlds." What, you might reasonably ask, is a virtual distributed world? It's hard to define, so David describes it for you:

> Let's say you're sitting, looking at your computer screen in Toledo, Ohio. A friend of yours is doing likewise, only she's in Albuquerque, New Mexico. But you're going to share a virtual world experience using your modems and our 3-D navigation software. You see a roller coaster. It's so real you can almost touch it. You move your computer mouse forward and experience the illusion of getting into the roller coaster. Your friend sees an image of you—we call it an "avatar" or "digital actor"—climbing aboard. You turn and see her avatar sitting in the seat next to you. Off you go on the virtual roller coaster ride of your life!

So what does this have to do with marketing? (That's what I asked David, just to keep him on track.) His answer was that people have to have somewhere to go on the information superhighway, and he wants to supply them with places to visit and events to experience: virtual shopping malls, virtual theme parks, virtual convention centers, virtual casinos, entire virtual cities—you name it. "This technology can collapse distance between people and between companies," David added.

My eyebrows hiked up a notch or two when he claimed that the technology to do all this is available today, without supercomputers and without anything more than regular telephone service. He says that companies won't need to have deep pockets in order to create virtual environments for their products. He's betting it all on developing software powerful enough to harness the latent power he feels isn't being fully utilized in today's personal computers.

He's currently working on a project he calls The World's Fair in Cyberspace, an Internet-based, 3D experience that will feature exhibitions designed by world-class content developers and advertising facilitated by major advertising agencies.

The Nautical Bookshelf: A Friendly Port in Uncharted Waters

The Nautical Bookshelf sells books about sailing from a cleverly designed Gophersite on the Internet. The Nautical Bookshelf offers a wonderful example of how to build an online commercial presence that is informative and easy-to-navigate, and that creates a sense of place and community from the very first visit.

Here's what visitors see on the main menu when they first access the site:

- An On-Line Guide to Nautical Books
- Frequently Asked Questions (FAQ) About Nautical Books
- Boating Tips
- How to Join Our Mailing List (It's Free!)
- Valuable On-Line Coupon

Here are excerpts from the first menu item file describing the service. Note the warmth and enthusiasm of the copy:

About Nautical Bookshelf's On-Line Resource Center

Ahoy, Matey! Welcome Aboard!

Whether you work for a corporation, military installation, government office, non-profit institution, college, university, or are an individual Internaut, we want to welcome you to our online resource center. In this Gopher server, we synthesize the challenges of cyberspace with the needs of boaters, sailors, and lovers of the sea. Even if you are not a boater, you will still find information on the sea to make your browsing worthwhile. Whether you are a confirmed "landlubber" or an "old salt," this resource center is for you!

Spend a Few Minutes. . . .

Give this center a chance—spend a few minutes browsing through the directories. You will find your efforts richly rewarded. . . . This server offers a wealth of information (including 17 practical boating tips) to help you become a better, safer, happier boater. . . .

Finding the Right Book Is Easy!

This resource center is at once an opportunity to gain information about boating—power and sail—and to buy nautical books using state-of-the-art computer technology. Purchasing a nautical book has never been easier! If you are looking for a specific title, you'll find the right book in seconds! The electronic catalog in this resource center constitutes a unique guide to nautical publications. Nothing quite like it exists at your local library, bookstore, marine store, or mail-order house. . . .

When you find a title you want, you can purchase that title from Nautical Bookshelf via e-mail, snail mail, or a toll-free number (see below). It's accurate, efficient, and, above all, FUN!!!!!!!!!!!!!

Talk to Us!

If you would like to comment on the nautical resource center, just send an e-mail message to *staff@nautical.com*. We will appreciate your support whether you send us your approval or constructive criticism. And we will reply promptly to your message.

Whatever your needs today, we want to wish you smooth sailing as you navigate this unique Gopher server.

Other items on the menu include free boating tips and techniques and an online coupon with a discount on book purchases.

You can visit The Nautical Bookshelf at *gopher.nautical.com*.

Quote.Com Provides Fast Financial Data on the Internet

Quote.Com offers online investment services. Their packages of services include wire services, news services, quotes, portfolio tracking, research tools, one-year price histories for stocks, commodities and mutual funds, Hoover's Reference Press Company Profiles, and annual reports (see Figure 18-3).

Figure 18-3. Quote.Com home page.

QuoteCom Home Page

Anyone with an e-mail address will be able to retrieve company profiles, wire service information, and quotes on more than 40,000 stocks, mutual funds, commodities, and futures. For under $10 a month, users can store a portfolio of up to 50 listed financial instruments.

Quote.Com's strategy of offering financial services on the Internet gives the company access to tens of thousands of investors, a niche market that is already computer savvy and hungry for information. Quote.Com delivers it in a convenient format.

You can access Quote.Com's services via e-mail at *info@ quote.com*, via FTP at *ftp.quote.com*, on the Web at *http://www. quote.com*, or through customer software available from Quote.Com.

Software.net Is a Cyber Software Shop

A Menlo Park, California-based company called CyberSource has started a company called Software.net, the world's first Internet-based computer software store. Software.net allows Internet users to browse, purchase, and retrieve software electronically, simply by pointing and clicking their mouses.

At the Software.net site, users can access a variety of software-related information, including product reviews and marketing materials. Over 6,500 software titles are available for purchase—the user can either enter a credit card number online or call an 800 number—and selected titles can be downloaded directly from the site upon purchase.

There are so many new software titles developed each month that even the largest computer retailers have a hard time keeping them all in stock. Software.net has the advantage of acting as a distributor for software without actually having to have all the titles it features in stock at all times. What Software.net really supplies is a convenient source for buyers seeking information about software. Because software is a digital product, the site may soon be selling more and more titles for immediate delivery via the Internet, saving on shipping costs and giving buyers an added incentive to buy from Software.net.

Visit the Software.net website at *http://software.net.*

Tabor/Griffin Communications: Gutenberg by the Gigabyte

The electronic journal HPCwire was started by former staff members of a magazine for the supercomputing industry called *Super-computing Review. Supercomputing Review* was sold to a computer publishing company, and the former publisher, Tom Tabor, started an electronic bulletin board called HPCwire (the HPC stands for High Performance Computing) as an online publication that had much the same flavor as the print version of the magazine. The bulletin board service was successful, but Tom found that although many users sampled the publication by dialing into the board, it was harder to get them to dial in again when a new issue was released. Readers would forget or be too busy—and dialing into the board required the user to be proactive.

Tom had a brainstorm and decided to shift the publication to an e-mail delivery format. According to Tom:

> We originally sent all the text for an issue of HPCwire to the subscriber's e-mailbox. But that was over eighty pages of text. So we quickly made a shift to only sending a table of contents with a brief outline of each article in that issue and a code number identifying each item.

The table of contents pages also includes the names of corporate sponsors and advertisers' headlines, both with code numbers. Subscribers select the articles or ad information they're interested in, and can transfer or download that data to their e-mailboxes in seconds.

HPCwire has turned the dynamics of publishing upside down, by creating a publication virtually free of printing and mailing costs, two of the biggest expenses in traditional publishing. Tom's newest project, *WEBster* the Cyberspace Surfer, is an electronically delivered e-zine (electronic magazine) covering the World Wide Web.

Titlenet Offers Book Publishers a Safe Place in Cyberspace

TitleNet was created by a company called Inforonics to help book publishers introduce their book catalogs to users of the Internet. TitleNet is paid for by the participating publishers who display their books on TitleNet's Gopher and Web servers.

The TitleNet site is an established area on the Internet. It is promoted regularly through contacts with selected Gopher servers at universities and libraries, which establish links to the TitleNet site. Inforonics also advertises its TitleNet services through monthly press releases to the publishing industry, the press, and the Internet community.

Books are ordered directly from publishers or from their designated resellers. Every title listed in TitleNet is linked to an order form that visitors can display on-screen. Orders may also be placed via phone, fax, or mail.

Inforonics provides publishers with reports on the level of visitor activity for their catalog, including the number of inquiries by title plus the number of requests for title information and order forms. Publishers are also able to gather information about users by inviting them to fill out a Web mailing list form linked to their catalogs.

You can visit TitleNet via Gopher at *gopher.infor.com*, or the World Wide Web at *http://www.infor.com*. Users who don't have

Internet connectivity can reach Titlenet from a PC with a modem and communications software at 508-486 8559 (for 2400 baud) or 508-486 0210 (for 9600 baud and higher). Just log in as "guest."

Walden University Is a School Without Walls

Walden University, based in Minneapolis, Minnesota, is an accredited "dispersed residency" doctoral program that gives mid-career professionals the opportunity to earn a doctorate, aided by computer technology, at their own location. As a true "university without walls," Walden has no campus, but provides many of the conveniences of a campus through its online Walden Information Network (WIN). WIN gives its students access to library information, faculty, advising, financial aid, interaction with other students, and direct access to the Internet. Ph.D.s are offered in Administration/Management, Education, Human Services, and Health Services.

Busy professionals seeking degrees have severe time limitations. Walden lets them pursue career goals according to their personal schedules. In competing with other degree programs, Walden has an edge in its ability to attract students from throughout the country.

There are openings and opportunities out there for you to create your company's future on the information superhighway. Find your opening. Make your opportunity. That's the promise—and the challenge—of an open, electronic economy.

Summary

In this chapter, we provided an overview of the emerging business opportunities on the information superhighway. We examined the relative ease of entry for a company to start a business in cyberspace and looked at three paths to success on the digital frontier. We explored a number of market niches that provide a good fit for the new-media environment. We evaluated the challenges that face entrepreneurs in this emerging business arena, and presented profiles of many companies that are meeting the test.

Chapter 18 Connection Section

Contact information for organizations and resources mentioned in or related to this chapter:

CDnow!, 215-646-6125

The Electronic Newsstand, 202-466-8688 or *info@enews.com*

EnviroKnow, 202-466-8688 or *enviroknow@enews.com*

Free Range Media, 206-340-9305

Hollywood Online, 310-581-4488

Id Software, developer of Doom and other interactive cyber-games, 214-613-3589

Footage.net, 508-369-9696 or *editor@footage.net*

Knowledge Adventure Worlds, 800-446-3636

Master-McNeil, 510-486-0947 or *info@naming.com*

The Nautical Bookshelf, 800-249-9446

Network Publishing, 801-377-9399

One World Interactive, 518-392-6928

Quote.Com, 702-324-7129

Soft.Net, 415-473-3067

Tabor/Griffin Communications, 619-625-0070

TitleNet, 508-486-8976 or *info@infor.com*

Walden University, 800-444-6795 or *request@win.waldenu.edu*

Conclusion

The Future of Cybermarketing

In the near future, the process of marketing will revolve more and more around creating, managing, and nurturing electronic relationships with customers. As John Houston at Modem Media puts it, "We're moving from 'broadcast' to 'personalcast'—developing direct, two-way electronic communication links with customers."

The Ideal Marketing Medium

If you could create the ultimate marketing medium, what characteristics would it have? I think most marketers would want to be able to reach a large number of prospects with a high volume of information, to customize that information for each user, to take the sales transaction from start to finish, and to do all of this at the lowest possible out-of-pocket cost. New-media marketing stacks up pretty well against traditional media when you use these factors as your benchmark. Here's a look at the advantages and disadvantages of the various marketing media.

Broadcast Advertising

Television and radio advertising offer a broad reach, but you're limited in the amount of information you can provide in a fifteen- or thirty-second spot. You can broadcast different ad spots in different cities, but other than that, customization is practically nil. You can't complete a sales transaction without adding another medium to the mix, such as telemarketing or mail, and broadcast time is typically quite expensive.

Cable Advertising

Cable television offers a variable reach, depending on the market you're after. Cable, like broadcast, offers a low volume of information, not much customization, and it can't complete the sales transaction without assistance from other media and the added expense that entails.

Direct Mail Advertising

This medium is popular with advertisers, largely because of its flexibility. Audience reach is highly variable, as is the amount of content you can include in a marketing package. Direct mail allows for a good deal of customization and offers the potential of a complete sales transaction. That's the upside. The downside is that direct mail carries all the expenses associated with paper-based marketing materials, including printing, packaging, and postage.

Newspaper, Periodical, and Directory Advertising

The reach of newspapers, magazines, and directories varies widely depending on the marketplace served. The amount of information that you can provide in an ad running in this form of media is comparatively low, and the capability of customizing that information for each consumer is typically not available. The ability to close the sales cycle is there (you can include a coupon in the ad that the user can send in with payment or bring in to your place of business), but this capability is underutilized. Pricing is based on reach, varying greatly from publication to publication.

In-Person Sales

Comparatively speaking, you can't reach nearly the same number of prospects with a sales force as with the other media listed here.

On the other hand, salespeople can offer as much information as the buyer needs to make a buying decision, can customize the presentation for each prospect, and can take a sales transaction from start to finish. Unfortunately, the price tag to achieve these capabilities is very high, and the cost to make a sales call on a single client rises every year.

Telemarketing

You can reach more prospects with telemarketing than through in-person sales, and the ability to customize the presentation is available, but is generally somewhat more limited than with an in-person sales call. The amount of information provided is determined by what the prospect will allow. Telemarketing transactions can be completed over the phone, and the cost per sale varies, depending on a number of factors, including the skill of the telemarketer.

New-Media Marketing

New-media marketing offers the best of all worlds. With communications media like the Internet and the World Wide Web, you can reach thousands, even millions of users for a relatively modest initial investment. You can include as much information as you like in your new-media marketing presentation, and you can make it easy for prospects to find the information they need through menu and search systems. Some new-media marketing options allow a sales transaction to be taken from start to finish online, and that capability will be enhanced over time.

Twenty Reasons Cybermarketing Is Inevitable

Today smart marketers recognize the importance of leveraging digital media to achieve marketing objectives. In the future, the importance of using the information superhighway to sell products and services will become clearer and more apparent. Here are some of the reasons:

• *More PCs in homes.* Over one-third of all U.S. households now have home PCs. Before long, that number will exceed 50 percent. At some point, we will reach a critical mass wherein computer-delivered information effectively competes with televisions, newspapers, and other forms of information delivery.

• *More PCs sold with modems pre-installed.* If more PCs come pre-equipped with modems, more users will be accessing online services and the Internet from their homes and offices.

• *Faster modems.* Faster modems allow users to access online services that are richer graphically and, consequently, more fun to use. Faster modems also allow business users to be more productive in transferring data and information. With faster modems, both groups will be likely to use their modems more often.

• *More PCs sold with CD-ROM drives pre-installed.* More computers with CD-ROM drives means more prospects who will be able to receive marketing information via CD-ROM.

• *More CD-ROM disc applications and faster CD-ROM drives.* More CD-ROM titles will inevitably cause more computer users to buy more CD-ROM drives. As manufacturers develop faster CD-ROM drives, the opportunity to package exciting video material into marketing-oriented discs will increase.

• *More software that makes it easier to use online services and the Internet.* As communications software improves, and word of this passes from one person to the next, more users will decide that it's time to go online.

• *More PCs sold with built-in access to online services and the Internet.* As mentioned earlier in the book, Microsoft will include access to its online service with Windows 95. Apple bundles e-World with the PCs it sells. And IBM started to include Internet access in OS/2 in November 1994. Developments such as these can only lead to a flood of new online service users.

• *More "fun stuff" to see and do online.* As there's more to see and do online, there will be more people to see and do it. Captivating information content will drive more consumers to spend more time in cyberspace.

• *More "serious stuff" to see and use online.* As reported earlier in the book, the base of business users of online services is already significant, far outdistancing the number of consumer users. Online developers are crafting new services, applications, and content for these users that will attract even more entrepreneurs, small business owners, and corporate managers to go online.

• *Better network security.* As security applications are developed which allow all kinds of risk-free interactions on the Internet and other networks, more consumers, business buyers, and corporate information systems managers will feel comfortable with doing business online.

• *A better legal framework for the digital frontier.* New laws protecting content providers and publishers are already working their way through Congress and the courts. As these proposals become law, it will accelerate the rush to digitize paper-based content and offer it online.

• *The likely success of one or more interactive TV trials.* With so many trials and pilot programs for interactive TV going on and so much technological firepower invested in this quest, there's a good chance that one or more of the players involved will find a way to make it work. A gradual nationwide roll-out of interactive services will follow, offering marketing opportunities for companies that want to reach and sell to consumers in new ways.

• *More bandwidth.* Digital wiring that can transmit a greater volume of data will allow users to access online services at faster, more satisfying speeds. They will also allow service providers to offer a greater range of content and communication services.

• *More international interconnectivity.* As international trade and open world markets continue to grow in importance, so will the technologies that facilitate international commerce. Online services will play a major role in the development of a truly international, interlinked marketplace.

• *Lowered barriers.* More and more individuals are finding that online commerce is a great way to do business. You don't have to be a big company. You don't have to belong to a particular country club. Age, race, ethnic background, disabilities, disadvantages—they don't mean much in cyberspace. That's why more and more business owners will see electronic marketing as their springboard to success.

• *Less expensive.* An obvious and powerful incentive to switch to new media is its lower cost. As marketers begin to understand the bottom-line benefits of cutting printing, packaging, and post-age costs, they will increasingly migrate to the least-cost market-ing solution: Cybermarketing.

• *Greater flexibility.* Marketers are growing to appreciate the flexibility that digital documentation affords them. They like the ability to make last minute changes. They like having the option of easily customizing sales materials for different groups of pros-pects.

• *Wired youth.* More and more graduates are coming out of universities and high schools already very familiar with digital tools like e-mail and multimedia. Likewise, the "Nintendo Gener-ation" has grown up with home computers and digital devices of all kinds. Digital media communication tools are part of their culture.

• *Less resistance.* The old guard will either give up their resis-tance to using new media, retire, or convert. Advertising on the Internet will be taken for granted. Consumers will expect and de-mand interactivity, more control, and more choices in content.

• *Satisfies real needs.* This is the most important reason of all for the continued expansion of the information superhighway. Digital media gives both consumer and business users the oppor-tunity to seek out and find information from more sources than ever before, to collaborate with others, and to say "Here I am and this is what I do."

The Marketplace of Tomorrow

You're in the middle of a short sales presentation with a potential buyer from Seoul, Korea, who opened a link into the "comm-window" of your terminal a few minutes ago. You see her image in one corner of the six-foot square flat panel display screen on the wall of your home office. (You're a commuter on the informa-tion superhighway.)

Your voices are captured, processed, and translated into each other's language. With a sweep of your wireless mouse, you un-fold a digital multimedia brochure on her screen. (The text of the brochure is also translated automatically.) Your personal intelligent agents, meanwhile, are exchanging basic data about each other's companies: phone numbers, fax numbers, e-mail, and physical addresses—all the little details. (You won't have to waste your time asking any of those questions before completing the call.)

The buyer originally located your company by browsing through the Open Vendormall, an electronic "yellow pages" listing of product suppliers based on SIC codes and universal product standards. She could have fired off a request for quotation through that system, but chose to place a videocall first to ask a few pointed questions and see who she'd be doing business with.

She asks for some pricing figures that aren't at your fingertips. "Jarvis?" (That's your name for your digital assistant.) "You called, sir?" he/it quickly responds. "Run into the databank and grab this month's pricing schedules—that's a good fellow." Jarvis is back in a microsecond with the relevant file.

The pricing looks right to the buyer, but she wants to see the product in action. You suggest a visit to your company's virtual display room, and she agrees, so you connect her screen and your own to the showroom. In the showroom it's more convenient to use avatars, so each of you sees a representation of the other on the screen. In the middle of the showroom an enlarged version of your product, a miniature jet engine designed to be used in golf carts, slowly rotates, suspended in air.

The buyer controls her avatar using a multipoint mouse. Her avatar reaches up to spin the engine in the opposite direction, then reaches inside and splits the image in two. You activate the representation so that she can see the engine's inner processes at work.

The buyer seems satisfied, and you return to videocall mode. She authorizes the purchase of two units for a test project. Before shipping, you'll need a deposit. "Will that be a digital cash transaction, or would you prefer we debit your corporate cybercard?"

The details are worked out, and you sign off. Your computer immediately goes to work processing the order and sending notification to all concerned parties. Best of all, your account is instantly credited (via electronic funds transfer) with the exact amount of your commission on the sale!

A Final Word From the Author

I sincerely hope you've enjoyed this excursion into the world of electronic commerce and interactive digital multimedia. If you found this book to be useful, then by all means tell your marketing associates (especially those who haven't yet considered venturing out onto the information superhighway).

If you have any ideas or information that you think should be included in future editions of *CyberMarketing*, please contact the publisher.

Glossary

Here are some words, buzzwords, and acronyms that will help you understand the worlds of the Internet, online services, and electronic commerce.

addresses (Internet) Internet *site* addresses exist in two forms: as a set of numbers *125.887.25.71* and as alphanumeric characters *microsoft. com.* An individual's *personal* address at this site could be represented as *bgates@microsoft.com.* ".com" at the end of an Internet address usually designates a commercial site; ".edu" is typically an educational institution; ".gov," a government agency; and ".net," a network services provider.

agent Also known as "intelligent agents," "personal agents," "knowbots," or "droids." Agents are search tools that automatically seek out relevant online information based on your specifications.

anchor Words or phrases in Web-based documents that when clicked lead to another page or resource. Synonymous with hyperlinks, anchors are typically highlighted to stand out from the rest of the document.

Archie Derived from the word "archive," Archie is a program that maintains a database of all the names of files and directories stored at public Internet archive sites worldwide. Archie allows you to quickly locate files that are available for downloading via FTP.

ASCII or American Standard Code for Information Exchange A worldwide standard (pronounced "ask-ee") in which numbers, letters, punctuation marks, symbols, and control codes are assigned numbers from 0 to 27. Easily transferred over networks, ASCII is plain, unadorned text without style or font specifications.

asynchronous connection A digital-to-analog or analog-to-digital connection; the type of connection a modem makes over a telephone line. (See also synchronous connection.)

ATM or asynchronous transfer mode An emerging network standard that allows the transmission of voice, video, and data over fiber-optic links.

authoring software Software for the creation of multimedia or hyper-text documents and presentations.

avatar An interactive representation of a human being in a virtual-reality environment.

backbone The primary high-speed network connections linking powerful computers on public and private networks.

bandwidth The ability of a transmission medium (e.g., fiber optic cable) to carry audio, data, video, or multimedia signals.

baud A unit of data transmission speed; or the maximum speed at which data can be sent down a channel.

BBS or bulletin board system A computer equipped with software and telecommunications links that allow it to act as an information host, or server, for remote computers.

bit Contraction of binary digit. The smallest unit of information a computer can hold. The speed at which bits are transmitted (bit rate) is usually expressed as bits per second (bps).

bozo filter Enables an e-mail recipient to automatically "zap" messages from predesignated undesirable sources.

bps or bits per second A measure of the speed with which data moves across a network. A typical modem moves data over phone lines at speeds of 4,800 to 28,800 bps.

browser Software for navigating information databases, especially the Internet's World Wide Web.

byte The number of bits used to represent a character.

CD-ROM or Compact Disc-Read Only Memory An optical disc from which information may be read from but not written to; can hold over 600 megabytes of multimedia data.

CD-R or Compact Disc-Recordable Device that allows user to record content onto a blank digital disc.

classified advertising (electronic) Simple, text-based online advertising, usually placed in common-sense categories (e.g., consulting services, office equipment, etc.)

client A computer that has access to services from a "server" over a computer network. When your modem dials up a research database, your system is the client and the system providing the information is the server, or host.

clipping services (electronic) Monitor news wires and other information sources for stories containing specified words, phrases, or symbols. These items are "clipped" and forwarded to electronic folders.

command line Whenever you can type in commands to the computer (either on your own computer or the system you are logged on to), you are at the command line.

configure   To change settings on hardware or software.

connect time fees or **connect charges**   Fees that are incurred while you are connected to an online service provider.

cross-posting   The practice of sending the same message to more than one Internet mailing list or discussion group. Typically frowned upon unless you're fairly sure that the posting is relevant for each list or group and that the circulation for each is substantially different.

cyberconsumers   Online shoppers and buyers.

cybermall   An electronic "site" shared by a number of vendors who often share the expense of the site. The site's provider will usually offer (for a fee) to help the vendor create and maintain its presence at the site.

cyberspace   The non-physical space where people interact with each other and with other computer systems via networks. Science fiction author William Gibson coined the term cyberspace to refer to a future world of computer networks linked to the human mind.

database   A system of related files and information.

dial-up connection   Links your computer to a host computer over standard telephone lines.

dedicated line   A permanent private telephone line between two locations; often used to connect a company's internal office network to an Internet service provider.

direct connection   A permanent connection between your computer system (either a single computer or a network) and the Internet. Sometimes called a leased-line connection because you lease the line from the phone company.

display advertising (electronic)   Online advertising with color, graphics, a variety of type styles, and more.

DNS or domain name system   A database of Internet names and addresses which translates names (ford.com) to official Internet Protocol numbers (365.121.) and vice versa.

download   To transfer a file from a remote computer to your computer's hard drive.

DSU or digital services unit   Used instead of a modem in a synchronous (digital-to-digital) connection to the Internet or to a private network.

electronic commerce   Electronic business transactions.

EDI or electronic data interchange   Allows computers to conduct structured paperless business transactions, such as ordering and invoicing, over telecommunications networks.

electronic forms   The electronic version of plain paper forms (i.e. order forms, application forms, survey forms, etc.).

E-mail or electronic mail   The most frequently used online service. Allows cybermarketers to exchange electronic messages with customers, prospects, or co-workers.

E-zines   Electronic publications distributed over computer networks.

FAQs or frequently asked questions   Answers to the questions commonly asked by new online users.

firewall   Security measures designed to protect a networked system from unauthorized or unwelcome access.

flame   An overtly angry or offensive message sent over the Internet; may be provocated by an actual or assumed breach of Internet "netiquette."

freeware   Software (often developed at universities and research labs) that you are free to retrieve and use at no charge. Freeware programs are typically located in software repositories on the Internet and other online services.

FTP or file transfer protocol   Allows cybermarketers to transfer files directly between a PC and a remote host system. You can download files and programs from thousands of servers throughout the Internet.

gateway   A computer link between two or more networks or databases.

GIF or graphics interchange format   A commonly used file compression format (pronounced "jiff") for transferring graphic files to and from online services.

Gopher   An Internet indexing system that allows users to browse and read multi-level menus of files stored at many different sites.

Gopherspace   The network of Gopher sites that span the Internet.

groupware   Software applications (like Lotus Notes) that facilitate shared work on documents and information. The next generation of groupware will enable individuals in different companies (for example vendors and their clients) to share information and work on projects together using groupware running on public networks.

GUI or graphical user interface   A software "front-end" that provides an attractive and easy to use interface between a computer user and a computer application. If you decide to develop an online system for your company's customers to access—and if you decide that the information presented in the system will go beyond simple text—you'll need to design a flexible and effective GUI.

hacker   Users who try to find ways to overcome computer and network security measures, either to demonstrate technical prowess or for illegal purposes.

hits   The number of times an online site is visited.

home page   The document displayed when you first open Mosaic. Also a company's primary electronic "page" of information on the World Wide Web. Similar to a book's cover and its table of contents.

host   A computer system acting as an information or communications server.

HTML or hypertext markup language   The computer language used to write, notate, and render documents within the World Wide Web. (Several software publishers are developing software that will allow users to create HTML documents directly from standard word processing programs.)

HTTP or hypertext transfer protocol   The protocol used to link hypertext documents on the World Wide Web. Precedes most World Wide Web site addresses (e.g., *http://marketplace.com*).

hypermedia   Refers to hypertext-based (see below) multimedia information.

hypertext   A system that provides electronic links from one online document to another. Clicking on highlighted words takes you to the next level in the related document.

inline images   Graphics contained within a Web document.

interactive   When feedback takes place between a system (i.e. a computer or a TV) and a user; or between an online service provider or vendor and a user; or between two users of a system.

IP or Internet protocol   Basic set of communication standards that controls communications activity on the Internet. An IP address is a number assigned to any Internet-connected computer.

IRC or Internet relay chat   An Internet system that allows Internet users to "chat" (via keyboard) in real time.

ISDN or Integrated Services Digital Network   A telecommunications standard that uses digital transmission technology to support voice, video, and data communications applications.

JPEG or joint photographic experts group   An image compression format used to transfer color photographs and images over computer networks.

Kiosk   A free-standing information and transaction server (like an automated teller machine). Often used for multimedia POS (see below) applications.

LAN or local area network   See network.

links   The hypertext connections between Web pages.

live   An object linked to another layer of information in a World Wide

Web file. For instance, clicking on a graphic of a building and seeing its floor plan.

login A name or code used to sign on to and gain access to an online service (e.g., agore for Al Gore).

lurk Read messages from discussion groups or newsgroups without contributing anything.

mailbot An e-mail address that returns information to customers.

mailing lists An Internet system for conducting ongoing "discussions" by sending copies of messages to all subscribers on a particular list.

metaverse A "metaphorical universe," a virtual, online representation of reality. (From the book *Snow Crash* by Neal Stephenson.)

MIME or multipurpose Internet mail extensions A messaging standard built on top of SMTP (see below) that allows Internet users to attach graphics, video, and voice files to e-mail.

modem "Modulator/demodulator"; an electronic device that changes computer signals into audio signals so they can be sent over regular phone lines and received by another modem that converts them back to digital signals.

Mosaic A World Wide Web browser developed at the National Center for Supercomputing Applications (NCSA); allows users to view multimedia files on the Internet.

MPC or multimedia PC A standard for multimedia computers and peripheral equipment (e.g., CD-ROM drives and sound cards) that ensures compatibility for all equipment with the MPC logo.

MPEG or moving pictures expert group Refers to a standard for video compression and desktop movie presentation. A special viewing application is needed to run MPEG files.

multimedia The use of multiple media to convey information.

menu A list of on-screen choices.

natural language The language we normally use to communicate with each other. Online systems that allow the use of natural language queries ("Which Canadian companies manufacture automobile safety glass?") are a significant advance over systems that require users to use computer language or codes.

NetFind An Internet software utility expert system designed to find e-mail addresses of other Internet users.

netiquette A loose set of customs and generally accepted rules for using online services and the Internet.

network A group of computers that are connected. Includes LANs (Local Area Networks, computers linked together in a single location), WANs (Wide Area Networks, computers linked over a wide area, like the Internet), VANs (Value-Added Networks, private or semi-private networks typically carrying commercial data traffic),

MANs (Metropolitan Area Networks, systems linking computers within a metro area, like the greater Chicago area MAN) and CANs (Campus Area Networks, linking computers within an industrial compound or university).

newbie or newbe   A novice Internet user.

node   A computer that is directly connected to a network.

offline   Any computer activity that takes place when your computer is not connected to another computer. For example, you may purchase a software program that allows you to quickly retrieve your e-mail from an online service so that you can read it offline in order to save on connection charges and phone charges.

one-off   A single evaluation copy of a CD-ROM disc created in advance of the production process.

online   Any computer activity that takes place when your computer is connected to another computer.

PEDs or portable electronic documents   Allow recipients to view digital files or documents in their original format whether or not they have a copy of the application it was created in.

POP or point of presence   A direct Internet connection.

POS or point of sale   When and where the customer is ready to do business.

post   To send an e-mail message to a public discussion group on the Internet.

POTS   "Plain Old Telephone Service." POTS is all you need to access most online databases and services.

PPP or point-to-point protocol   An Internet connection enabling a company to use phone lines and a modem to connect to the Internet (without having to connect to an Internet host computer). PPP connections are rented from Internet service providers.

prompt   A symbol or symbols (often $ or % or >) displayed on your screen when a computer system is waiting for input from you.

protocol   A set of standards used to define patterns of electronic communication. Operating rules governing the format, timing, and other aspects of data transmissions on networks.

public-key cryptography   A method of scrambling data so that only the sender and recipient can read it. The user creates a pair of encryption keys—one public and the other private. Any message encrypted with the public key can only be decrypted with the private key—and vice versa.

ripscrip   Remote Imaging Protocol Script Language, a simple format for transmitting graphics over a variety of networks that is used on bulletin board systems nationwide. Both sender and receiver must have ripscrip software.

router   A device that transmits data between two networks that use the same communications protocols.

search engine   Programs or functions that help users find information in text-oriented databases.

server   A computer system managing and delivering information for "client" computers accessing the system.

set-top boxes   A computer-based control unit, like a cable converter box, that sits on top of a TV set and brings interactive services into consumers' homes.

SGML or standardized generalized markup language   An international standard for the publication and delivery of electronic information. It is used in industries that create large volumes of mission-critical documentation, including the aircraft, automotive, defense, electronics, government systems, publishing, research, and telecommunications industries.

shareware   Software programs available on public networks and BBSs which allow you to try the software and pay a fee only if you continue to use the product.

SIG or signature file   A short message tacked on to the end of your e-mail messages that identifies you as the sender. It may include contact data such as your phone number, fax number, address, information about your company—even a short inspirational or humorous statement.

SLIP or serial line Internet protocol   A method of Internet connection enabling companies to use phone lines and a modem to connect to the Internet without having to connect to a host. SLIP connections are rented from an Internet service provider.

SMPT or simple mail transfer protocol   A messaging standard that runs over TCP/IP (see below) and allows users to send and receive e-mail over the Internet. SMPT defines mail format and routing protocols so that users of different kinds of systems (PC, Macs, UNIX) can send mail to each other.

spam   To distribute a message across Internet conference areas or newsgroups without regard for the topic of discussion of the group.

synchronous connection   An analog-to-analog or digital-to-digital connection. Businesses often use higher-speed synchronous connections to link an office network to the Internet. (See also asynchronous connection.)

sysop or system operator   A person who runs a bulletin board system.

T-1 and T-3   High-speed data line connections.

TCP/IP or transmission control protocol/Internet protocol   The basic protocol controlling applications on the Internet. You normally need the TCP/IP "stack" in your software in order to fully utilize Internet search and file transfer tools.

Telnet A communications function that allows you to access and control a remote computer on an interactive basis.

trading partners Relationships between customers, vendors, and distributors linked through electronic commerce and EDI.

URL or uniform resource locator The addressing system for the World Wide Web, and a proposed addressing standard for all Internet services. A Web site's address is known as its "URL." The URL contains information about the method of access, the server to be accessed, and the path of any directories or files to be accessed on the server.

USEnet newsgroups The Internet plays host to over 9,000 general and special interest newsgroups that provide up-to-the-minute news and discussions on practically every topic imaginable. You can participate in newsgroups that relate to your industry or market.

VAN or value-added network See networks.

Veronica A search utility that helps you find what you're looking for on Gopher servers around the world. Instead of looking through a series of menus, Veronica allows users to enter key words to locate the Gopher site holding the desired information.

videotex An early prototype of today's online systems designed to deliver text and interactive services to video terminals. Some videotex systems are still in use.

video-on-demand Allows TV viewers to select movies or other video content through the use of a set-top control box and have it immediately delivered to their screen. One of the most likely early applications for interactive television.

virtual reality A format for interacting with computer systems that seeks to mirror the way we normally operate in the real world. It may include the use of three-dimensional graphics, a sense of perspective, a sense of motion, or other factors to convey the appearance of reality or of an imagined reality.

WAIS or wide area information server Somewhat like an electronic reference librarian. WAIS uses plain English (or "natural language") commands to simultaneously search through multiple Internet databases, returning documents, pictures, and sounds that appear to be relevant to the search. WAIS is an invaluable tool for Internet market research.

Web, World Wide Web, WWW or W3 A hypertext browsing and searching system on the Internet that uses HTTP to link multimedia files and documents.

web browser Software that allows a user to access and view HTML documents on the World Wide Web. Mosaic is one example of a Web browser.

Index